Linguistics for Intercultural Education

Language Learning & Language Teaching (LL&LT)

The LL&LT monograph series publishes monographs, edited volumes and text books on applied and methodological issues in the field of language pedagogy. The focus of the series is on subjects such as classroom discourse and interaction; language diversity in educational settings; bilingual education; language testing and language assessment; teaching methods and teaching performance; learning trajectories in second language acquisition; and written language learning in educational settings.

For an overview of all books published in this series, please see
http://benjamins.com/catalog/lllt

Editors

Nina Spada
Ontario Institute for Studies in Education
University of Toronto

Nelleke Van Deusen-Scholl
Center for Language Study
Yale University

Volume 33

Linguistics for Intercultural Education
Edited by Fred Dervin and Anthony J. Liddicoat

Linguistics for Intercultural Education

Edited by

Fred Dervin
University of Helsinki

Anthony J. Liddicoat
University of South Australia

John Benjamins Publishing Company
Amsterdam / Philadelphia

The paper used in this publication meets the minimum requirements of
the American National Standard for Information Sciences – Permanence
of Paper for Printed Library Materials, ANSI z39.48-1984.

Library of Congress Cataloging-in-Publication Data

Linguistics for Intercultural Education / Edited by Fred Dervin, Anthony J. Liddicoat.
  p. cm. (Language Learning & Language Teaching, ISSN 1569-9471 ; v. 33)
Includes bibliographical references and index.
1. Intercultural communication. 2. Multicultural education. 3. Language and languages--
Variation. 4. Cross-cultural orientation. 5. Language and education. 6. Language and
    culture. I. Dervin, Fred, 1974- editor of compilation. II. Liddicoat, Anthony,
    1962- editor of compilation.
P94.6.L55   2013
407.1'1--dc23   2012042206
ISBN 978 90 272 1307 5   (Hb ; alk. paper)
ISBN 978 90 272 1308 2   (Pb ; alk. paper)
ISBN 978 90 272 7235 5   (Eb)

John Benjamins Publishing Co. · P.O. Box 36224 · 1020 ME Amsterdam · The Netherlands
John Benjamins North America · P.O. Box 27519 · Philadelphia PA 19118-0519 · USA

Table of contents

Introduction

Linguistics for intercultural education

Fred Dervin and Anthony J. Liddicoat
University of Helsinki / University of South Australia

1. Introduction

The rationale for this book addresses the urgent need to find ways of improving intercultural education in a world where, on the one hand, hypermobility leads to unprecedented encounters between people from different countries, while, on the other, forms of rejection of and attacks on the 'Other' increase on a daily basis. The possibilities afforded by, and the problems resulting from, increased contacts across linguistic and cultural boundaries have led educators and education authorities to seek ways of educating for diversity. The issue of intercultural learning has been tackled in many and varied publications, especially in the fields of education (for example, Abdallah-Pretceille 1986; Cushner 1998; Silva 2002; Genovese 2003; Nesbitt 2004; Majhanovich, Fox & Pasalic Kreso 2009; Grant and Portera 2010; Marginson & Sawir 2011) and language education/applied linguistics (for example Ager, Muskens & Wright 1993; Bolten 1993; Byram 1997, 2008; Cerezal 1999; Corbett 2003; Byram, Nichols & Stevens 2001; Alred, Byram & Fleming 2002; Sercu, Bandura, Castro & Davcheva 2005; Piller 2011; Preisler, Klitgard & Fabricius 2011). In spite of the extensive literature on the subject, there is still much which needs to be done to address the ways in which language education can contribute to educating for diversity.

One of the problems which faces the field of intercultural education is the diversity of ways of understanding the basic concepts that it addresses. One manifestation of this is the diversity of terms used to name the field: intercultural, multicultural, cross-cultural, transcultural, etc. For example, several journals are dedicated to intercultural education, but they are not all labeled "intercultural". In fact the vast majority of journals use the adjective multicultural: e.g. *International Journal of Multicultural Education, The Journal of Multiculturalism in Education* and *Multicultural Education and Technology*. Of the main journals in the field, only the International Association for Intercultural Education (IAIE) has the term "intercultural" in the name of the journal they publish, *Intercultural Education*. This diversity of terms emphasises an initial problem with the notion of intercultural education: there often seems to be some confusion between terms, and this has an impact on how the issues are conceptualised, tackled and researched. In spite of the significance of the differences in terminology for conceptualising the field, the range of terms used does not seem to reflect clear differences in understanding. A quick look at the aims and scope of two of the abovementioned journals, *Intercultural Education* and *International Journal of Multicultural Education*, reveals that the reasons for using the terms "intercultural" or "multicultural" are not explained and that, in spite of the differences in name, their aims are in a way very similar:

> *Intercultural Education* is a global forum for the analysis of issues dealing with education in plural societies. It provides educational professionals with the knowledge and information that can assist them in contributing to the critical analysis and the implementation of intercultural education. Topics covered include: terminological issues, education and multicultural society today, intercultural communication, human rights and anti-racist education, pluralism and diversity in a democratic frame work, pluralism in post-communist and in post-colonial countries, migration and indigenous minority issues, refugee issues, language policy issues, curriculum and classroom organisation, and school development.

> *International Journal of Multicultural Education* (IJME) is a peer-reviewed open-access journal for scholars, practitioners, and students of multicultural education. Committed to promoting educational equity, cross-cultural understanding, and global awareness in all levels of education, IJME publishes reports of empirical research, typically in qualitative research orientation; literature-based scholarly articles that advance theories and scholarship of multicultural education; praxis essays that discuss successful multicultural education programs or practical instructional ideas and strategies; and reviews of visual arts, professional and children's books, and multimedia resources (primarily websites and films).

In these statements the area of inquiry seems to be very similar in spite of the different ways of naming the field and the various terms appear to be used interchangeably. *Intercultural Education* uses the adjective 'multicultural' once to describe its area of focus and the *International Journal of Multicultural Education* uses 'cross-cultural'. Although the significance of the overlapping use of terms is debated, Grant & Portera (2010) argue that because there is no consensus amongst practitioners and scholars on their meaning this is not so important. Nonetheless, we see the lack of semantic and epistemic clarity in the use of terms as problematic for developing clear conceptualisations of the field. In this volume, we have chosen to use the adjective 'intercultural' and propose in the following discussion to clarify ways of understanding and working with the term.

2. A different approach: Linguistics for intercultural education?

In language education the issue of intercultural education is often tackled through the concepts of culture or identity (see infra) which are investigated quantitatively and qualitatively using approaches such as content analysis, narrative analysis, ethnography, certain forms of discourse analysis, etc. In such approaches, the most reported classroom practices include such techniques as simulation activities, role-plays, self-reflexive essays, ethnographic exercises, critical incidents, etc. These are often accompanied by content or narrative analyses, which are used to examine the data produced. In such ways of working, the analysis of language has tended to be overshadowed by many disciplinary fields.

The focus of this book is to investigate ways in which language can be used as the focus for intercultural learning. To date, linguistic approaches have not been systematically or coherently used to deal with intercultural education in research or in classrooms, while such fields as anthropology, sociology, psychology and philosophy have had a clear influence on theory, practices and research directions. The lack of linguistic approaches in intercultural education is in many ways surprising. Some of the well-known authors from language learning and teaching or applied linguistics (for example, Byram, Corbett, Kramsch, Risager, Sercu) have laid a lot of emphasis on language in their understanding of intercultural learning. The same is also true for the journal *Language and Intercultural Communication,* which is indirectly related to intercultural (communication) education. Yet researchers in the area do not use linguistic tools to research intercultural phenomena in education or to propose ways of improving teaching and learning in the same way as 'linguistics' journals such as *Intercultural Pragmatics* and *Journal of Multicultural Discourses,* which deal with intercultural communication more generally.

What we endeavour to present in this volume is a linguistically oriented focus applied to intercultural learning in formal educational contexts. We thus aim to give language a more central place in intercultural education and propose to bring together language education, linguistics and the 'intercultural' as a coherent focus. The relationship between these elements has varied over time and most recently, linguistics has played a more reduced role in developing theory, methods and practice in language education, especially where views of the nature of language teaching and learning have moved beyond simple code-based views.

3.   What is the "intercultural" in "intercultural education"?

We now return to the term 'intercultural' to develop an understanding of how it is to be understood here. In language education, the learner has now become a real "subject"– a subject who is at the centre of learning and teaching; a subject who is taught to be responsible for his/her learning; a subject who interacts; a subject who is required to be both performer and analyser of language in use. The emergence of an intercultural perspective in language education has had a signifi-cant role to play in allowing these changes. Many researchers such as Abdallah-Pretceille (1986, 2003), Auger (2007) Byram (1997, 2008), Holliday (2010), Kramsch (1993) and Zarate (1986) have called for systematic integration of work on intercultural communication and the development of intercultural capabilities in language classrooms. Though their approaches and theoretical backgrounds often differ, their main message seems to be the same: language educators need to move away from an educational approach which consists of building up facts about a "target culture", comparing "cultures" and analysing the cultural routines and meanings of a particular group of people to one in which the language learner as language user and intercultural mediator are foregrounded. This movement is away from an overemphasis on national or ethnic identities and cultural differ-ences seen from an objectivist perspective to a more (inter-)subjective focus on the learners themselves as participants in diversity.

This is where a critique of intercultural education is needed because it is nec-essary for practitioners and scholars to position themselves within what often appears as a conceptual 'jungle'. There are indeed different ways of approaching intercultural education, which depend on how the intercultural is understood. If we decompose the word, there are two obvious components: the prefix *inter-* and the root *culture*.

Let us begin with what Latour (2008: 3) called the "tired old notion of culture". There is an increasing agreement that intercultural education has surrendered to the concept of culture as a fixed static entity, especially in terms of national culture (Abdallah-Pretceille 2003; Barbot & Dervin 2011; Dervin 2008, 2011; Holliday 2010; Finch & Nynäs 2011). This means that much of the work on intercultural education ignores recent developments in the understanding of culture which have resulted from critique of the concept in many disciplines, especially by an-thropologists (see Abu-Lughod 1991; Hannerz 1999; Wikan 2002). Intercultural education has therefore sought to develop approaches to teaching culture which have often not considered the ways in which culture is theorised. The idea of culture as national culture has been particularly pervasive.

National cultures have had a particular salience in wider discourses of nationhood. Since the rise of Modernity in eighteenth century Europe and the acceleration of globalization ever since (Pieterse 2004), the "imagined communities" (Anderson 1999) that constitute worldwide nations-states have created and "marketed" boundaries between "cultures" (Brubaker 2004:66). The anthropologist Pieterse (2004:224) even asserts that this has led to a strong "boundary fetishism" in international politics, everyday discourses on the Other (tourism, advertising) and even in research worlds. Culture has thus had a role to play in differentialist views of the world and people. Breidenbach & Nyìri (2009:9) argue that "culture – or rather, cultural difference – is now held to be the main explanation for the way the human world functions". The field of anthropology, as the study of humankind, has played a leading role in creating this understanding of "culture": Tommy Dahlén reminds us that nineteenth and twentieth century structural functionalism contributed to "viewing culture as a stable value system, governing human action and manifested in social institutions such as family, corporations and government" (1997:159). Such views have given rise to particular ways of understanding culture in language teaching not only in Europe (French *civilisation* and German *Landeskunde*), but more widely (Japanese *nihonjijou*) and are still widely used in intercultural education, whether in general education or language learning and teaching.

Recent criticisms of the concept of culture (though they are not so new) constitute important steps in reviewing the way we conceptualise intercultural education. In her 2010 book, Anne Phillips emphasises the fact that "culture is the catch-all explanation for everything" (Phillips 2010:63). The concept of culture can be used to present uncritical, solid, static and sometimes "pathologizing" (Briedenbach & Nyíri 2009:322) visions of people when it is used as an agent (*cultures meet, cultures clash…*). Phillips also asserts that "in popular usages of the term, there is a tendency to call on culture when faced with something we cannot otherwise understand" (2010:65). Gerd Baumann (1996:4) has demonstrated how the phrases "in my culture we do" or "in our culture we don't" are used strategically by people to explain their behaviours or thoughts (see also Abdallah-Pretceille 2003). Politically this has led to extreme cases such as "cultural defence" where cultural traditions are used for purposes such as legitimizing crimes (Phillips 2010:86). For Bayart (2005), such an understanding of culture – sometimes termed *culturalism* – commits three errors: it maintains that culture is a corpus of timeless and stable representations, that boundaries between cultures are clear-cut and that culture is endorsed by coherent political orientations. When culture is understood in this way what is represented as a cultural practice then "misrepresents what is frequently a contested activity as if it were slavishly followed by all those associated with particular cultural groups" (Phillips 2010: 5).

The contestation around culture raises the question of whether the "cultural" should continue to be the basis for developing understandings of the intercultural. A clear-cut answer to this question would be both counterproductive and counterintuitive. Although there are problems around understandings of culture as a concept, it can be nonetheless powerful as a way of understanding human diversity. Anthropology has spent considerable thought on resolving the problems in the use of culture as a concept. The Norwegian anthropologist T. H. Eriksen (2001: 141) proposes one solution: "Instead of invoking culture, if one talks about local arts, one could simply say "local arts"; if one means language, ideology, patriarchy, children's rights, food habits, ritual practices or local political structures, one could use those or equivalent terms instead of covering them up in the deceptively cosy blanket of culture". Another option is to emphasise the role of the social actor in understanding culture. This position is related to the argument that there is today a consensus on the fact that there is great "internal diversity" in all societies beyond so-called *multiculturalism* (that is, the presence of foreigners, Dahlén 1997: 174) – and that this diversity applies to every single person not just the Other:

- social codes are contested, power relationships altered (Bhatia 2007: 61);
- people live in "a web of cultural references and meanings" (Phillips 2010: 61);
- people are urged to "continuously reconstitut(e) themselves into new selves in response to internal and external stimuli" (Ewing 1990: 258) (see also Gaulejac 2009: 47).

For anthropologists and many other representatives of the human and social sciences, these criticisms of the concept of culture are widely accepted. According to Ewing (1990: 262; see also Chauvier 2011), anthropology is now interested in "inconsistencies" and pays more attention to the "experiencing actor" rather than a static "subjectivity-less" cultural representative. That is, the focus has shifted from cultures as things to human beings as the social enactors of culture.

The criticism of the concept of culture and the proposals put forward by anthropologists, amongst others, is of interest to and importance for intercultural education and it should trigger changes in the way we deal with culture in classrooms and research. If interculturality is about people from different countries meeting, and if the concept of culture as it has been understood is losing its credibility to analyse such situations, there is a need to search for different options for understanding what is a basic concept for the field. Many researchers have adopted a critical perspective on culture (Abdallah-Pretceille 1986, 2003; Dervin 2008,

2011; Holliday 2010; Piller 2011) and have proposed that the intercultural is more about constructing a relationship through negotiating images of the Self and the Other, cultures, languages, etc. rather than using these elements as explanatory static elements. According to Piller (2011:172) "Culture is sometimes nothing more than a convenient and lazy explanation". In intercultural education, therefore, there is a need to pay more careful attention to how culture is understood for the purposes of teaching and learning and how it is represented to learners. We need to move beyond seeing cultures as discrete, static entities and see cultures as varied, subjective and power-based constructions of lived experience.

Returning to the morphology of the intercultural, the contested understandings of culture are an important indication that understandings of the prefix 'inter-' should be given greater importance in the treatment of interculturality. The idea of *inter*culturality is that it involves intermediary positions – between individuals and between groups – and that cultures are deployed for social purposes. Abdallah-Pretceille (2003:20) emphasises that for researchers and practitioners it is important to "understand the intention of people when they refer to their culture or more precisely to certain cultural elements". This is precisely what Piller, amongst others, has proposed to do to renew interculturality:

> Just as research on language and gender has moved away from a focus on difference ("women's language vs. men's language") to an interest in the social construction of a gendered identity (e.g. Crawford 1995; Talbot 1998; Romaine 1999), I am suggesting that a social construction approach would also offer new insights in the field of intercultural communication. Instead of asking how Germans and Americans, for instance, use different communication styles, it might be much more useful to ask how cultural and national identity is 'done,' i.e. how it is constructed in ongoing interactions. (Piller 2000:21)

Interculturality is then a process of construction through interaction in which subjectivities and variation are not to be understood as "noise" which obscures the object of study but rather as its constituent parts. An increasing number of scholars argue that culturalism gives a vision of cultures that is too objectivist-differentialist and that it corresponds to "analytical stereotyping" (Sarangi 1994). The shift from a culturalist view to an intercultural view has consequences for the practices of intercultural education. This is why methodologies which consist of soft content analysis, which merely paraphrase what the Other or the Self have to say to serve as evidence of culture, need to be questioned. In attempting to move intercultural education beyond superficial ways of understanding the intercultural, methods such as participant-observation, self-reflexive essays, role-plays, simulations, and even sojourns abroad have been used for allowing learners to develop what Byram (2008) calls "intercultural competence". Such activities are proposed as opportunities for students to develop reflexive and critical skills yet, how the students build up these skills through such activities is often less well explored. In what follows we are presenting what linguistics can do for intercultural education.

In this book, we have retained the concept of culture as a core element of the intercultural in spite of the problems which exist. In using this term however we wish to signal a view that cultures are fluid, malleable, subjective constructs and that is not only the conceptualisation of culture that is contested but the realties represented by cultures themselves.

4. Language and intercultural education

An important starting point for considering how linguistics can contribute to intercultural education is to consider the role of language in intercultural education. While *culture* may be an obvious reference point, language in some sense lies in the background, being the unnamed dimension of the intercultural. In some approaches to intercultural education, language has in fact been overlooked or neglected. Sarangi (1994) gives a good example of how a situation involving a difficult 'intercultural encounter', in this case during a job interview, can easily pass as a 'clash of cultures' (the interviewer is English; the interviewee from an Asian country) while the linguistic competences of the actors (the Asian interviewee does not speak English as a first language, the Englishman does not articulate ideas well) can account for a lot of what is happening during the interaction.

The removal of language from the focus on intercultural education often results in a trivialising of the intercultural project. For example, Australia's *Multicultural Education Program* had an ambivalent relationship to language – it was made available as a component of education, but much of the focus of work did not recognise a role for language, especially in understandings of intercultural education for the monolingual, monocultural mainstream. The focus for the mainstream was tolerance and acceptance of the interculturalism of others rather than the development of the interculturality of the Self (Liddicoat 2009). This way of understanding the intercultural focused on cultural products – food, dress, folkloric practices – disassociated from their context and rendered into the language of the majority, as Jupp (2000) terms it a "pasta and polka" version of the other.

The possibility of excluding language from the focus of intercultural communication in part comes from a limited conceptualisation of language as code, as grammar rules and vocabulary items. This problem has derived from the ways language education has understood language and which has sometimes been adopted uncritically into thinking about intercultural education. Rather than focusing on the superficial features of linguistic codes, it is important to consider more deeply the role of language as a constituent part of human life. The essential role of language is not the production of linguistic forms but rather the creation, communication and interpretation of meanings. When considered as social practices of meaning making and interpretation, language becomes not an optional extra for but a constituent part of intercultural education. It is the medium through which cultures are created, enacted, transmitted and interpreted and in which "doing being intercultural" occurs (Axelson 2007). It is also the medium through which teaching and learning are constituted. That is, diversity is not encountered directly for the student of intercultural communication; it is mediated through practices of the languages involved.

Intercultural education is fundamentally an investigation of the intersections of language and culture in that language and culture shape processes of meaning making and interpretation. In intercultural education, these processes exist at multiple levels. The language(s) and culture(s) of the student influence and inform the practices on meaning making and interpretation which the student brings to each encounter with diverse others. Equally, the language(s) and culture(s) of these others influence and inform their own processes of meaning making. Learning therefore happens at the interstices of languages and cultures and through the recognition of the place of languages and culture in processes of learning. This is more than saying simply that language is the vehicle for "culture". It is to argue that language is constituent not only of cultures, but of perceptions of cultures (our own and others') and the processes by which we make sense of ourselves and others.

In understanding language in the context of intercultural education, it is therefore necessary to begin with an elaborated theory of language, seeing language as "open, dynamic, energetic, constantly evolving and personal" (Shohamy 2007: 5) and as encompassing the rich complexities of communication viewed as interactionally-grounded and involving "participants' contingent, emergent and joint accomplishment" of meaning (Kasper 2006: 305). This involves intercultural education with questions of voice, identity and co-construction between participants and the expression of Self through language. Language is then not so much a thing to be studied as a way of seeing, understanding and communicating about the world and each language user uses his or her language(s) differently to do this. In this sense, language is both personal and communal and as personal and communal it takes its place in the constitution of intercultural education.

Seeing intercultural education as an activity which is fundamentally based in language means that there is a demonstrable capacity for linguistics to contribute to intercultural education. However, the role of linguistics itself needs to be problematized in such an endeavour. Understanding language as a complex, personalised and contingent meaning-making system has implications for conceptualising what linguistics is as a contributor to intercultural education and where and how linguistics can be engaged.

5.   What linguistic approaches can benefit intercultural education?

Linguistics as the science of language has an ambivalent relationship with educational contexts in which language is relevant. In fact, there are many ways in which linguistics has been conceived which in themselves render such a relationship problematic. Much linguistics has focused on language as an autonomous system and in so doing has specialised in a focus on the linguistic code, which, as we have argued above, is not the most salient point of connection between language and intercultural education. The point of intersection between linguistics and intercultural education lies in understandings of language as a communicative and interactive system and the implications of such understandings for what can be said about language.

As linguistics has often defined language as a communication system as its object of study (for example Saussure (1916) claimed that linguistics was the science of speech communication), this bringing together of linguistics and intercultural education would appear *prima facie* to be unproblematic. However, linguistics has often held only a rudimentary understanding of what communication entails and has tended not to give much attention to what it means by communication and its definitions have tended to remain underdeveloped (Curnow 2009; Haugh & Liddicoat 2009). For Saussure, communication was a simple process in which an active speaker encodes a message for a passive listener – an unproblematic exchange of meaning through language. Harris (2003) has argued that Saussure's conceptualisation of language as the science of speech communication is untenable because Saussure adopted a model of communication "which explains communication as the transference of thoughts from one person's mind to another person's mind" (Harris 2003:25). In such a view, meaning itself is unproblematized and unproblematic – it emerges complete and entire from the linguistic code, rather than involving subjective, contextualised interpretation. Even such a minimal view of languages as a communication system is not undisputed within linguistics. Chomsky and his colleagues (Fitch et al. 2005; Hauser et al. 2002) have argued that communication itself is incidental to grammar as an organising principle and thus as the focus of linguistic study. The points of connection between linguistics and intercultural education can therefore be obscured by some of the ways in which linguistics has defined its own area of focus. In order to engage with linguistics in the context of intercultural education, therefore, it is necessary to consider how linguistics, broadly understood, allows for the possibility of dealing with the complexities of language understood as a medium for the creation, communication and interpretation of meanings.

From the middle of the twentieth century, approaches to the study of language began to consider the place of context in understanding language. In particular they have recognised that the relevant contexts for understanding how language is used in communication go beyond linguistic context and that there is a need to consider complex relationships between language and the world beyond language. The idea that language is influenced by the extralinguistic context is not new, Wegener (1885) had already recognised that language provides only part of what is needed for communication and that speakers need to fill in the rest from their knowledge of the world. Malinowski (1923) further developed the idea of communication as contexted language use and argued that for the necessity of considering two different types of context: context of situation (micro-context) – the "*hic et nunc*" environment in which language is used (see Dubois 1969: 116) – and context of socioculture (macro-context) – the experiential, social, institutional and ideological background knowledge shared by participants – in linguistic communication.

Linguistic approaches in which social and cultural linguistic contexts have been explicitly addressed often began in other disciplines and were then adapted into linguistics or they are forms of linguistics influenced by ideas from other disciplinary areas and represent an expansion of linguistics beyond a narrow concern with language structures. Some of these approaches are considered to be part of the mainstream in linguistics others have remained more at the boundaries between linguistics and other disciplines. Many of these approaches are put into practice in the chapters that compose this volume.

An early articulation of a view of linguistics that begins to articulate the socioculturally contexted nature of language is use can be seen in Hymes' (1966) formulation of communicative competence. Hymes' conceptualisation, drawn from anthropology, sees language use in communication as highly embedded in context and requiring knowledge of cultural frames of reference. Communicative competence has been highly influential in models of language education (for example Canale & Swain 1981), although somewhat ironically it has produced ways of teaching and learning languages in which culture has been somewhat marginalised. Nonetheless, the idea of communicative competence as something beyond grammatical competence has been influential as a starting point for coming to see the intercultural in language education (for example Byram 1997; Liddicoat 2011).

A further impetus for rethinking the ways in which linguistics deals with language came from philosophy, also in the 1960s, with the development of Speech

Act theory (Austin 1962; Searle 1969) and the emergence of pragmatics as an area of enquiry in linguistics. Speech Act theory introduced into linguistics the idea of seeing language as action and thus a new understanding of what constituted linguistic communication which gave rise to ways of understanding language use as cultured, most notably from work in cross-cultural pragmatics (Blum-Kulka, House & Kasper 1989). The emergence of pragmatics has also had an impact on understandings of language acquisition and as seeing language acquisition in the light of intercultural communication. Much research in pragmatics for language learning has focused on the idea of culturally appropriate language use, however, recent work has also begun to consider what pragmatics contributes to deepening understandings of the relationship between language use and culture.

A further way of understanding language as action emerged from Sociology in the form of Conversation Analysis which sought to locate language structure within processes of micro-level social organisation (Sacks 1992). Conversation Analysis views language as fundamentally located within a social context which both shapes and is shaped by language. Moerman (1996: 150) argues that "Social rules and cultural values are learned, enforced, and manipulated – indeed, they exist – only on the social occasions in which they are oriented to and used", however, apart from Moerman's work (1988), researchers have tended to focus on the social rather than on the cultural in language use. In language education, this focus on the social has been manifested mainly through descriptions of the ac-quisitional and communicative processes of language users (Gardner & Wagner 2004) and CA's current role seems to be one of researching aspects of intercultural learning rather than as a resource for teaching.

The idea of language as social has also been developed through Systemic Functional Linguistics which sees language as a social semiotic, as a resource for making meanings (Halliday 1978). From this social semiotic perspective, the lan-guage learner can be seen as a maker of meaning and as drawing on and develop-ing understandings of context of culture and context of situation in their language use. The language learner therefore comes to be seen as having a *voice* in using their new language and as engaging with multiple contexts and multiple cultures in the language use (Kramsch 1993, 2008).

Some approaches to language as a social phenomenon have also appeared in specific academic contexts and have not yet found a voice in others. This is the case with for example *theories of enunciation/utterance* and the highly interdisci-plinary *dialogism* in the French-speaking world. Starting from the argument that researchers are not interested in finding some "truth", "French" discourse analysis, from which the aforementioned methods are derived, looks into representations that cross discourses. The basic idea is that any utterance consists of two parts: a *dictum* (what is said) and a *modus* (how it is said) (Bally 1965: 36). The dictum cannot be verified against truth because, on the one hand, it emerges from the inter/subjective worlds of the speakers, and on the other, it is constructed through a modus (Ducrot 1993:113). In other words, the modus is "the subject's reaction to a representation that they construct themselves in their discourse" (Vion 2001:144). French enunciation/utterance theories, inspired by language philosophers such as Austin and Searle and also by Bakhtin and Jakobson, propose that discourse is marked by various unstable enunciative traces (Marnette 2005:19), that is, by different voices. Enuniciative/utterance analyses allow the researcher to examine and question the agency and/or positioning of people taking part (in)directly in acts of interaction: the *speaker* (the person who is physically speaking, the *enunciators* (people who are involved in negotiated discourses) and the *co-enunciators* (interlocutors or "voices" that are included in discourses). Analysing enunciation consists in identifying the "linguistic means (…) through which speakers position themselves, inscribe themselves in the message (implicitly or explicitly) and situate themselves in relation to it" (Kerbrat-Orecchioni 2002:33). This allows a dynamic approach to identity and "culture as an alibi" in intercultural communication (Dervin 2008).

Dialogism, which is complementary to theories of enunciation, is based on the central idea that there is interdependency between the "self" and the "other" (Marková et al. 2007:1). As a consequence, "there can be no ego without others, no voice without other voices and no self discourse without other discourses" (Linell 2009:36). The concept of voice is central in this approach, which allows a direct link with theories of enunciation. According to Hermans (1999:110), "voices function like interacting characters in a story, involved in a process of question and answer, agreement and disagreement". These voices allow the researcher to identify specific identity strategies and construction in specific contexts (macro and/or micro) of interaction (see Perrin 1999; Dervin 2008; Orvig & Grossen 2004). Many linguistic traces can help speakers to 'voice': direct, indirect and/or hybrid represented discourses (often called speech, see Rosier 1999). The use of some pronouns can also help to manipulate voices. In French for example the pronoun *on* is fascinating in this sense as it can trigger unstable and difficult to identify voices (Boutet 1994). Finally, negation is also a dialogical mark (Ducrot 1993).

The impact of linguistics on education to date, whether autonomous linguistics of more socially and culturally oriented linguistics has often been to describe the target of learning – to identify the forms, functions, uses, etc. of language to be learnt or to describe the ways in which learners' language deviates from that of native speakers. That is, linguistics, which sees itself as a quintessentially *descriptive* discipline has, when applied to language education become the source of *prescriptions*, of statements of norms (Liddicoat & Curnow 2003). However, in intercultural education, the roles and scope for linguistics goes beyond the articulation of native speaker norms and provides possibilities for analysis of language as meaning and its articulation with "culture" both as a resource for learning and as an account of what learners do in and through language.

6.   A proposal: Four emphases

The chapters in this book use a range of approaches to linguistic analysis and address quite different contexts of interculturality. Within this diversity, there emerge four main ways in which linguistics has been shown to have a role in intercultural education: as affordances for learning, as processes for learning, as processes of evaluation, and as accounts of teaching. These four emphases are in reality overlapping and closely interrelated and many of the chapters provide accounts of more than one of these. The four ways of using linguistics identified here represent a useful way of thinking about the possibilities for linguistics as a component part of intercultural education and provide a starting point for further consideration of a linguistic perspective on interculturality.

One role that linguistics can play in intercultural education is to identify elements of language that can be used as affordances for learning about the relationships between language and culture (in its non-essentialist form, see Dervin 2012; Holliday 2010) as they are manifested in communication. As language is a constituent part of culture, linguistic features can provide points of departure for reflection on similarities, differences and instabilities between practices and on the ways that languages and cultures are co-constructed. There is potential for linguistic analyses at a range of levels from word to text to provide such starting points (see Liddicoat 2009 for some of these possibilities). In this case, linguistics itself is not taken as a constituent part of intercultural education but rather the relevant research lies outside the domain of education. Research in linguistics, which is carried out to elucidate features of language, can become a resource for other purposes that lie beyond purely linguistic objectives and analyses. If linguistics is to provide such a starting point, however, it needs to consider the interrelationships between languages and cultures as a constituent part of analyses.

In this volume, the results of research on language in use – pragmatics, discourse analysis – in particular shows ways in which language analyses can provide affordances for learning. In the chapters by McConachy and Cohen and Sykes the results of pragmatics research provide a starting point for engaging learners with investigations into the deeper associations of language and culture and the consequences of these for acting within a linguistically and culturally diverse world. Wang and Rendle-Short use insights from Conversation Analysis to identify ways in which English and Chinese differ in the use of conversation routines in certain contexts. The chapters show that the identification of linguistic practices which demonstrate differences, similarities, and/or instabilities in cultural conventions of use can be used as a way of gaining entry into an appreciation of the ways in which language is cultured and the consequences of this for interacting in contexts of linguistic and cultural diversity.

It is unsurprising that pragmatics and discourse analysis should be represented in such a way in this volume as it has been in research in pragmatics that relationships between languages and cultures have been most operationalised. In fact, the language-culture relationship has been a central part of pragmatics research for a considerable time, first in the traditions of cross-cultural pragmatics (e.g. Blum-Kulka, House & Kasper 1989) and discourse analysis (Kerbrat-Orecchioni 1993) in which the realisation of various speech acts in different cultures has been a dominant focus, and interlanguage pragmatics (e.g. Kasper & Blum-Kulka 1993) with its emphasis on the acquisition of pragmatic capabilities, to the more recent emergence of ethnopragmatics (Goddard 2006; Traimond 2004), which has focused more on what language in use can reveal about underlying cultural constructs. However, the scope of linguistic input into intercultural education is not simply limited to issues of pragmatics and there is research emerging in other fields of linguistics that can provide useful insights for developing intercultural education, such as syntax (e.g. Enfield 2002), semantics (Goddard 2005), discourse analysis (e.g. Scollon & Scollon 2001; Traverso 2001) or textlinguistics (Connor 2004). Such studies do not in themselves necessarily present a project of intercultural exploration in the sense in which it has been used in this book but rather have the potential to identify particular loci of interest around which intercultural learning can be constructed.

A second role for linguistics that emerges through the chapters in this book is as a learning process within education itself. Intercultural education involves the development of reflective and analytic capabilities which can be used to developing insight into and mindfulness of the ways in which languages and cultures are at play in human life. Intercultural education also includes increasingly, influenced by critical pedagogy, a critical component which should lead language learners to commit to combat inequality and forms of prejudice, oppression and discrimination (Dervin & Keihäs 2012; Räsänen 2009). As participants in linguistic and cultural diversity, individuals need to be both performers in sociality and analysers of the performance of themselves and others as they mutually construct interactions, and through them, relationships (Liddicoat & Scarino 2010) but also power structures (Shi-xu 2001). Various forms of linguistics provide elements for the analytic repertoire that individuals bring to intercultural encounters. McConachy's chapter shows how a metapragmatic analysis of language in use can be a way of coming to understand deeper cultural issues underlying ways of using language. The learners in this study work through an analysis of speech acts, comparing and contrasting their first language practices and understandings with those of the target language to gain insights into deeper issues of the relationships between language and culture. Sykes and Cohen describe a process of strategy learning that develops critical attention to interactions providing additional interpretive dimensions for analysing, understanding and responding to the linguistic productions of others and to understanding other's evaluations of self. In this case, the learning process described is not so much in the context of the classroom learning, but rather the educational component is a preparation for analytic engagement in interactions beyond the classroom. Wang and Rendle-Short describe a way of using Conversation Analysis to develop awareness of differences in the interactional significance of similar utterances in the cultural contexts of different languages. They reveal that the development awareness of the processes of language use gives learners greater control over the practices of the diverse individuals they encounter. These chapters show that developing the resources available to intercultural actors to analyse the language(s) and discourses they run into in interactions with others opens new ways of understanding and engaging with linguistic and cultural diversity – both opening one's own practices to critical awareness and focusing understanding on potentially unfamiliar ways of acting and power differentials.

Thirdly, the studies in this volume demonstrate how linguistics can provide ways of evaluating the intercultural capabilities of students through studies of their language use. The intercultural is expressed through acts of language – communication, interaction, text – and these productions can be treated as constructions and enactments of intercultural perspectives by students, in interaction with others, which can be elucidated by linguistic analysis. These chapters examine the ways in which participants in intercultural interactions construct their experience of diversity as meaningful. These constructions provide texts for analysis that demonstrate underlying values, assumptions and interpretations. Trémion's study shows that attention to the ways in which utterances are constructed can reveal the forms of (co)construction and enactment of intercultural understanding which are drawn on by students. The study shows how attention to the language used to represent self and other as an expression of intercultural understanding can reveal how students understand and respond to diversity and that understandings of diversity go far beyond declarative knowledge about the other. This study also reveals how analysis of students' productions can reveal the opportunities and constraints that an educational program can place on how diversity is encountered and made meaningful. In their chapter, Cuenat-Egli and Bleichenbacher show how a linguistic analysis can be used to examine the ways in which linguistic and intercultural capabilities work together. They identify the ways in which the language used by a plurilingual individual can enable or constrain the possibilities in expressing intercultural understandings and how the plurilingual person's overall linguistic repertoire provides options that can be drawn upon in constructing and expressing an intercultural world view. Byrd-Clark and Stratilaki's chapter examines the ways in which language learners' discourses about plurilingualism and pluriculturality can reveal (inter)subjective representations of distance and proximity between languages. These representations form a part of the communicative context in which additional languages are learned and used. While Trémion, Cuenat-Egli and Belichenbacher and Byrd-Clark and Stratilaki have used linguistic to analyse the content of students' language for insights into intercultural understanding, Wang and Rendle-Short's study focused more on what the analysis of the structures of language can reveal. They show that subjecting students' language to analysis can reveal underlying assumptions about how aspects of language use are understood as meaningful contributions to interaction and reveal the extent to which learners are conscious of diversity in linguistic practice.

Finally, linguistics can be used to analyse the processes of teaching to understand how the language used by teachers (and students) provides particular affordances for learning. These studies can be seen as continuing a long tradition of classroom discourse analysis that has sought to investigate how ways of interacting in classrooms construct the possibilities for learning (e.g. Marton & Tsui 2004). The chapters in this volume, however, have moved beyond the superficial linguistic features of classroom interaction to examine critically how interactions enact understandings of the nature and value of diversity and provide opportunities for exploration of new understandings. Cole and Meadows show how attention to language can provide an account of the processes of teaching that construct the intercultural for learners. Close attention to language can reveal the cultural contextualisation of teachers' linguistic productions and identify the messages about cultures and people that are produced and reproduced through the act of teaching – and thus reveal power imbalance. Harbon and Maloney show how teachers' responses to students' understandings of linguistic and cultural diversity can open up or limit possibilities for introducing complexity into interpretations of linguistic and cultural diversity. They argue that the common Initiation-Response-Feedback pattern of teacher talk often works to close down possibilities and to ratify particular ways of understanding diversity as normative while other ways of structuring talk show more creative possibilities.

What these four ways of working with linguistic have in common is that they do not seek to describe language for its own sake but rather analyse language to understand that which lies beyond language. In this way, the chapters in this volume construct not only an understanding of the way linguistics can contribute to intercultural education but also provide an account for how intercultural education understands linguistics. The view of linguistics presented here is one that rejects the idea of autonomous linguistics (Derwing 1979) in which language seen as independent of other aspects of human life or even of its contexts of use. The view of linguistic here is one which highlights the interrelationships that exist between language and other aspects of human experience. It shows that linguistics as a discipline can provide useful ways of connecting with the intercultural as it is presented in and through language. In this sense, it responds to Sériot's question about the use of linguistics in dealing with the intercultural: "If café conversations inform us that all the Scots are mean or that Corsicans are lazy, will we one day stop using linguistics to justify such fantasies which psychoanalysis can better deal with?" (Sériot 2004: 43).

7.   About this volume

This book is composed of eight chapters, which look at the use of linguistics both in the language classroom and in researching this context. Each chapter reflects one or several role(s) that linguistics can play in intercultural education.

The volume is divided into two parts: (1) Developing intercultural competence through the use of linguistics; and (2) Linguistics for studying interculturality in education.

The first part of the volume opens with *Avoiding the essentialist trap in intercultural education: Using critical discourse analysis to read nationalist ideologies in the language classroom*, written by **Deborah Cole** and **Bryan Meadows**. In this chapter, special emphasis is given to the important argument that intercultural education tends to rely on essentialized notions. The authors argue that perpetuating such notions not only poses many problems for learning but is also counterintuitive. Based on two data sets and using the principles of Critical Discourse Analysis (CDA), Cole and Meadows propose what they consider to be a way out of essentialism. CDA thus becomes a tool which allows an alternative intercultural education to emerge, which is more equitable and ethical.

In the second chapter **Mirjam Egli-Cuenat** and **Lukas Bleichenbacher** deal with intercultural competence in the international mobility of Swiss teacher trainees. Here they discuss the problems of linking the learning objectives of linguistic *savoir-faire* as they are described by the *European Language Portfolio* and the *Common European Frame of Reference* (CEFR) and intercultural competence. Based on Jean-Claude Beacco's (2004) *"proposition de référentiel pour les compétences culturelles"*, the authors discuss how linguistic discourse analysis can contribute to the development of intercultural competence in formal language learning and teaching.

A place for pragmatics in intercultural teaching and learning, written by **Troy McConachy**, demonstrates how Japanese learners of English as a foreign language are able to develop intercultural awareness while dealing with pragmatics in a language classroom by means of a textbook. The chapter illustrates how learners can be led to examine their own cultural assumptions through linguistic analysis. The chapter also investigates the role of the teacher's discourse in raising intercultural awareness by guiding students' analyses.

In a similar vein, **Andrew D. Cohen** and **Julie M. Sykes** examine the application of language learner strategies in the learning of pragmatics in Spanish as a foreign language. Pragmatic behaviour is presented by the authors as one of the central aspects of intercultural education. Based on two online Spanish-speaking environments designed to support the learning of pragmatic behaviour, the study shows some differences in the ways the students used pragmatic strategies in both environments.

In the next chapter **Yan-Yan Wang** and **Johanna Rendle-Short** look at the use of Chinese Mandarin *ni hao ma* (how are you?) in an oral Chinese language test, by using both intercultural pragmatics and Conversation Analysis (CA). The authors are interested in how tertiary language learners develop their intercultural competence and use it in a test of social interaction. The emphasis is on a conversation analysis of telephone openings. They investigate two groups of Chinese Mandarin learners, one of which had received intercultural training in the use of the *ni hao ma* phrase and the other not and examine the differences in understanding of the two groups. In similar terms to the previous article, their study illustrates how language learners and educators can be reflexive about the discourses produced by the Self and the Other, and also about the hidden cultural assumptions of those discourses.

The second part of the volume is entitled Linguistics for studying interculturality in education.

Lesley Harbon and **Robyn Moloney**'s chapter is entitled *Language teachers and learners interpreting the world: Identifying intercultural development in language classroom discourse.* Revisiting their research projects on intercultural language education in Australia the authors note that they have given little space to linguistic aspects of the 'intercultural'. They argue that the use of linguistics in intercultural education can provide teachers with valuable tools. As a "remedy", Harbon and Moloney analyse classroom data by examining evaluative exchanges (I-R-E exchange, Sinclair & Coulthard 1975, 1992) and turn-taking. Through their analysis, the authors demonstrate that, amongst other things, variations on the evaluative exchange may impact on interculturality.

Using a 'French' discourse analytic approach, **Virginie Tremion**'s contribution is based on a famous online intercultural exchange programme entitled *Cultura*. During the exchange, the students were asked to compare their "cultures" and explore the links between culture and communication. In the chapter, Tremion examines how the construction of *alterity* occurs in the discourse of the students in *Cultura*. She also presents the potential problems posed by the programme as it tends to lead the students to culturalist and essentialist discourses.

The final chapter of the volume was written by **Julie Byrd Clark** and **Sofia Stratilaki**. Entitled *Complex and symbolic discursive encounters for intercultural education in plurilingual times,* the chapter aims to define linguistic competence in relation to intercultural education by providing a historical overview of how linguistic competence has been conceptualized in Europe and contextualizing multilingualism and the 'intercultural' through the examination of a case study on French-German bilinguals in prestigious institutional school environments.

These papers, drawing on different theories and methods, give an insight into the ways in which linguistics can address core issues relating to intercultural education. They demonstrate that a focus on language provides new possibilities for the development of intercultural education by showing how the intercultural is embedded within the linguistic act of communication.

Acknowledgements

The editors would like to thank the following people who reviewed the chapters: Nathalie Auger (University of Montpellier, France), Juliane House (University of Hamburg, Germany), Marjut Johansson (University of Turku, Finland), Celeste Kinginger (PennState University, USA), Andy Kirkpatrick (the Hong Kong Institute of Education, Hong Kong), Jonathan Newton (University of Wellington, Australia), Bert Peeters (Macquarie University, Australia), Ingrid Piller (Macquarie University, Australia), Patricia Pullin (University of Zurich, Switzerland), Beata Webb (Bond University, Australia), Alain Wolf (University of Norwich, England).

References

Abdallah-Pretceille, M. (1986). *Vers une pédagogie interculturelle.* Paris: Economica.
Abdallah-Pretceille, M. (2003). *Former et éduquer en contexte hétérogène.* Paris: Economica.
Abu-Lughod, L. (1991). Writing against culture. In R. Fox (Ed.), *Recapturing anthropology* (pp. 137–162). Santa Fe, NM: School of American Research.

Ager, D., Muskens, G. & Wright, S. (Eds.). (1993). *Language education for intercultural communication*. Clevedon: Multilingual Matters.

Alred, G., Byram, M. & Fleming, M. (2002). *Intercultural experience and education*. Clevedon: Multilingual Matters.

Anderson, B. (1999). *Imagined communities*. New York, NY: Verso.

Auger, N. (2007). *Constructions de l'interculturel dans les manuels scolaires*. Fernelmont: E.M.E.

Austin, J. L. (1962). *How to do things with words*. Cambridge, MA: Harvard University Press.

Axelson, E. (2007). Vocatives: A double-edged strategy in intercultural discourse among graduate students. *Pragmatics, 17*(1), 95–122.

Bally, C. (1932/1965). *Linguistique générale et linguistique française*. Berne: Francke.

Barbot, M.-J. & Dervin, F. (Eds.). (2011). Rencontres interculturelles et formation. *Éducation Permanente*. No. 186.

Baumann, G. (1996). *Contesting culture: Discourses of identity in multi-ethnic London*. Cambridge: Cambridge University Press.

Bayart, J.-F. (2002). *The illusion of cultural identity*. Chicago, IL: University of Chicago Press.

Beacco, J.-C. (2004). Une proposition de référentiel pour les compétences culturelles dans les enseignements des langues. In J.-C. Beacco, S. Bouquet & R. Porquier (Eds.), *Niveau B2 pour le français: Textes et références* (pp. 251–287). Paris: Didier.

Bhatia, S. (2007). *American karma: Race, culture, and identity and the Indian diaspora*. New York, NY: New York University Press.

Blum-Kulka, S., House, J. & Kasper, G. (Eds.). (1989). *Cross-cultural pragmatics: Requests and apologies*. Norwood, NJ: Ablex.

Bolten, J. (1993). Interaktiv-interkulturelles Fremdsprachlernen. In H. P. Kelz (Ed.), *Internationale Kommunikation und Sprachkomptenz* (pp. 99–139). Bonn: Dümmler.

Boutet, J. (1994). *Construire le sens*. Bern: Peter Lang.

Breidenbach, J. & Nyíri, P. (2009). *Seeing culture everywhere*. Washington, DC: University of Washington Press.

Brubaker, R. (2004). *Ethnicity without groups*. Cambridge: Harvard University Press.

Byram, M. (1997). *Teaching and assessing intercultural communicative competence*. Clevedon: Multilingual Matters.

Byram, M. (2008). *From foreign language education to education for intercultural citizenship: Essays and reflections*. Clevedon: Multilingual Matters.

Byram, M., Nichols, A. & Stevens, D. (2001). *Developing intercultural competence in practice*. Celevedon: Multilingual Matters.

Canale, M. & Swain, M. (1981). Theoretical bases of communicative approaches to second language teaching and testing. *Applied Linguistics, 1*, 1–47.

Cerezal, F. (Ed.). (1999). *Enseñanza y aprendizaje de lenguas modernas e interculturalidad*. Madrid: Talasa.

Chauvier, E. (2011). *Anthropologie de l'ordinaire*. Toulouse: Anacharsis.

Connor, U. (2004). Intercultural rhetoric research: Beyond texts. *Journal of English for Academic Purposes, 3*(4), 291–304.

Corbett, J. (2003). *An intercultural approach to English language teaching*. Clevedon: Multilingual Matters.

Curnow, T. J. (2009). Communication in introductory linguistics. *Australian Journal of Linguistics, 29*(1), 27–44.

Cushner, K. (1998). *International perspectives on intercultural education.* Mahwah, NJ: Lawrence Erlbaum Associates.

Dahlén, T. (1997). *Among the interculturalists: An emergent profession and its packaging of knowledge.* Stockholm: Stockholm University Press.

Dervin, F. (2008). *Métamorphoses identitaires en situation de mobilité.* Turku: Humanoria.

Dervin, F. (2011). *Les identités des couples interculturels. En finir vraiment avec la culture.* Paris: L'Harmattan.

Dervin, F. (2012). *Impostures interculturelles.* Paris: L'Harmattan.

Dervin, F. & Keihäs, L. (2012). *Uusi kulttuurienvälisyys.* Jyväskylä: FERA.

Derwing, B. L. (1979). Against autonomous linguistics. In T. A. Perry (Ed.), *Evidence and Argumentation in Linguistics* (pp. 163–189). Berlin: de Gruyter.

Dubois, J. (1969). Énoncé et énonciation. *Langages, 13*, 100–110.

Ducrot, O. (1993). À quoi sert le concept de modalité? In N. Dittmar & A. Reich (Eds.), *Modalité et acquisition des langues* (pp. 111–129). Berlin: Walter de Gruyter.

Enfield, N. (2002). Ethnosyntax: Introduction. In N. Enfield (Ed.), *Ethnosyntax: Explorations in grammar and culture* (pp. 3–30). Oxford: Oxford University Press.

Eriksen, T. H. (2001). Between universalism and relativism: A critique of the UNESCO concept of culture. In J. Cowan, M.-B. Dembour & R. Wilson (Eds.), *Culture and rights. Anthropological perspectives* (pp. 127–148). Cambridge: Cambridge University Press.

Ewing, K. P. (1990). The illusion of wholeness: Culture, self, and the experience of inconsistency. *Ethos, 18*(3), 251–278.

Finch, J. & Nynäs, P. (2011). *Transforming otherness.* New York, NY: Transactions.

Fitch, W. T., Hauser, M. D. & Chomsky, N. (2005). The evolution of the language faculty: Clarifications and implications. *Cognition, 97*(2), 179–210.

Gardner, R. & Wagner J. (Eds.). (2004). *Second language conversations.* London: Continuum.

de Gaulejac, V. (2009). *Qui est je?* Paris: Seuil.

Genovese, A. (2003). Per una pedagogia interculturale: Dalla stereotipia dei pregiudizi all'impegno dell'incontro. Bologna: Bononia University Press.

Goddard, C. (2005). The lexical semantics of culture. *Language Sciences, 27*(1), 51–73.

Goddard, C. (2006). Ethnopragmatics: A new paradigm *Ethnopragmatics. Understanding Discourse in Cultural Context* (pp. 1–30). Berlin: Mouton de Gruyter.

Grant, C. A. & Portera, A. (2010). *Intercultural and multicultural education: Enhancing global interconnectedness.* London: Routledge.

Halliday, M. A. K. (1978). *Language as social semiotic. The social interpretation of language and meaning.* London: Edward Arnold.

Hannerz, U. (1999). Reflections on varieties of culturespeak. *European Journal of Cultural Studies, 2*(3), 393–407.

Harris, R. (2003). On redefining linguistics. In H. G. Davis & T. J. Taylor (Eds.), *Rethinking linguistics* (pp. 17–68). London: Routledge.

Haugh, M. & Liddicoat, A. J. (2009). Examining conceptualisations of communication. *Australian Journal of Linguistics, 29*(1), 1–10.

Hauser, M. D., Chomsky, N. & Fitch, W. T. (2002). The faculty of language: What is it, who has it, and how does it evolve? *Science and Education, 298*, 1569–1579.

Hermans, H. J. H. (1999). Dialogical thinking and self-innovation. *Culture Psychology, 5*, 67–86.

Holliday, A. (2010). *Intercultural communication and ideology.* London: Sage.

Hymes, D. H. (1966). Two types of linguistic relativity (with examples from Amerindian eth-nography). In W. Bright (Ed.), *Sociolinguistics* (pp. 114–167). The Hague: Mouton.

Jupp, J. (2000). Immigrant society. In R. Nile (Ed.), *The Australian legend and its discontents* (pp. 326–338). St. Lucia, Qld: University of Queensland Press.

Kasper, G. (2006). Speech acts in interaction: Towards discursive pragmatics. In K. Bardovi-Harlig, C. Félix-Brasdefer & A. Omar (Eds.), *Pragmatics and Language Learning* (Vol. 11, pp. 281–314). Honolulu, HI: National Foreign Language Resource Center, University of Hawai'i at Manoa.

Kasper, G. & Blum-Kulka, S. (Eds.). (1993). *Interlanguage pragmatics.* New York, NY: Oxford University Press.

Kerbrat-Orecchioni, C. (1993). Variations culturelles et universaux dans les systèmes conversa-tionnels. In J.-F. Halté (Ed.), *Interactions: L'interaction, actualités de la recherche et enjeux didactiques* (pp. 61–90). Metz: Centre d'Analyse Syntaxique de l'Université de Metz.

Kerbrat-Orecchioni, C. (2002). *L'Énonciation. De la subjectivité dans le langage.* Paris: Armand Colin.

Kramsch, C. (1993). *Context and culture in language education.* Oxford: Oxford University Press.

Kramsch, C. (2008). Voix et contrevoix: L'expression de soi à travers la langue de l'autre. In G. Zarate, D. Lévy & C. Kramsch (Eds.), *Précis de plurilinguisme et du pluriculturalisme* (pp. 35–38). Paris: Éditions des archives contemporaines.

Liddicoat, A. J. (2009). Communication as culturally contexted practice: A view from intercul-tural communication. *Australian Journal of Linguistics, 29*(1), 115–133.

Liddicoat, A. J. (2009). Evolving ideologies of the intercultural in Australian multicultural and language education policy. *Journal of Multilingual and Multicultural Development, 30*(3), 189–203.

Liddicoat, A. J. (2011). Language teaching and learning from an intercultural perspective. In E. Hinkel (Ed.), *Handbook of second language teaching and research* (Vol. 2, pp. 837–855). New York, NY: Routledge.

Liddicoat, A. J. & Curnow, T. J. (2003). Language descriptions. In A. Davies & C. Elder (Eds.), *Handbook of applied linguistics* (pp. 25–53). Oxford: Blackwell.

Liddicoat, A. J. & Scarino, A. (2010). Eliciting the intercultural in foreign language education. In A. Paran & L. Sercu (Eds.), *Testing the untestable in foreign language education* (pp. 52–73). Clevedon: Multilingual Matters.

Linell, P. (2009). *Rethinking language, mind, and world dialogically.* Charlotte, NC: Information Age Publishing.

Majhanovich, S., Fox, C. & Pasalic Kreso, A. (Eds.). (2009) *Living together: Education and inter-cultural dialogue.* Dordrecht: Springer.

Malinowski, B. (1923). The problem of meaning in primitive languages. In C. K. Ogden & I. A. Richards (Eds.), *The meaning of meaning* (pp. 296–336). New York, NY: Harcourt Brace and World.

Marginson, S. & Sawir, E. (2011). *Ideas for intercultural education.* New York, NY: Palgrave Macmillan.

Marková, I., Linell, P., Grossen, M. & Salazar Orvig, A. (2007). *Dialogue in focus groups: Explor-ing socially shared knowledge.* London: Equinox.

Marnette, S. (2005). *Speech and thought presentation in French: Concepts and strategies.* Amster-dam: John Benjamins.

Marton, F. & Tsui, A. (Eds.). (2004). *Classroom discourse and the space of learning*. Mahwah, NJ: Lawrence Erlbaum.

Moerman, M. (1988). *Talking culture: Ethnography and conversation analysis*. Philadelphia, PA: University of Pennsylvania Press.

Moerman, M. (1996). The field of analyzing foreign language conversation. *Journal of Pragmatics, 26*(2), 147–158.

Nesbitt, E. (2004). *Intercultural education: Ethnographic and religious approaches*. New York, NY: Academic Press.

Perrin, L. (1999). La fonction des reprises diaphoniques locales dans le dialogue. In J. Verschueren (Ed.). *Pragmatics in 1998: Selected papers from the 6th International Pragmatics Conference* (Vol. 2, pp. 448–461). Antwerp: International Pragmatics Association.

Phillips, A. (2010). *Gender and culture*. Cambridge: Polity.

Pieterse, J. N. (2004). *Globalization and culture: Global mélange*. Lanham, MA: Rowman & Littlefield Publishers.

Piller, I. (2000). Language choice in bilingual, cross-cultural interpersonal communication. *Linguistik Online, 5* (1). Retrieved from http://www.linguistik-online.com/1_00/PILLER. HTM.

Piller, I. (2011). *Intercultural communication*. Edinburgh: Edinburgh University Press.

Preisler, B., Klitgard, I. & Fabricius, A. (2011). *Language and learning in the international university: From English uniformity to diversity and hybridity*. Clevedon: Multilingual Matters.

Räsänen, R. (2009). Teachers' intercultural competence and education for global responsibility. In M.-T. Talib, J. Loima, H. Paavola & S. Patrikainen (Eds.), *Dialogs on diversity and global education* (pp. 29–49). Bern: Peter Lang.

Rosier, L. (1999). *Le discours rapporté: Histoire, théories, pratiques*. Paris-Brussels: Duculot.

Sacks, H. (1992). *Lectures on conversation*. Oxford: Basil Blackwell.

Salazar Orvig, A. & Grossen, M. (2004). Représentations sociales et analyse de discours produit dans des *focus groups*: Un point de vue dialogique. *Bulletin de Psychologie, 57*(3), 263–272.

Sarangi, S. (1994). Intercultural or not? Beyond celebration of cultural differences in miscommunication analysis. *Pragmatics, 4*(3), 409–427.

Saussure, F. (1916). *Cours de linguistique générale*. Paris: Payot.

Scollon, R. & Scollon, S. W. (2001). *Intercultural communication: A discourse approach* (2nd edn.). Oxford: Basil Blackwell.

Searle, J. R. (1969). *Speech acts: An essay in the philosophy of language*. Cambridge: Cambridge University Press.

Sercu, L., Bandura, E., Castro, P. & Davcheva, L. (2005). *Foreign language teachers and intercultural communication: An international investigation*. Clevedon: Multilingual Matters.

Sériot, P. (2004). Oxymore ou malentendu? Le relativisme universaliste de la métalangue sémantique naturelle universelle d'Anna Wierzbicka. *Cahiers Ferdinand de Saussure, 57*, 23–43.

Shi-xu. (2001). Critical pedagogy and intercultural communication: Creating discourses of diversity, equality, common goals and rational-moral motivation. *Journal of Intercultural Studies, 22*(3), 279–293.

Sinclair, J. M. & Coulthard, M. (1975). *Toward an analysis of discourse*. London: Oxford University Press.

Shohamy, E. (2007). *Language policy: Hidden agendas and new approaches*. London: Routledge.

Silva, C. (2002). *L'educazione interculturale: Modelli e percorsi*. Pisa: Edizioni del Cerro.

Traimond, B. (2004). *La mise à jour: Introduction à l'ethnopragmatique*. Pessac: Presses Universitaires de Bourdeaux.

Traverso, V. (2001). Interactions ordinaires dans les petits commerces: Éléments pour une comparaison interculturelle. *Langage et société, 95*(1), 5–31.

Vion, R. (2001). Modalités, modalisations et activités langagières. *Marges linguistiques* (pp. 239–251). Saint-Chamas: M.L.M.S. Éditeur.

Wegener, P. (1885). *Untersuchungen über die Grundfragen des Sprachlebens*. Halle: Max Niemeyer.

Wikan, U. (2002). *Generous betrayal*. Chicago, IL: The University of Chicago Press.

Zarate, G. (1986). *Enseigner une culture étrangère*. Paris: Hachette.

PART I

Developing intercultural competence through the use of linguistics

Avoiding the essentialist trap in intercultural education

Using critical discourse analysis to read nationalist ideologies in the language classroom

Deborah Cole and Bryan Meadows
University of Texas-Pan American / Farleigh Dickinson University

Even though intercultural educators recognize that essentialism is detrimental to their goals, their delivery of course content to students continues to be criticized for being mired in essentialized notions of "nation" and "culture". Holliday (2011) argues that we construct essentialist discourses and practices to protect nationalist ideals and standards because doing so benefits the researchers, teachers and students who also benefit from the maintenance of global, national, and local inequalities. It is thus very difficult to articulate and practice alternatives to "nationalist standard practices" (Meadows 2009), though we may be well aware that continuing to perpetuate essentialist visions of the world is unethical. Our goal in this chapter is to articulate one step out of this "essentialist trap". We demonstrate how the tools of linguistics, specifically Critical Discourse Analysis (CDA), can be used to surface three discursive processes (*objectification, prescription,* and *alignment*) which are commonly used to reproduce essentialism in language instruction. Awareness of these processes sheds light on how discourse in typical language classrooms constructs monolithic, essentialized views of languages and cultures. Discourse data from an Indonesian language classroom demonstrates how these very same processes can alternatively operate to circumvent the limitations on diversity posed by nationalism. We argue that when students and teachers acquire the ability to make use of CDA to identify linguistic practices in the classroom as products of common, underlying discursive processes, they also acquire the grounds for imagining and enacting alternatives to nationalist essentialising. Such awareness, we contend, can lead to an intercultural education that is more equitable, ethical, and timely.

1. Introduction

The field of Intercultural Education continues to struggle with a glaring and em-barrassing paradox: We say we are aware of the dangers of essentialism but we teach and write and think as though discrete categories of culture and language exist (Dervin 2011; Holliday 2011; McSweeney 2002). Resting on the assumptions that groups of people can be clearly delimited and that group members are more or less alike (Bucholtz 2003: 400), nationalist essentialism generates exaggerated portrayals of inter-national diversity as well as intra-national homogeneity. Con-sistently, contemporary social scientific inquiry challenges these monolithic por-trayals, exposing diversity where nationalist homogeneity is otherwise prescribed (Holliday 2011; Hymes 1974; Tai 2003; Wolfram 1991) and identifying contiguity across otherwise discrete nationalist borders (Gupta & Ferguson 1997; Irvine & Gal 2000; Risager 2007). Nationalist essentialism is particularly problematic for Intercultural Education because by projecting a social landscape that naturalizes inter-national diversity and intra-national homogeneity, it narrows the range of what counts in the language classroom. This narrowing process leads students away from legitimate engagement with linguistic and cultural diversity – exactly what students need to develop their intercultural competence.

The current situation, where educators recognize the limits of essentialism but nevertheless reinforce it, has been called neo-essentialism by Holliday (2011: 69). As Holliday puts it, essentialized nationalist objects "are seductive because they are convenient for theory building in the academy, and provide accountable so-lutions in intercultural communication training" (ibid.: 15–16). In conventional thinking, language classrooms are successful when they prepare students for en-counters with coherent "national peoples", who are proprietors of a single "na-tional language". The reasons for language educators to continue to work within this nationalist paradigm (Risager 2007) seem to outweigh any serious consider-ation of other options. For example, teachers cannot be expected to teach multiple versions of a language in the space of a semester (or even over the course of a degree); only a limited number of any language's varieties are even represented in textbooks; teachers themselves are only familiar with a limited number of vari-eties; and students often expect to learn "standard" varieties for use in particular national contexts. A practical solution remains to be formalized in the field, and our intent with this chapter is to articulate how the tools of linguistic analysis, which raise metalinguistic awareness, can enable teachers and students to begin to step out of the essentialist trap.

Following recent thinking in the field of Intercultural Education (Liddicoat 2006; Risager 2007; Tai 2003), we will advocate for the rich inclusion of cultural and linguistic diversity in language classrooms. Liddicoat (2006), for example, describes a language unit wherein students developed a heightened sensitivity to the complex ways the *tu/vous* distinction in French is employed in social interactions through an exposure to its use in varied contexts. Importantly, Liddicoat found that when this exposure to variation of use in different contexts was paired with prompts to participate in critical reflection, students began to see their own language practices in English from the perspective of French. Thus, in coming to understand the complexity of successfully employing French's *tu/vous* distinction, these students began to decenter from the norms of their L1, acquiring a level of intercultural competence that transcends essentialist thinking. In a similar vein, we advocate for exposing language students to the target language's phonetic diversity to raise their awareness of the phonological complexity that is not only inherent in any language but which is so often erased (through essentialism) in language teaching.

Our chapter is organized as follows. We begin with a review of *nationalist standard practices* and why they are problematic for Intercultural Education. This is followed by a brief introduction to the area of linguistics that interests us here, i.e. Critical Discourse Analysis, or CDA. We then introduce three discursive processes which are prevalent in metalinguistic talk in language classrooms and which can be revealed through CDA: *objectification*, *prescription*, and *alignment*. Our orientation to these processes includes a discussion of how they are commonly deployed to enforce essentialized notions of languages and cultures. We then turn to data from a *Bahasa Indonesia* (Indonesian) language classroom where these same three processes serve to denaturalize the idea of an essentialized national language and instead work to reveal intra-national diversity. We conclude by discussing some practical implications of how the explicit use of CDA in the language classroom can widen the range of what counts in language instruction and facilitate the goals of Intercultural Education.

2. Nationalist standard practices and intercultural education

The nationalist paradigm is a condition of nationalist ideology (Billig 1995), an ideology that serves as a social-organizational resource available to individuals in microinteractions to bring order to pervasive cultural and linguistic diversity. Although nationalism is rendered in multiple ways in practice, there are two consistent arguments that undergird it: (a) humanity is divisible by nature into discrete nationalist units (i.e., nations), and that (b) each nation, in order to secure its own liberty, is best administered under a political state which faithfully reflects the national character (hence, the nation-state) (Anderson 2006; Billig 1995; Gellner 2006; Kedourie 1994). When we cast nationalist entities as ideological products, we are justified in giving attention to the kind of social practices that maintain them (Bourdieu 1977; Young 2009). We offer the term, *nationalist standard practices*, to refer to those social practices in language classroom settings that presuppose, reinforce, and elaborate singular notions of nation. The critique of language classrooms as sites of nationalist reproduction is not new (Bourdieu & Passeron 1977; Golden 2004; Meadows 2009). In offering the term nationalist standard practices, we bring to the ongoing conversation a way to perceive nationalist essentialism as a contextualized social process that brings order to pervasive cultural and linguistic diversities.

Nationalist standards take shape in language classrooms in two ways. First, the nationalist standard subject, which is an idealized monocultural individual (Alptekin 2002; Davies 2004; Kramsch 2003; Rampton 1990), is advanced according to tropes of authenticity. Second, the nationalist standard language, or *Standard* (Silverstein 1996, 2003), understood as a collection of linguistic features associated with an authentic nationalist center, is advanced according to tropes of correctness (Lippi-Green 2011; Preston 2005; Wiley & Lukes 1996). Following the equation that links each nation to a unique language (Blommaert & Verschuren 1992; Heller 2008; Woolard 1998), a nationalist standard subject is an idealized native speaker of a nationalist standard language. The problem with nationalist standard practices, as we see it, is not so much that they simplify the linguistic field (because this appears to be necessary in any language classroom setting), but that they make the possibility for choosing to engage with linguistic diversity difficult to see and therefore difficult to implement. In other words, nationalist standard practices not only move linguistic diversity out of earshot, they function hegemonically.

Further, in fixating on language and culture as products of idealized native speakers, nationalist standard practices function in language classrooms to promote a monoglossic imaginary at the expense of focusing on the processes by which the shifting heteroglossic and hetero-cultural realities of social communities are actually constructed. Scholars in intercultural studies emphasize the importance of cultivating student awareness of the social processes underlying such shifts in linguistic and cultural categorization. Abdallah-Pretceille (2007: 481) explains, "it is culture in action, and not culture as an object, which is at the heart of intercultural reasoning." Likewise, Hannerz (1999) underscores the importance of process-awareness in Intercultural Education when he writes, "an emphasis on process may entail subversion of a kind of mystique of cultural difference which seems to be an important part of cultural fundamentalism" (p. 402) and a barrier to "cultural choice and mobility" (p. 405).

Since it is in discursive practice that nationalized "cultures" and "languages" are recognized and reified, language (or linguistic practice) is at the very heart of the matter. As Dervin and Liddicoat explain in the introduction to this volume (see p. 9),

> [T]he 'intercultural' is more about constructing a relationship through negotiating images of the Self and the Other, cultures, languages, etc. rather than using these elements as explanatory static elements…This is more than saying simply that language is the vehicle for 'culture.' It is to argue that language is constituent not only of cultures, but of perceptions of cultures (our own and others') and the processes by which we make sense of ourselves and others.

This stance leads us directly to the empirical analysis of discourse to account for how individuals use talk to manage a nationalist landscape populated by discrete national cultures and languages. We will argue that once students have an awareness of the processes that build and contain their nationalist social worlds, they are positioned to take agency over those processes.

3.   The uses and utility of critical discourse analysis[1]

Critical Discourse Analysis is an ideal tool to lead students through an exploration of the discursive practices at the center of intercultural encounters. From early on, CDA has been crafted as an approach to the analysis of discourse that aims to uncover the ideological components of texts (Blommaert & Bulcaen 2000; Kress & Hodge 1979; van Dijk 2001) and to put in perspective the contribution of texts to the perpetuation of (or challenge to) commonsense ideologies (e.g., nationalism, racism, Orientalism, sexism, etc.). Since ideologies circulate covertly because they are "perceived to be locked within the system described" and "not acknowledged as part of the act of describing" (Holliday 2011:57), we need a method of social scientific inquiry to make visible the particular linguistic processes and selections by which Standard is reified and its alternatives are (unconsciously) rejected. CDA is just the tool we need: It can be used to identify and account for the monoglossic effects teacher talk can have on heteroglossic realities, and it can make visible the processes whereby social ideologies, from their privileged positioning, shape commonsense understandings of social practices.

Scholars who do CDA do not promote a single theory or method, but rather encourage approaching linguistic analysis through an inter-disciplinary lens. Our

---

1.   This sub-heading explicitly tropes on the title of one of Michael Silverstien's (1998) seminal papers on language ideology, "The uses and utility of ideology".

take on CDA draws explicitly on scholarship in linguistic anthropology, an area that has made important advances to our understanding of the relationship between language practice and *language ideology* (e.g. Hill 2008; Mendoza-Denton 2008; Silverstein 2003). This approach involves comparative analyses of ideologically-laden statements in discourse observed within their ethnographic contexts in multiple locations over time. Critical discourse analytic studies within this tradition have uncovered rich and robust evidence of universal semiotic processes that humans in all sociolinguistic projects make use of to construct essentialized boundaries between groups (Bucholtz & Hall 2004; Irvine & Gal 2000). Such processes include "linking processes" (like *iconicity* and *fractal recursivity*), which pick out matches between linguistic forms and types of speaker and "leveling processes" (like *erasure* and *highlighting*), which "simplify… the sociolinguistic field" (Park 2010: 24).[2] The repeated identification of these processes in discourse in a wide range of languages around the world has provided many researchers in the past decade with the analytical tools for better understanding how humans construct groups of "us" and groups of "them" in a wide range of locations and speech events. The processes we propose below build on and advance this productive research.

We are advocating for teachers and students to become aware of the processes by which language ideologies function so they can use them to monitor their own discourse. CDA is about disrupting the commonsense that is realized by means of discourse. This is accomplished by deconstructing segments of discourse and interrogating each component of the text for its contribution to realizing *a* "commonsense." Ideologies each function covertly in textual production and consumption to realize particular forms of commonsense. In the setting of language classrooms, nationalist essentialism is a prominent ideology that shapes the conventional practice. Teachers can use CDA to tackle this commonsense and then, by extension, to make visible alternative versions of commonsense. The

---

2. *Iconicity* refers to speakers' tendencies to identify apparently motivated connections between language forms and types of speaker (e.g. slow speech = slow person). *Fractal recursivity* refers to the process of mapping such iconic identifications onto other behaviors or features of the identified group (e.g. slow speech + slow person can be mapped onto ideas about slow-moving cultural behaviors as a whole which can then be used to justify identifications of a group of people as rural, backward, uneducated, etc.). *Erasure* refers to the fact that language ideologies ignore certain facts about speakers and language (e.g. groups who may indeed value slower speech, finding it more polite or hospitable, may also speak quite quickly in certain contexts and/or particular members of such a group may speak quickly on a regular basis). *Highlighting*, which "go[es] hand in hand" (Park 2010: 24) with *erasure*, is the process of picking out particular features in the sociolinguistic field for focus (e.g. rate of speech, rather than intonation or stress patterns, for example).

analysis of ideology in discourse requires special attention to what does not appear in the textual data at hand because ideology rules out certain options at the level of presupposition. Thus, teachers must also question the arguments that are presupposed in their own metalinguistic talk (i.e., that which is taken for granted). Conversely, ideologies can also appear indirectly in texts. One example is the subtle evaluatory work of adjectives. The selection of one adjective over another often reflects an ideology or worldview vis-à-vis the object being described (e.g., weird vs. eccentric). Thus, teacher analysts will want to give attention to their word choice in their metalinguistic talk.

Our presentation of CDA in this chapter is strategically focused on specifying a method for raising metalinguistic awareness of the discursive processes particular to teacher talk so that teachers may uncover the language ideologies that shape their own discourse. Understanding such processes is useful in accounting for the visions of nation that language teachers realize in their metalinguistic talk in front of their students. Our goal is to encourage teachers to analyze their own classroom discourse according to these three processes, looking specifically at how their metalinguistic talk either legitimizes or delegitimizes the diversity of voices/subjectivities/positions present in the target communities that they construct for students in their speech. We will argue that the expansion of voices in the language classroom benefits Intercultural Education for two reasons: (1) it brings to the forefront the discursive construction of social groupings (e.g., national ones) and the political processes that determine who and what counts as legitimate, and (2) it engages students with the diversity of voices that exist in social reality, rather than an idealized nationalist imaginary.

4. Objectification, prescription, and alignment in essentialized language instruction

In this section, we present *objectification*, *prescription*, and *alignment* and provide concrete examples of how these processes can function to advance a nationalist agenda in language classrooms. In doing so, we demonstrate how a CDA approach allows us to identify the ways in which teacher discourse can function to constrict heteroglossia in language classrooms. The examples we use come from our own experiences and should resonate with readers as familiar practice. In pointing to how these processes allow teachers to link essentialized language categories to essentialized cultures, to essentialized nations in a valorization of the Centre, we hope to offer some clarity on how essentialism is constructed in language classroom discourse.

The first process we see at work in essentializing classroom discourse is *objectification*, a metalinguistic ability that humans share and which is clearly and constantly at work in the language classroom where the object of study is in fact language.[3] Objectification is realized linguistically by segmenting linguistic practice into nominalized bits and then placing these bits in relational frames that appear to fix meaning (e.g. "*lack* means *without*" or "*sans* se dice *sin*"). Doing this allows teachers to equate one formal piece of language with another in their metalinguistic classroom talk. However, as a primary tool for language educators to teach lexical items and semantic content, relational frames of the form "A means B" are somewhat problematic for realizing the goals of Intercultural Education. This is because such relational frames point students towards decontextualized, objectifiable meanings, and the process of teaching them contradicts current understandings of meaning as co-constructed and contextually-dependent. To be clear, we do not deny that degrees of permanence and stability in linguistic practice are self-evident and necessary for language instruction. It would of course be inconceivable to provide instruction without holding up linguistic forms in discrete individual units. However, when forms are continuously (and only) equated without any qualification, other viable options that could potentially complete the relational equation never have a chance to emerge (e.g. *lack* can also mean "need" or "require").

When we recognize that conventional language classrooms are constructed against a nationalist backdrop, we can see how the process of objectification can advance nationalist standard practices, particularly as part of the discourse of correctness. Traditionally, successful language students are those who can appropriate a way of speaking, listening, and/or writing that is tied to a nationalist type (e.g., American English, Japanese, Canadian French, etc.). Through objectification, teachers may restrict student attention to specific forms of meaning that are associated with nationalist standard ideals. Other forms of meaning that students may actually encounter in interactional contexts in their target language environment are never mentioned. An example from the Rio Grande Valley where both authors have taught illustrates this point. Along the border of the United States and Mexico nearing the southern tip of Texas, the word "barely" is used to mean

---

3.   Objectification appears implicitly in all of the oft-cited definitions of language ideology. For example Michael Silverstein's early definition of language ideologies as 'sets of beliefs about language articulated by users as a rationalization or justification of perceived language structure and use' (Silverstein 1979: 193) or Irvine and Gal's (2000: 35) definition as 'the ideas with which participants and observers frame their understanding of linguistic varieties and map those understandings onto people, events, and activities that are significant to them'.

"recently". Thus, "I barely turned in my homework" is meant to be interpreted as "I just turned it in" not "Circumstances almost prevented me from turning it in."

Our point is not that someone teaching English as foreign language to students in France would need to know this usage, but rather that examples of variable meanings and functions for linguistic forms abound and that objectification of linguistic forms using the relational frames that typify language instruction is one of the discursive processes by which essentialism can (and does) occur. It is worth noting that this "regional" usage of the word "barely" would not occur in any of the standard language teaching resources to which foreign language teachers of English have access precisely because its usage to mean "recently" is not representative of a nationalist standard subject. The relational frame "*barely means recently*" is therefore, from the perspective of nationalist standards, "incorrect". Once linguistic practices are packaged into formal objects, a teacher is then in position to promote some forms over others. Objectification is thus intimately tied to the process of *prescription*.

Prescription is the explicit direction from a position of authority to shape linguistic and cultural practice to determine what counts as legitimate language.[4] Again, prescription is constantly at work at in the language classroom where student utterances are corrected and prescribed by the teacher (Collins 1991; Lippi-Green 2011) even though the notion of linguistic correctness is never grounded in an objective source (Crystal 2006; Milroy & Milroy 1985) and is subject to socio-political struggle (Voloshinov 1986). Prescription can act in support of nationalist standard practices when correctness is tied to nationalist visions of singularity and authenticity. With respect to teacher practice, we have found the Initiation-Response-Evaluation (IRE) participation framework (Sinclair & Coulthard 1975) as a productive site to prescribe nationalist ideals of standard. The routine aspect of this framework is particularly effective in developing a student disposition toward a singular, nationalist standard way of being and speaking.

When teachers have a single form of practice in mind, they privilege specific ways of describing the world. Place names, for example, can be overtly nationalist. Traveling around the city of Tucson in the state of Arizona in the U.S. where we have both studied, one hears two different pronunciations of the city's name: [tu.san] and [tuk.son]. The former follows English language phonological patterns and the latter follows Spanish phonological patterning. In Meadows' visits

---

4. This process too has long been implicitly present in definitions of language ideologies in that language ideologies protect the interests of particular sociolinguistic groups at the expense of others (Hill 2008; Park 2010). *Prescription* can be seen in Irvine's (1989: 255) inclusion of the "loading of moral and political interests" in her definition of language ideologies and Spitulnik's inclusion of "the construction and legitimation of power" (1998: 164) in hers.

to language classrooms in this region, however, [tu.san] is the only pronunciation permitted. The justification teachers give for this singular pronunciation is "that's how people say it." As part of prescribing student usage, discursive arguments such as this privilege a one language=one culture=one nation equation which is violated by the presence of multiple pronunciations. In this example, Spanish language phonology is not commiserate with "American" locations and is thus erased in the language classroom for being "incorrect", though it may well be encountered outside the classroom. It is important to note, however, that combating such essentialism can be problematic, as students may themselves be oriented towards the nationally prescribed forms. Ullman (2010), for example, observed that Spanish speaking immigrants to Tucson in her ESL classroom were well aware that their own use of the Spanish variant made them vulnerable to harassment from the U.S. border patrol who may ask them, "Where are you from?". Her students wanted and needed access to the English phonological pattern to avoid deportation and looked to the teacher to prescribe the "correct" form.

Prescription is thus also linked to *alignment*, a process by which speaker/hearers selectively link linguistic, cultural, and geographic variables to create and maintain sociolinguistic categories (like national subjects and standard languages).[5] We witness this clearly on occasions when language teachers shuttle between first-person singular and plural pronouns (I → we) in order to position themselves within a mainstream, nationalist center (e.g., *I wanted to get the store clerk's attention, so you know, in America we say "excuse me" or clear our throat*). Pronouns are powerful rhetorical tools to position discourse participants, both locally to the given context but also globally to contexts on a macro-scale (Benveniste 1996), and the metonymic potential of pronouns is especially potent in nationalist discourse (Billig 1995; Wodak, de Cillia, Reisigl, & Liebhard 2009). The effect of an instructor's blended use of singular and plural first-person pronouns thus brings into alignment the individual self with the nationalist collective, projecting the instructor's subjectivity to a massive scale. In fact, under the nationalist paradigm, teachers' pedagogical authority hinges on their ability to align themselves with a nationalist center (Bourdieu & Passeron 1977).

---

5.   The construction of national linguistic identities through alignment processes was articulated in much earlier work on language ideologies, notably by Silverstein (1979, 1996). In recent anthropological theory, Agha (2003, 2005) has coined the terms *symmetric* and *asymmetric role alignment* to refer to ways speakers and hearers construct their ethnolinguistic identities with or against the complex of voices within their semiotic universes. We draw directly on Agha's formulation in our use of the more general term *alignment*. We feel this more general term also covers the often forgotten option of "non-alignment", as discussed by Eriksen (2001) and Holliday (2011).

We see the nationalist paradigm in the way that teachers and students recognize one another as embodiments of nationalist essences. When self and other (re)presentation is understood as a singular alignment between one way of speaking and a national way of being, classroom discourse draws attention away from the subjective and context-bound nature of interculturality. A language classroom that instead acknowledges the diversity of linguistic forms available to language learners provides students with options for making choices about the different identities and locations with which they may want (and need) to align at different times. We turn now to a data set that highlights how the very same processes of objectification, prescription, and alignment may be redirected to broaden the field of legitimate linguistic and cultural practice to make voices from the Periphery audible in classroom discourse. We offer these data as an example of what language classrooms can look like when nationalist essentialism is rejected.

5.   Objectification, prescription, and alignment in an alternative to nationalist essentialism

The data in this section demonstrate how the processes of *alignment*, *objectification*, and *prescription* are used by a teacher to denaturalize nationalist standards through *stylization* (Coupland 2001) or active engagement with multi-voicedness (i.e. polyphony). This alternative expands the range of appropriate talk and legitimizes student engagement with the now audible linguistic diversity that ideologies of essentialized national languages obscure. These data illustrate the ubiquity of the discursive processes we identify: *Objectification*, *prescription* and *alignment* are not particular to nationalist standard practices. Further, and perhaps more importantly, they provide an example of what can be done in the intercultural language classroom to deconstruct nationalist standards by making evident the inherent variation present in any human language.

These data were recorded in Yogyakarta, Central Java in 2002 during a weekend retreat for incoming university freshmen to an Indonesian language and literature program. They provide an example of exposing students to phonetic variation in Bahasa Indonesia (Indonesian). The particular workshop excerpted here focused on methods for reading and understanding Indonesian poetry. *Regulative* and *instructional* discourse (Bernstein 2000) were in Indonesian. In revealing the "three secrets" of successful poetry reading, the instructor and professional storyteller We Es Ibnoe Sayy, switches between accents and styles of Indonesian. The English translation represents contrasts between Standard and Other-than-Standard Indonesians with font changes for different styles of speaking. Colloquial lexical items, signaled in bold, are translated as lexical and phonetic variations found in

American English varieties. Lines 18 and 20 are in italics as the instructor is quoting from Chairil Anwar's poem *"Doa"* (prayer).[6] Periods (.) indicate intonational boundaries and question marks (?) indicate a rise in pitch.

Teacher:

(1) kalau baca puisi	if [you] read poetry
(2) begini wajar atau **nggak**.	[is] like this proper or **ain't** [it].
(3) kalau orang **ngomong**.	if a person [be] **talkin**.
(4) wajar itu seperti **ngomong** biasa	proper is like **talkin** normal
(5) ini **lho** baca puisi itu.	this **right here** is reading poetry.
(6) kalau asalnya tegal ya.	if his origin [is] tegal yes.
(7) ya ada dialek tegal	yes there is [a] tegal dialect
(8) yang mungkin yang ya pengaruh ya	that maybe that yeah affects [it] yeah
(9) **ora** apa apa lah **kaya gic**.	[is] **no problem like dis**.
(10) **nek ora bisek**	**if [you] can no do [it]**
(11) **ajak kayak guek** ya.	**jus [do it] like me** yeah.
(12) **gitu**.	**like that**.
(13) kalau dia aslinya dari sumatera utara	if he['s] originally from northern Sumatra
(14) ya. **kita orang**	yes. **us folks**
(15) memang biasalah	of course [it is] normal
(16) **ngomong**nya begitu.	his **talkin** like that.
(17) tidak apa-apa itu.	that [is]n't [a] problem.
(18) *kepada pemeluk teguh*.	*to the firm embracer*.
(19) ya?	yes?
(20) *tuhanku. dalam termangu*.	*my lord. in [a] daze*.
(21) mungkin pengaruh dialek	maybe the influence of dialect
(22) **nggak** apa-apa.	**ain't** [a] problem.
(23) tetapi kemudian?	but then?
(24) dalam nada itu tadi. apa.	in that intonation just then. what.
(24) wajaran itu wajar seperti **ngomong**.	properness is proper like **talkin**.

Objectification occurs primarily in this passage through the use of intonational and phonetic variation to index different dialects. This particular type of objectification, which links salient linguistic features to sociocultural personas, is common, widespread, and well documented (Lippi-Green 2011; Mendoza-Denton 2008; Urciuoli 1996). As the poetic texts under discussion in this classroom are

---

6. The third person singular pronouns *dia* and *nya* translated as 'he' and 'his' are actually neutral with respect to gender. For a "thicker description" of this discourse event as advocated in Holliday (2011), see Cole (2004).

written and well known, there is no room for the students to engage lexical or syntactic variation when reading poetry. The instructor instead draws on the phonetic variation present in spoken Bahasa Indonesia and uses it to talk about Indonesian itself, in the process making audible the very variation that nationalist standard practices prescribe against.

In fact, and perhaps ironically, the whole thrust of this teaching moment is prescriptive, but in a way that turns on its head Indonesians' well-known and widely circulated motto *Menggunakan Bahasa Indonesia dengan baik dan benar* (Trans. 'Use Indonesian well and correctly').[7] Here the instructor prescribes the reproduction of Other-than-Standard variants in a formal university setting where his use of these styles and colloquial lexemes is unusual. The instructor argues that what is "proper" should be dictated by the shifting contexts, specifically by imagining the varied authors and audiences the students will engage when they read. Thus the alignment that emerges here is multiple and shifting reflecting the reality of Indonesian as a living language. Rather than presenting Indonesian as a single, discrete system linked to a singular, imagined national citizen, the instructor aligns with different voices from various regions in a performance that denaturalizes nationalist standard and its accompanying ideologies. These data thus demonstrate how *objectification, prescription* and *alignment* can also be used to highlight the very intra-national diversity that nationalist standard suppresses.

6. Discussion

Instructor discourse in the above data set denaturalizes essentialized boundaries by revealing the linguistic diversity always present within any "imagined nation" (Anderson 2006). His objectification of variation in the classroom presents a more complex, and thus more accurate, model of the linguistic landscape in which the students will eventually find themselves. By acknowledging and actively promoting this complexity in his metalinguistic talk in front of students, the teacher models a skill we might well want our interculturally trained language students to possess: a sensitivity to their sociolinguistic environment that includes a willingness to adapt their voices phonetically to adopt different versions of a language for communicating with each of the particular individuals they meet.

---

7. See Mohamad (2002) on the history and politics of standardizing Indonesian and Cole (2010) and Goebel (2008) on Indonesian ideologies of linguistic diversity.

The reader may object that the example we have presented has only demonstrated that we have shunted essentializing practices to the level of intra-national cultural groups rather than solving our essentialist problems. For isn't to imagine that everyone from Northern Sumatera has the same accent an essentializing move? Of course it is. We are not arguing that the utility of being able to identify *objectification, prescription*, and *alignment* processes in discourse is that they will automatically enable us to stop essentializing, as any grouping of even two individuals requires some degree of essentialism. Instead, we argue that the usefulness of this critical approach to discourse is in helping us to recognize moments when discursive processes are used to promote nationalist standard practices and when they are used to denaturalize them. We argue, then, that the essentialism in the featured classroom promotes interculturality, demonstrating how we might "alternat[e] between an attitude that discriminates and a thinking process which reconstructs universality" (Dervin 2011:9).

Applying Critical Discourse Analysis to this classroom further suggests that once prescription is revealed as context dependent, the door is open for discussing the variety of "propers" that students negotiate and manipulate outside the classroom (e.g., proper with their grandparents, proper with their friends, proper at the bar, proper at work, etc.). This sets the stage for negotiating the degree to which standard versions of languages should be the only ones legitimized in the language classroom. The denaturalization of Standard that occurs when linguistic diversity is audible in the language classroom also reveals alignment options and enables critical reflection about whom we align ourselves with when we limit ourselves to using one particular language variety in class. As language learning is by its very nature "a process of appropriation of others' voices" (Meadows 2010:98), we argue that the ability to recognize the discursive processes by which we limit or expand the vocal options we make available to students presents a way out of our continued participation in essentializing discourse and practice.

Simply acknowledging that linguistic variation exists "somewhere out there" is not enough. For successful Intercultural Education to happen, a shift in conventional wisdom is required. We argue that the solution to combating the limitations posed by nationalist essentialism is to embrace cultural and linguistic diversity in language classroom settings. A nationalist standard should not be the *only* vision for language classrooms, but one of many made available to students. Intercultural Education benefits when language classrooms create opportunities for students and teachers not just to recognize, but to engage legitimately with linguistic and cultural variation.

7. Conclusion

The problem facing intercultural language education is precisely the kind of essentializing that occurs in language classrooms dominated by the nationalist paradigm, that of reducing the complexity of languages and speakers to an imagined nationalist standard. When given over to nationalist essentialism, students are not given the opportunity to legitimately engage in linguistic and cultural diversity. They are not afforded the opportunity to see nationalist communities as contextually-dependent, discursive constructions in social practice. And they become participants in reinforcing the very linguistic, cultural, and ideological boundaries that have historically maintained and continue to perpetuate the unequal distribution of resources across human groups globally (Holliday 2011; Phillipson 1992). As the danger of nationalist essentialism lies in its ability to reduce the complexity of voices to which students are exposed thus ill-preparing them for intercultural encounters, it is important for classroom participants to be able to identify the specific linguistic processes by which "the norms imagined by nation… prevent these voices of complexity from being recognized" (Holliday 2011:61). Confronting the trap of nationalist essentialism thus requires close examination of the discursive practices that undergird it.

Like Holliday (2011:2), we see the charge of Intercultural Education as moving beyond a "sensitivity to the essentially different behaviours and values of the other and to cultivate individuals who may employ the ability to read culture which derives from underlying universal cultural processes." We offer Critical Discourse Analysis (CDA) as a valuable tool to help classroom participants acquire the ability to reflexively recognize and explicitly articulate the discursive processes by which language is used to shape both Self and Other communities. Without this ability, Intercultural Education will remain mired in essentialist and neo-essentialist practices, constantly "fall[ing] back on prescribed national cultural description" (Holiday 2011:15). CDA provides the means for teachers and students to challenge the commonsense of nationalist standard practices, thus opening the door to the heteroglossia that was there all along. We have demonstrated how the methods of CDA makes visible the processes of *objectification*, *prescription*, and *alignment* which serve in the interest of nationalist standard practices by reducing the range of legitimate sociolinguistic practices available to language students. We have also demonstrated how these same processes can serve in the interest of Intercultural Education to engage with the realities of linguistic and cultural diversity and raise awareness of the discursive context-bound construction of communities.

We position our chapter as a starting point for teachers. We suggest that one way to achieve the goals of Intercultural Education is to encourage students to practice dialectal variety as a way of engaging diversity and denaturalizing nationalist standard practices. This openness to variation sets the groundwork for student projects investigating and presenting on dialects and cultural practices specific to different regions rather than nations (e.g., the study of Japanese languages, in the plural). The benefit of this type of education is not that all of the students in the class will become proficient in multiple varieties, but that everyone in the class becomes aware of the reality of the particular, that every situation will be different, and that an intercultural perspective remains open to the emergent qualities of each encounter.[8] Intercultural Education is not about telling students how to behave appropriately in unfamiliar places with unfamiliar people, but rather to provide students with the analytical tools they need to figure out how to act in each emerging encounter.

References

Agha, A. (2003). The social life of cultural value. *Language & Communication, 23*(3–4), 231–273.

Agha, A. (2005). Voice, footing, enregisterment. *Journal of Linguistic Anthropology, 15*(1), 38–59.

Alptekin, C. (2002). Towards intercultural communicative competence in ELT. *ELT Journal, 56*(1), 57–64.

Anderson, B. (2006/1983). *Imagined communities: Reflections on the origins and spread of nationalism,* rev. edn. London: Verso.

Abdallah-Pretceille, M. (2007). Interculturalism as a paradigm for thinking about diversity. *Intercultural Education, 17*(5), 475–483.

Benveniste, E. (1996). The nature of pronouns. In P. Cobley (Ed.), *The communication theory reader* (pp. 63–69). London: Routledge.

Bernstein, B. (2000). *Pedagogy, symbolic control and identity: Theory, research, critique,* rev. edn. London: Rowman and Littlefield.

Billig, M. (1995). *Banal nationalism.* London: Sage.

Blommaert, J. & Bulcaen, C. (2000). Critical discourse analysis. *Annual Review of Anthropology, 29,* 447–466.

Blommaert, J. & Verschueren, J. (1992). The role of language in European nationalist ideologies. *Pragmatics, 2*(3), 35–375.

Bourdieu, P. & Passeron, J. (1977). *Reproduction in education, society and culture* (Trans. R. Nice). London: Sage.

Bourdieu, P. (1977). *Outline of a theory of practice* (Trans. R. Nice). Cambridge: Cambridge University Press.

---

8. See Cole (2007) for a brief sketch of using this approach in linguistics courses.

Bucholtz, M. (2003). Sociolinguistic nostalgia and the authentication of identity. *Journal of Sociolinguistics, 7*(3), 398–416.

Bucholtz, M. & Hall, K. (2004). Language and identity. In A. Duranti (Ed.), *A companion to linguistic anthropology* (pp. 369–394). Malden, MA: Blackwell.

Cole, D. (2004). *Performing 'unity in diversity' in Indonesian poetry: Voice, ideology, grammar, and change.* Unpublished Ph.D. dissertation. Tucson, AZ: University of Arizona.

Cole, D. (2007). Online voice tools can help us teach and learn about language attitudes (and be attentive to prescriptivism in academic written English). *Anthropology News, 48*(6), 11.

Cole, D. (2010). Enregistering diversity: Adequation in Indonesian poetry performance. *Journal of Linguistic Anthropology, 20*(1), 1–21.

Collins, J. (1991). Hegemonic Practice: Literacy and standard language in public education. In C. Mitchell & K. Weiler (Eds.), *Rewriting literacy: Culture and the discourse of the other* (pp. 229–253). New York, NY: Bergin & Garvey.

Coupland, N. (2001). Dialect stylization in radio talk. *Language in Society, 30,* 345–375.

Crystal, D. (2006). *The fight for English: How language pundits ate, shot, and left.* Oxford: Oxford University Press.

Davies, A. (2004). The native speaker in applied linguistics. In A. Davies & C. Elder (Eds.), *The handbook of applied linguistics* (pp. 431–450). Malden, MA: Blackwell.

Dervin, F. (2011). A plea for change in research on intercultural discourses: A 'liquid' approach to the study of the acculturation of Chinese students. *Journal of Multicultural Discourses, 6*(1), 37–52.

Eriksen, T. (2001). Between universalism and relativism: A critique of the UNESCO concept of culture. In J. Cowan, M. Dembour, & R. Wilson (Eds.), *Culture and rights: Anthropological perspectives* (pp. 127–148). Cambridge: Cambridge University Press.

Gellner, E. (2006/1983). *Nations and nationalism.* Ithaca, NY: Cornell University Press.

Goebel, Z. (2008). Enregistering, authorizing and denaturalizing identity in Indonesia. *Journal of Linguistic Anthropology, 18*(1), 46–61.

Golden, D. (2001). "Now, like real Israelis, let's stand up and sing": Teaching the national language to Russian newcomers in Israel. *Anthropology & Education Quarterly, 32*(1), 52–79.

Gupta, A. & Ferguson, J. (1997). Beyond 'culture': Space, identity, and the politics of difference. In A. Gupta & J. Ferguson (Eds.), *Culture, power, place: Explorations in critical anthropology* (pp. 33–51). Durham, NC: Duke University Press.

Hannerz, U. (1999). Reflections on varieties of culturespeak. *European Journal of Cultural Studies, 2*(3), 393–407.

Heller, M. (2008). Language and the nation-state: Challenges to sociolinguistic theory and practice. *Journal of Sociolinguistics, 12*(4), 504–524.

Hill, J. (2008). *The everyday language of white racism.* Chichester: Wiley-Blackwell.

Holliday, A. (2011). *Intercultural communication and ideology.* London: Sage.

Hymes, D. (1974). *Foundations in sociolinguistics: An ethnographic approach.* Philadelphia, PA: University of Pennsylvania Press.

Irvine, J. & Gal, S. (2000). Language ideology and linguistic differentiation. In P. Kroskrity (Ed.), *Regimes of language: Ideologies, polities, and identities* (pp. 35–84). Santa Fe, NM: School of American Research.

Irvine, J. (1989). When talk isn't cheap: Language and political economy. *American Ethnologist, 16*(2), 248–267.

Kedourie, E. (1994/1960). *Nationalism,* fourth expanded edn. Malden, MA: Blackwell.

Kramsch, C. (2003). From practice to theory and back again. In M. Byram & P. Grundy (Eds.), *Context and culture in language teaching and learning* (pp. 4–17). Clevedon: Multilingual Matters.

Kress, G. & Hodge, R. (1979). *Language as ideology*. London: Routledge.

Liddicoat, A. (2006). Learning the culture of interpersonal relationships: Students' understandings of personal address forms in French. *Intercultural Pragmatics, 3*(1), 55–80.

Lippi-Green, R. (2011). *English with an accent: Language, ideology, and discrimination in the United States,* second edn. London: Routledge.

McSweeney, B. (2002). Hofstede's model of national cultural differences and their consequences: A triumph of faith – a failure of analysis. *Human Relations, 55,* 89–117.

Meadows, B. (2009). *Nationalism and language learning at the US/Mexico border: An ethnographically-sensitive critical discourse analysis of the reproduction of nation, power, and privilege in an English language classroom.* Unpublished Ph.D. dissertation. Tucson, AZ: University of Arizona.

Meadows, B. (2010). 'Like my tutor and stuff, people I would talk to': Laying claim to imagined national communities in learner discourse. *Critical Inquiry in Language Studies, 7*(2–3), 88–111.

Mendoza-Denton, N. (2008). *Homegirls: Language and cultural practice among Latina youth gangs.* Malden, MA: Blackwell Publishing.

Milroy, J. & Milroy, L. (1985). *Authority in language: Investigating language prescription and standardization.* London: Routledge.

Mohamad. G. (2002). Forgetting: Poetry and the nation, a motif in Indonesian literary modernism after 1945. In K. Foulcher & T. Day (Eds.), *Clearing a space: Postcolonial readings of modern Indonesian literature* (pp. 183–211). Leiden: KITLV Press.

Park, J. (2010). Naturalization of competence and the neoliberal subject: Success stories of English language learning in the Korean conservative press. *Journal of Linguistic Anthropology, 20*(1), 22–38.

Phillipson, R. (1992). *Linguistic imperialism.* Oxford: Oxford University Press.

Preston, D. (2005). How can you learn a language that isn't there?. In K. Dziubalska-Kolaczyk & J. Przedlacka (Eds.), *English pronunciation models: A changing scene* (pp. 27–58). Bern: Peter Lang.

Rampton, B. (1990). 'Displacing the native speaker': Expertise, affiliation, and inheritance. *ELT Journal, 45*(2), 97–101.

Risager, K. (2007). *Language and culture pedagogy: From a national to a transnational paradigm.* Clevedon: Multilingual Matters.

Silverstein, M. (1979). Language structure and linguistic ideology. In R. Clyne, W. Hanks, & C. Hofcauer (Eds.), *The elements: A parasession on linguistic units and levels* (pp. 193–257). Chicago, IL: Chicago Linguistic Society.

Silverstein, M. (1996). Monoglot 'standard' in America: Standardization and metaphors of linguistic hegemony. In D. Brenneis & R. Macaulay (Eds.), *The matrix of language: Contemporary linguistic anthropology* (pp. 284–306). Boulder, CO: Westview.

Silverstein, M. (1998). The uses and utility of ideology: A commentary. In B. Schieffelin, K. Woolard & P. V. Kroskrity (Eds.), *Language ideologies, theory and practice.* Oxford: Oxford University Press.

Silverstein, M. (2003). The whens and wheres – as well as hows – of ethnolinguistic recognition. *Public Culture, 15*(3), 531–557.

Sinclair, J. & Coulthard, R. (1975). *Towards an analysis of discourse: The English used by teachers and pupils.* Oxford: Oxford University Press.

Spitulnik, D. (1998). Mediating unity and diversity: The production of language ideologies in Zambian broadcasting. In B. Schieffelin, K. Woolard, & P. Kroskrity (Eds.), *Language ideologies: Practice and theory* (pp. 163–188). New York, NY: Oxford University Press.

Tai, E. (2003). Rethinking culture, national culture, and Japanese culture. *Japanese Language and Literature, 37*(1), 1–26.

Ullman, C. (2010). "I live in Tuuk-SON": Rethinking the contexts of language learning along the Mexico-U.S. border. *TESOL Journal, 1*(4), 509–519.

Urciuoli, B. (1996). *Exposing prejudice: Puerto Rican experiences of language, race, and class.* Boulder, CO: Westview Press.

van Dijk, T. (2001). Critical discourse analysis. In D. Schiffrin, D. Tannen, & H. Hamilton (Eds.), *The handbook of discourse analysis* (pp. 352–371). Malden, MA: Blackwell.

Voloshinov, V. (1986/1973). *Marxism and the philosophy of language* [Trans. L. Matejka & I. R. Titunik]. Cambridge, MA: Harvard University Press.

Wiley, T. & Lukes, M. (1996). English-only and standard English ideologies in the US. *TESOL Quarterly, 30*(3), 511–535.

Wolfram, W. (1991). *Dialects and American English.* Englewood Cliffs, NJ: Prentice Hall.

Wodak, R., de Cillia, R., Reisigl, M., & Liebhart, K. (2009/1999). *The discursive construction of national identity,* second edn. Edinburgh: Edinburgh University Press.

Woolard, K. (1998). Language ideology as a field of inquiry. In B. Schieffelin, K. Woolard, & P. Kroskrity (Eds.), *Language ideologies: Practice and theory* (pp. 3–47). Oxford: Oxford University Press.

Young, R. (2009). *Discursive practice in language learning and teaching.* Malden, MA: Wiley-Blackwell.

Linking learning objectives of linguistic *savoir-faire* and intercultural competence in mobility experiences of teacher trainees

Mirjam Egli Cuenat and Lukas Bleichenbacher
University of Teacher Education St. Gallen

This paper presents a small-scale study to determine how the categories of Beacco's (2004) proposals for intercultural competence compare with linguistic competence as specified by the CEFR. Implementing a broad intercultural perspective such as defined by Byram (1997, 2008 *inter alia*) into foreign language education is clearly a great challenge for curriculum planners and teacher educators. The Council of Europe's (CoE) *Common European Framework of Reference* descriptors of communicative competence, widely used in curriculum design and teacher education across Europe, are benefitting from a high pedagogical and political legitimacy (Policy Forum CoE 2007). Hence, the formulation of intercultural learning objectives, related as closely as possible to the well-known level descriptions of linguistic proficiency of the CEFR, could be a valuable way of promoting the intercultural dimension on a broad basis. Beacco's reference descriptions of cultural competences ("*référentiel de compétences culturelles*" 2004) is very promising yet not well known in this regard. In our chapter, we will focus on his description of linguistic *savoir-faire* linked to intercultural competence of teacher trainees spending time abroad, as an emblematic curricular element promoting intercultural and plurilingual competence.

We will first review and assess previous work and debates on the linguistic correlates of intercultural competence, with a focus on communicative activities (*savoir-faire*). We then test our insights against a corpus of interviews which encapsulates the intercultural experiences of a small group of foreign exchange students at a Swiss teacher education college, combining approaches from discourse analysis, conversational analysis and interactional sociolinguistics, such as proposed, for instance, by Brown & Lewinson (1988), Bronckart (1997), Traverso (2004), and Kasper & Omori (2010). Through the analysis of our data, our aims are to pinpoint meaningful and concrete discursive features corresponding to a selected sample of Beacco's descriptors, and to show, more generally, how linguistic analysis can contribute to enroot, in a systematic way, the dimension of intercultural competence in foreign language learning and teaching.

1. Introduction

Implementing a broad intercultural perspective such as defined by Byram (1997, 2008 *inter alia*) into foreign language education is, in today's world, both a necessity, but also clearly a great challenge for curriculum planners and teacher educators. The Council of Europe's (CoE) *European Language Portfolio* and the *Common European Frame of Reference* (CEFR) descriptors of communicative competence, widely used in curriculum design and teacher education across Europe, now benefit from a high pedagogical and political legitimacy (Council of Europe 2000, 2007). Hence, the formulation of intercultural learning objectives, related as closely as possible to the well-known level descriptions of linguistic proficiency of the CEFR, could be a valuable way of promoting the intercultural dimension on a broad basis. Beacco's (2004) approach, published in French, though very promising in this regard, is not yet well known. In our chapter, we will focus on the description of linguistic *savoir-faire* linked to intercultural competence of teacher trainees spending time abroad, as an emblematic curricular element promoting intercultural and plurilingual competence. Our main questions are the following:

- Is it possible to link the reference levels in the CEFR with descriptors of intercultural competences?
- In other words, is it possible to describe the relationship between linguistic competences as formulated by the CEFR and descriptors of intercultural competences clearly enough to formulate learning objectives where both dimensions are expressed?
- If so, which linguistic phenomena can be linked (i.e., seen to represent) the described competences?
- And, more generally, in what way can linguistic discourse analysis contribute to enroot, in a systematic way, the dimension of intercultural competence in foreign language learning and teaching?

In Section 2 we will present the challenge of articulating objectives of linguistic and intercultural competences in the context of language learning and teaching, and discuss one possible solution, namely Beacco's 'reference description of cultural competences' ("*référentiel de compétences culturelles*"). We will assess the difficulty and the risk of this task in the light of what has been presented before, and study one aspect of the reference description in more detail. In Section 3 we will describe the approach we chose in order to make the selected competences more tangible at the linguistic surface of discourse. In Section 4 we present data from a small corpus compiled among guest students studying for one semester in a Swiss teacher training institution. Based on some exemplary analyses of conversational interactions, we demonstrate how specific discourse analytic methods can be used to pinpoint the joint development of linguistic and intercultural competence in the context of education.

2.   Articulating objectives of linguistic and intercultural competence

2.1   Linking linguistic and intercultural competence in the context of language learning: A tricky issue

Commentators disagree on the importance of intercultural competence in the context of foreign language education, though most tend to agree with Christ (2007) that its role is a central rather than just an auxiliary one. A major problem is that the academic concept of intercultural competence is itself difficult to grasp. Among various scholarly contributions, the most influential model is that proposed by Byram & Zarate (1994), where the notion of intercultural competence is divided into six components on a continuum that encompasses factual knowledge, practical skills, and attitudes that can lead towards humanitarian action, designated by the terms *savoir, savoir comprendre, savoir apprendre/savoir-faire, savoir-être* and *savoir s'engager*; the same notions reappear, albeit in a slightly different organization, in Byram's more recent model of "intercultural citizenship" (2008). Foreign language competence is not included in this conceptualization, as Sercu (2005: 3f.) points out: "Communicative competence itself can in fact be considered a sixth *savoir*, namely *savoir communiquer*". A likely reason for the researchers' endeavours to conceive the progression of intercultural competence as independent from foreign language proficiency lies in the continued refusal, in much recent work in applied linguistics, to consider the native speaker (and, one could add, the representative of a 'native culture') as the only appropriate model for a learner (see, for instance, Alred et al. 2003: 4). Likewise, if models based on a binary opposition between L1 and L2, or culture of origin and target culture, are disregarded in favour of the notion of a "third space" or "third place" (Kramsch 2009: 244), which is only constructed once intercultural (rather than just transcultural) encounters actually take place, it becomes less clear which foreign language one is supposed to measure the proficiency in. Hu and Byram (2009: xx) criticize approaches which devote no attention whatsoever to language, and also those in which "the foreign language level" and "the stages of intercultural subjectivity [...] are placed in direct relationship with each other". In sum, what they question is any kind of direct, necessary, and bidirectional link between the two sets of competence – a critique which warrants an assessment of Beacco's model, since it is precisely this that the model proposes. In the following section, Beacco's model is presented in more detail.

2.2   J.-C. Beacco's proposal for a 'reference description of cultural competences'

Following the principle of 'reference descriptions' leading to the formulation of testable learning objectives and the creation of 'identifiable objects of teaching', in his 2004 chapter, Beacco puts forward an inventory of cultural competence descriptors for foreign language education.[1] These descriptors, on the one hand, are given their corresponding language competence levels from A1 to C2, according to the Common Frame of Reference (CEFR); on the other hand, they are matched with language competence descriptors.

Beacco's reference guide has to be seen in the larger context of moves coordinated by the Council of Europe to concretely link the CEFR descriptors for the five skills (listening, reading, spoken interaction, spoken production, and writing) with the linguistic material of different languages (see Beacco & Byram 2007: 33 and 73 for a discussion of the usefulness of reference descriptions). While these skills are seen as valuable for learning any foreign languages, a series of reference descriptions for different languages (such as English, French and German) were subsequently produced with support from the Council of Europe, in order to assist curriculum designers in defining learning objectives in a given language. During the compilation of the B2 reference description for French, Beacco proposed to add the dimension of cultural as well as intercultural competence to the communicative goals. However, Beacco repeatedly highlights his awareness of the difficult nature of this enterprise, one of many problems being the fact that intercultural competence cannot be uniquely accounted for by using linguistic categories.

Beacco distinguishes between five dimensions of cultural competence; however, his categories do not map easily onto Byram's and Zarate's *savoirs* mentioned above. Beacco proposes the dimension of *action* (roughly corresponding to *savoir-faire*), the *ethnolinguistic dimension* (awareness of the pragmatic norms of the target language, especially linguistic politeness), the *dimension of explicitly*

---

1.   There are other interesting proposals for the description of intercultural (communicative) competences including a learning progression, elaborated in the context of European projects, for instance the evaluation grid of the Leonardo project "INCA", the descriptions of the ECML project "ICCinte" (Lázár et al. 2007), and those of the Socrates project "LOLIPOP". Except for the last (for a critical discussion, cf. Schneider et al. 2009: 79ff.), the grids are not matched with the CEFR reference levels.

intercultural communication (discussed in detail below), the *interpretative dimension* (how well the language learner can interpret, in a wide sense, L2 texts and realities), and finally the *educational dimension*, which is concerned with exploiting intercultural experiences with the aim of influencing learners' attitudes (much like *savoir-être*) towards more openness, while avoiding a simple 'relativist multiculturalism' (Beacco 2004: 281). The French reference descriptions, for instance level B2 (Beacco et al. 2004), also contains lists of the linguistic material relevant for any specific intercultural competence, for instance expressions of politeness and the words needed to discuss culturally relevant topics (Chapter 9: 327).

In this chapter, we have chosen to focus on *explicitly intercultural communication* for several reasons: Firstly, interactions that are explicitly about intercultural matters are common at any stage of an intercultural experience, including those created as the result of student mobility, and among any constellation of participants. Secondly, they take place even in contexts that are not explicitly educational, for example in informal meetings between students from different countries, with or without representatives of what Beacco calls the 'target society'. Finally, the notion of interaction plays a larger role in explicitly intercultural communication than in Beacco's ethnolinguistic and interpretative dimension, because it is primarily concerned with face-to-face interactions, and thus with the extent to which metacultural discourse is actively co-constructed in varying kinds of conversations, whether spoken or mediated. In Table 1, the descriptors for explicitly intercultural communication are illustrated.

In this table, as well as throughout Beacco's chapter (see Beacco 2004: 267ff.), the descriptors of levels of intercultural competence and the relevant linguistic features are characterized by similar patterns of progression on different levels; this is also true in the explicitly intercultural communication domain. The intercultural progress that is relevant to the kind of explicitly intercultural communication at hand encompasses the ability to describe one's own and to foreign cultures, to assume own or foreign cultural viewpoints, and to mediate between different cultures from a vantage point of critical distance.

On the linguistic side, there is an increase in the complexity of the situations in which the learner is expected to function, combined with a decrease in their predictability. Hence, in the domain of face-to-face encounters, the learner moves from simulated conversations (A1) and everyday interactions (B1, B2) to debates in academic contexts (C2). Likewise, at levels B2 and above, there is an emphasis on demanding, monologic and more argumentative text types, such as autobiographical narratives or extensive written work. Also, at higher levels (B1 and above), intercultural communication should be possible even if one's interlocutors are less benevolent or even openly critical, and the learners should be able to manage controversial debates where their point of view may appear isolated (see Section 3

Table 1. Selected descriptors for intercultural and linguistic competences at CEFR levels B1–C1 (based on Beacco 2004: 270f.; our translation)

Level	Intercultural competences	Linguistic competences
B1	Participating successfully in interactions about a different culture, in one's L1 and L2, with benevolent interlocutors. Describing aspects of one's own and different cultures.	Being able to use the relevant vocabulary and speech acts, to adopt a neutral tone, and to argue from a cultural point of view.
B2	As above, though also with critical interlocutors. Ability to question metacultural arguments given by representatives of a different culture.	Producing monologic analyses in discourse. Showing awareness of one's interlocutors' attitudes and ideologies. Arguing in a quite nuanced way from a cultural point of view. Producing autobiographical narratives.
C1	Producing more or less favourable accounts of one's interlocutors' society without threatening their faces. Being able to mediate between a different culture and one's own without demonstrating one's affiliation with the different culture.	Presenting the results of one's analyses in professional, academic or official contexts, a scientific register, and from a cultural, socio-political and historical point of view. Contributing to conversation where one needs to compensate for one's minority status.

below). As regards the learner's freedom to exploit their plurilingual repertoire, at levels A1–B1 the learners may use their first language or other languages, as appropriate, both actively or passively, whereas at level B2 and above, the descriptors refer to the target language only. Finally, the main objectives of *explicitly intercultural interaction* are always geared to mediation. The allophone ('foreign') speaker either seeks for a deeper access to a target language community or tries to convey knowledge about his or her own community of origin, in a context that involves members of the target language community. Moreover, the same speaker can try to convey knowledge about the target language community to someone else, either a member of his or her own community, or a third party (ibid.: 268).

3.   Materials and method

Our hypothesis is that the discursive analysis of examples of *explicitly intercultural communication* matching Beacco's descriptions can help to create a more concrete link between levels of linguistic and intercultural competence. A detailed discourse analysis of concretely realized examples of oral and written discourse corresponding to the linguistic activities described by the CEFR descriptors is also the means theoretically privileged by Beacco for specifying the linguistic material of the CEFR-Levels in a specific language (Beacco 2004: 5). Hence the textbook accompanying the French B2 reference level offers a series of methodological suggestions for the individual users in order to be able to characterize a wider range of discourse genres not covered by the reference description (e.g. Traverso 2004 for the discursive analysis of interaction). In a similar vein, we make use of discourse analysis to assess how Beacco's rather abstract descriptors of linguistic and intercultural competence can be applied to actual discourse, with the aim of pinpointing its linguistic components more precisely. By doing so, our aim is to complement and systematize the inventory of discourse phenomena given for French competence descriptors, e.g. at CEFR level B2. In specific, we studied the following phenomena that we consider fundamental in the fields of pragmatics (Brown & Levinson 1988), discourse analysis (Bronckart 1997), conversation analysis (Traverso 2004) and interactional sociolinguistics (Rampton 1995); see also Kasper & Omori (2010):

- Cohesion, use of discourse markers, topic development
- Structuring and co-construction of discourse sequences
- Linguistic politeness (face work)
- Style shifting and code-switching

The data were collected in the context of a student exchange programme of primary school teacher training students in their early twenties who came to a teacher training college in German-speaking Switzerland for one semester. Two students, Amélie and Hugues, come from a similar institution in the French-speaking part of Switzerland, Britta is from Germany and Karin from the Netherlands. All students have a knowledge of German at least at B1, though none is functional in Swiss German, the variety used for all informal functions in the area. While the courses they attended were mainly in English, German was the default language of the teaching internship which was part of their programme of study at the Swiss host institution. To establish contact with our informants, we participated as lecturers in one of the students' regular classes, taught by an experienced foreign language methodology lecturer, who also acts as the institution's student and staff mobility coordinator. In this class, the students were instructed to self-assess their plurilingual and intercultural competence using different instruments, and to reflect on their experiences in discussions, which were videotaped. We also met the students individually for an observation of their performance during their teaching internships, and for a semi-structured interview about their personal and professional experiences while in German-speaking Switzerland. As a starting point, we considered Beacco's descriptors for the linguistic correlates of explicitly intercultural communication for the CEFR levels B1, B2 and C1, the relevant levels for the students (see Table 1 above). In the following section, this framework is applied to our analysis of the students' discourse.

4.   Analysis

Our analyses are mainly taken from the semi-structured interviews with three of the four learners, while the last example is taken from one of the meetings in class. We start with Amélie, the L1 speaker of French, whose overall performance both in German and English as foreign languages is situated broadly at the B1 level, and then move on to Britta, the L1 speaker of German with an English competence at least at level B2. Their performance is then contrasted with that of Hugues, the French L1 speaker who is at C2 in English (these ratings are ours (the authors')). Finally, we add some observations of a classroom interaction where Karin, the L1 speaker of Dutch, their teacher, and the two of us were present.

4.1   Amélie: Linguistic competences lacking in L2, intercultural competence appearing in L1

Excerpt 1 (M = Mirjam Egli Cuenat, A = Amélie; German/French original in italics followed by our translation)

M: *und eh, eh, Sie selber erm, sind sie in einem einem in einem multikulturellen Umfeld aufgewachsen?*
     and er, er, you yourself, er, did you grow up in a a in a multicultural environment?

A: *nein*
     no

M: *zuhause*
     at home

A: *nein nein*
     no no

M: *nicht*
     not

A: *meine zwei Eltern sind, also kamen, also, aus Genf*
     my two parents are, well come, well, from Geneva

M: *ja*
     yes

A: *aber wir wohnen im Waadtland*
    but we live in Vaud

M: *ja*
    yes

A: *aber ja meine Grossvater, er, kam, aus erm, Thurgau*
    but yes my grandfather, he, came, from erm, Thurgau

M: *ja*
    yes

A: *und also seine Nachname ist <typical German-speaking surname> ja also*
    and well his surname is <typical German-speaking surname> yes well

M: *also (laughter) sie haben ein wenig Schweizerdeutsch*
    well (*laughter*) they have a bit of Swiss German

A: *ja also meine Grosseltern kommen aus Sch- ja also Sch- diese Teile*
    yes well my grandparents come from Sw- es well Sw- these parts

M: *okay, haben sie mit ihnen Schweizerdeutsch gesprochen?*
    okay, did they speak Swiss German to them [their children]?

A: *sie haben nicht mit meine Eltern gesprochen weil also, meine Grosseltern, also*
    mein Grossvater eh f- finde findet das schrecklich, er, er
    they didn't speak to my parents because well, my grandparents, well my
    grandfather erm f- finds it terrible, erm, erm

M: *also seine eigene Muttersprache findet er schrecklich*
    so he finds his own native language terrible

A: *ja also er war also er hat im Genf ge- also erm gewachsen*
    yes well he was, well he has g- well erm grown in Geneva

M: *ist aufgewachsen*
    has grown up

A: *ja und dann ist er also hat er in Zürich gearbeitet ja*
    yes and then he was well he worked in Zurich yes

M: *mhm*

A: *ja also er wollte nicht diese Sprache, erm, an meine Mutter lernen*
    yes well uhm he didn't want to learn [sic] this language, erm, to my mother

M: *mhm aber er selber war er auch oder ist er auch zweisprachig?*
    mhm but he himself is he also, or was he also bilingual?

A: *ja-*
    yes

M: *ah*

A: *also er, ah, so, ja, er hat so, ja so, ja*
    well he, er, well, yes, he was like, yes like, yes

M: *es ist ein bisschen kompliziert*
    it's all a bit complicated.

Excerpt 2

M: *haben sie denn jetzt das Gefühl jetzt wo sie in der deutschen Schweiz sind – seit ein paar Monaten – haben Sie sich irgendwie angepasst an die deutsche Schweiz*
do you have the impression, now that you've been in German-speaking Switzerland – for a few months – have you adapted in some way to German-speaking Switzerland

A: *ja also, erm, ff- (pause) ich mein, also eh erste Mal, erm also ich weiss nicht was sagen aber erm* yes well erm ff- (pause) I mean well eh first time, erm well I don't know what to say but erm

M: *Sie können es auch auf Französisch sagen XX*
you can also say it in French XX

A: *erm wenn ich jemand über Schwyzerd- ehm über ja also über Schwytzerdütsch Kultur spreche eh also versteh nicht so viel also maintenant que j'ai vécu en Suisse allemande*
erm if I somebody talks about German-sp- erm about yes well about German-speaking culture eh well don't understand much, well now that I've lived in German-speaking Switzerland

M: *mhm*

A: *Röstigraben*[2] *(laughter)*

M: *oui*
yes

A: *(laughter) je comprends moins enfin je vois moins euh le Röschtigraben, la différence enfin (laughter)*
(laughter) no I understand less, in fact I can see it less, the "Röstigraben", the difference *(laughter)*

M: *ah avant il vous paraissait plus important*
ah, before you found it more substantial

A: *en fait avant euh je voyais je voyais les Suisses allemands différents*
in fact before, uhm, I found I found the German-speaking Swiss different

M: *ah*

A: *et je comprends pas je comprenais pas parce que je n'ai pas vécu ici*
and I don't understand, I didn't understand because I didn't live here

M: *oui*
yes

C: *et donc je, il y avait le Röstigraben, enfin, mais maintenant je, je comprends mieux, enfin, ouais, je comprends mieux eh la culture suisse allemande*

---

2. "Rösti" is a typical Swiss German potato dish, which has given the name to the concept of the "Röstigraben" ('Rösti gulf'), a folk designation of the linguistic and (supposed) cultural barrier between German- and French-speaking Switzerland.

and so I, there was the "Röstigraben", in fact, but now I, I understand better, in fact, yes, I understand Swiss German culture better

M: *mhm*

A: *et euh il y a m il y a plus c- cette barrière*
and uh, there is erm, there isn't this barrier anymore

M: *ouais et euh qu'e qu'est-ce que vous comprenez mieux vous dites que vous comprenez mieux la culture suisse allemande, c'est quoi alors, ça m'intéresse*
yes and er what what do you understand better, you've said that you understand Swiss German culture better, so what is this, this interests me

A: *(laughter) par exemple l'écologie ici il y a beaucoup enfin il y a beaucoup plus de vélos on trie les déchets, enfin je fais ça aussi à la maison mais c'est vrai que chez nous en Suisse romande on fait moins*
(laughter) for instance ecology, here there are in fact there are many more bikes, people separate waste, in fact I also do that at home but in the end where I live in French-speaking Switzerland we do it less

M: *mhm*

A: *maintenant je comprends mieux enfin je suis en vélo aussi, je trie les déchets il y a des choses comme ça qui sont différentes maintenant que je vis avec. Mais c'est vrai que maintenant que je vis ici mais c'est vrai que, je me rappelle plus des préjugés qu'on a sur les Suisses allemands*
now I understand better, in fact I also ride a bike, I also separate my waste, there are things like that which are different, now I cope with them. But it's true that now that I live here, but it's true that I can't remember the prejudice anymore that we have against the German-speaking Swiss

M: *vous ne vous rappelez plus (laughter)*
you can't remember it *(laughter)*

A: *je dois demander à ma mère (laughter)*
I have to ask my mother *(laughter)*

M: *et elle peut vous dire*
and she can tell you

A: *oui*
yes

M: *mhm*

C: *XX*

M: *donc vous avez l'impression d'avoir changé*
so you have the impression that you have changed

The interviewer started the interview in German, her L1. Amélie was first asked whether she had grown up in a multicultural environment, which she denied, but then added that her grandfather had migrated from German-speaking to French-speaking Switzerland. Asked about the grandfather's attitudes towards German as his L1, Amélie attempted to sketch the biography of his migration in more detail. However, reaching the limits of her L2 proficiency when asked about her grandfather's bilingualism, she gave up, and the interviewer ratified her difficulty, expressing her understanding: 'it's all a bit complicated'.

Compared to Beacco's descriptor of B2 (see above), when speaking German, there is an obvious lack of differentiated vocabulary and fluency, resulting in corrections and an abundant use of backchannels by the interviewer. Even with a very cooperative interlocutor, the speaker is hardly able to go beyond a rather one-dimensional, naïve and factual representation of her linguistic and cultural background and hence of her relationship to the target culture. The use of discourse markers structuring the discourse across turns as well as within the turns is very basic and linear; she uses no other coordinating expressions than "also" ('in fact'). Moreover, there is some ambiguity in the use of anaphoric expressions, such as "meine Eltern" ('my parents') vs. "meine Mutter" ('my mother'); it is far from clear if both parents have Swiss German origins.

The excerpt in her L1, on the other hand, shows that she is able to co-construct a more differentiated view of cultural difference and change. Amélie appears unable to answer a question about cultural adaptation, but when the interviewer encourages her to use French, she states that her perception of the difference in mentalities between the two language groups has changed. She refers to a common stereotype of German speakers having higher environmental awareness, but then uses the term 'prejudice' herself and seems at a loss to reconstruct how she conceived of German speakers before her exchange semester, claiming that she would need to ask her mother about the prejudice. In describing this change of mind, she uses complex discourse structuring and flexible manipulation of language, including markers such as "enfin" ('in the end') and "mais c'est vrai" ('but it's true that'), which are indicative of a critical rethinking and reformulation of her ideas. Her success in describing the process is reflected by the interviewer's acknowledgement, "so you have the impression that you have changed", which contrasts strikingly with the communicative breakdown at the end of the previous excerpt. Hence, Amélie is co-constructing this more complex perception and change of identity with the interlocutor, and the interaction shows clear linguistic and discursive traces of this. To sum up, the analyses show quite an interesting case: In French, her language of origin, Amélie explains a change of perception which cannot be verbalized in German, the target language, due to a lack of linguistic competence, even if the interlocutor is very benevolent and cooperative. The analysis shows that for this kind of intercultural competence, there is a need for a certain linguistic-discursive competence: a broader vocabulary, flexibility for developing thematic strands, and for co-constructing analytical sequences – a competence which can be linguistically described. This notion of necessary

conversational flexibility linked to the capacity to talk about intercultural problems, to make oneself understood, and to proceed from there in one's learning
process is very much compatible with the discourse analytic approach by Pekarek
Doehler et al. (2008), who describe competences of discourse organisation in
interaction (abbreviated *CODI*), trace their development, construct oral competences as 'teachable objects' and seek to evaluate them, while creating a direct link
to descriptors of the CEFR.

4.2   Britta: Contesting the interviewer's account of the target culture

In her interview, Britta demonstrates an English proficiency of B2 to C1, and uses
the appropriate vocabulary and structures to answer a number of questions about
different aspects of her stay in Switzerland At this level, according to Beacco's
descriptors, she should also be able to comment on more problematic aspects of
her intercultural experience. The interviewer asks her about any negative experiences during her semester abroad in Switzerland. Somewhat unwillingly, she
mentions that she is experiencing some of her Swiss acquaintances as rather reserved, and not displaying enough initiative for her to get to know them beyond
a superficial stage:

Excerpt 3 (B = Britta, L = Lukas Bleichenbacher)

B: mh because you you sometimes see students walking around and you just say
      'hi' and then that's all because they they you do you do a class er lesson together
      but I don't know anything about these students for example. (*chuckles*)

L: mhm, ja, ja it's something it's something one one frequently says that there is
      about about Swiss Swiss people there is –

B: yeah but it also depends on the person because it's nothing erm, it it also
      happens in in Germany, we have courses together and you don't know who you
      were, each other, that happens but it also happens the other way round. So you
      should not really think like black and white, I don't like this, I don't like this.

Britta mentions the reservedness of some Swiss students as a negative experience.
Somewhat unnecessarily, the interviewer immediately ratifies and agrees with her
statement, since it is in line with a well-known auto- and heterostereotype about
the Swiss. The interviewer tries to make Britta comfortable: 'you're entitled to
this opinion; many other newcomers to Swiss society have made similar experiences'. However, once Britta realizes that her opinion has been linked to the notion of stereotyping, she first qualifies and then almost withdraws it. She shows
awareness of how by default, stereotypes can cause problems in communication,

and highlights her disapproval of them. In her answer, she rejects the notion of generalization across individuals ("it also depends on the person") and 'nations' ("it also happens in Germany"), and the emphatic repetition of "I don't like it" suggests that her refusal of the simple stereotype 'the Swiss are reserved' is a viewpoint she feels strongly about (which she also underlines in other parts of the interview), rather than just a well-sounding phrase to make the interviewer happy. Britta's meta-intercultural discourse is both personal and logically well-founded, with a correct and reasonably complex use of different conjunctions and coordinators ("and", "because", "but", "also", "so") that juxtapose and contrast different viewpoints. Most strikingly, she is absolutely capable of containing the double potential face threats to the interviewer, first in that he is Swiss like the people she complains about, and secondly when she rejects his interpretation of her criticism: her disagreement is prefigured by an initial agreement ("yeah"), and she goes at length to discuss precisely why she rejects the interviewer's suggestion. In sum, her performance fully corresponds to both the intercultural and linguistic competence that Beacco outlines at level B2 and partly C1, where reasonably complex metacultural discourse mirrors the ability to mark distance towards the interlocutor's opinions about his own community, as well as to question opinions on her own, without the risk of threatening the interlocutor's face – and, more generally, a willingness to reject simple stereotypes.

4.3   Hugues: Flexible manipulation of codes, assuming and quoting different viewpoints

The third student, Hugues, has a similar background to Amélie's, but a much higher competence in both English and German as foreign languages. From the outset of the interview, Hugues' answers are appropriately detailed, well-structured, and display a high degree of accommodation; for instance, he draws meaningful intercultural comparisons at an early stage in the interview, before having actually been asked to do so, because he obviously anticipates the interviewer's intentions and interests. Later on, he is asked to analyze an intercultural aspect of the host society that does not involve himself as a foreigner, but the children in kindergarten whom he teaches during his teaching practise. Since there is a fair percentage of children from immigrant backgrounds, who speak little to no German at home, the question arises whether in kindergarten, it makes sense to use the Swiss German dialect (the community language, or 'L' variety in German-speaking diglossic situation in Switzerland), or rather Standard German, the language of schooling (which is also the potential L2 target variety of the immigrant children's parents). The question is controversial in public discourse; while most specialists are clearly in favour of using the Standard, there are political moves in some Swiss cantons to ban the Standard from pre-school education. For the following excerpt, it is important to understand that Hugues is a newcomer to this debate, and is unlikely to ever have thought about these issues either in his private life, or even as a part of his education in his home institution (since diglossia is virtually non-existent in French-speaking Switzerland). When asked, Hugues rapidly offers an accurate and concise account of the kindergarten's policy, the official guidelines, and the conflicting debates surrounding the issue. Then, the interviewer asks him to consider the issue from the young learners' point of view:

Excerpt 4 (H = Hugues, L = Lukas Bleichenbacher)

L: which which is easier for the kids if if it's just that that argument, I mean what what do they understand and speak better themselves, is it is it actually Swiss German or High German, or does it depend?

H: it depends on the kids because you have the you have these kids er with really erm both parents erm from the Balkan or wherever, so they're not that much in contact with *Schweizerdütsch*, I mean I guess their only contact with *Schweizerdütsch* is here in the kindergarten so but at home they speak their mother tongue or maybe a bit German but the German the parents learnt arriving here so.

L: might be High German as well or a mixture.

H: yeah. And yeah so for instance the teacher has "*wer ist dran*" and the kids "*I bi dra I bi dra I bi dra*", so it's not the point is not having them speak High German but just being in contact and hearing, and memorizing as much as possible. Because I think if you only start in the first grade it's like learning a second language already, and this transition must be like smooth from the kindergarten.

Despite the slightly simplistic nature of the interviewer's question, and his rather informal style, as seen in the second comment "Might be…", Hugues presents the problem in an accurately complex way, by depicting a possible scenario for the linguistic background of some of the immigrant children (and simultaneously acknowledging, with the phrase "I mean I guess", that he is only speculating). In his second turn, he initially accommodates to the interviewer's informality ("Yeah. And yeah so for instance …"), but then independently steers his discourse onto a more educational and academic level. He does so first by quoting relevant typical answers in the appropriate variety: the teacher's question "*wer ist dran*", 'whose turn is it', is given in Standard German, whereas the pupils often respond in Swiss German with "*I bi dra*", 'it's my turn' ("*Ich bin dran*" in Standard German), using code-switching between three varieties strategically to illustrate his observation. He then accounts for the children's linguistic performance in accurate, and increasingly more complex vocabulary, ("being in contact", "hearing", "memoriz-ing", "transition … smooth"), and concludes by questioning the commonly held view that Swiss and Standard German are not different languages. All these clearly point to Beacco's notion of the "scientific register"; Hugues' performance in this explicitly intercultural interaction qualifies as clearly on the level of C1, not just because he fulfills the linguistic criteria outlined by Beacco with respect to his skilled shifting between different appropriate styles, but also because he does so with a fluency and competence that enable him to function on a par with a fully proficient user of English. He displays the corresponding intercultural competence by accommodating, much like Britta in the previous example, to his interviewer's style of speaking and his interests, but also by skillfully deepening the level of metacultural analysis according to his needs, from a wider cultural and socio-po-litical perspective. In terms of intercultural competence, he does not just display openness to aspects of the host culture in general. Rather, he demonstrates a de-tailed knowledge and appreciation of the complex multicultural society among the children in the kindergarten, and accounts for the savoir-faire (teaching in the Standard while remaining open to the dialect) that is necessary to ensure in-tercultural understanding – not on a theoretical level, or even his own or an adult teacher's viewpoint, but from the perspective of the young learners themselves. Thereby he also fulfills Beacco's C1 criterion of being able to mediate between cultures, without demonstrating affiliation to the different cultures.

4.4   In-jokes in the classroom: Linguistic sensitivity without intercultural sensitivity

Our analysis so far has shown that Beacco's descriptors are indeed both useful and relevant for the combined assessment of linguistic and intercultural proficiency, provided one extends their application beyond the classical dichotomy of source and target culture, to include scenarios with the use of English as a lingua franca, rather than just German as the host language of the community. In the analysis of our last excerpt, we assess to what extent a fluent and engaged debate, which is ex-plicitly intercultural in Beacco's sense, just like the examples analyzed above, fails to result in any insightful metacultural analysis. The scene was recorded during a classroom seminar towards the end of the international students' stay, in which they were asked to reflect in a general way on different aspects of their stay, and specifically on their in-group interactions. As an example, the students mention that they indulge in a number of inside jokes, and they are then asked to describe these further. As an example, Hugues quotes a Physical Education instructor who finished a lesson by saying that the students "can go and have a *douche*", rather than "shower" ("*Dusche*" in German), unwittingly using an English word that a proficient English user would understand as a reference to feminine hygiene (most likely in the context of obscene bantering):

Excerpt 5 (H = Hugues, L = Lukas Bleichenbacher, T = Teacher, B = Britta, K = Karin)

H: and most of them [the in-jokes] are related to the fact of the er weird English of some of our teachers with with a mix of German

L: mhm

H: of course it's the same was with the sport, it was 'and now you can have a shower', especially 'douche' in English has an another meaning, and that's what's really funny. So most of them are based on content, language, funny things.

T: I realize we've been speaking about the follow ups on Monday, sometime you mentioned the the quality or the sound of High German that people around you produce, the man from <place name>, the lady from <place name>, the lady at the cashier in <shop name>, so that comes back nearly every week or every two weeks, so I think you are very sensibilized in this er kind of field, in listening exactly, imitating, sharing, and also kidding about.

B: it's not like we want to be mean or something but but we just recognize and of course it's funny especially for me, when strictly speaking most of the time when people say 'I speak High German now' and then I'm like 'what, what is this?' and –

K: and especially if they use –

B: t's only hard to understand –

K: but it's funny when they start 'okay today I speak High German'

H: '*also Grüezi mitenand*' (*laughter*)
'well, hello everybody' (*laughter*) [Hugues is quoting a typical formal Swiss German greeting that would be used by teachers even before teaching or lecturing in the Standard]

K: and then it goes five minutes like that 'uh-oh, High German, High German' (*laughter*) then it goes two minutes in High German, then in Swiss German again.

H: (*miming*) you should hold up a sign. (*laughter*)

T: 'Only High German please'

In this conversation, the international students use a variety of metalinguistic ob-servations, but also stylized crossings (Rampton 1995) into different varieties (L2 English, Swiss Standard German, Swiss German) to create a sense of community which pokes mild fun at those members of the host community who lack their international and academic backgrounds. The relaxed and inspiring classroom atmosphere created by their teacher enables the students to refer to a mildly obscene in-joke at the expense of their teacher's colleague. The teacher, however, does not perceive this as a face threat against a member of her institution; instead, she compliments the students for their acute sense of linguistic analysis that she has often witnessed during the discussions of their joint field trips (the "follow-ups"). Britta reacts to this maybe unexpected flattering by minimizing the possible threat to the PE instructor in question, but then goes on to refer to another source of hilarity: a perceived frequent failure of local German speakers to speak adequate Standard German for any extended period of time. This leads to a series of rapid, comic imitations of such speakers, and even the teacher joins in by suggesting, jokingly, that the international students might sport a sign reading "Only High German please", to display to dialect speakers whenever necessary. Despite the light-hearted tone, what the members of the class actually co-construct is an account of a country inhabited, to some extent, by linguistically deficient people. In doing so, they fail to analyze these phenomena with the same care they demonstrated during the interviews and also to display much tolerance towards people juggling with different varieties – despite the fact that they are fully aware of how similar the others' task is to their own, and also that of the children in their future multicultural classrooms. Strikingly, while the discursive strategies employed by the students in this excerpt (such as strategic code-switching or a differentiated use of discourse markers) are as complex as in the interviews discussed above, this is not the case for the intercultural competence: neither mediating between cultures nor critical distance is apparent, nor even (except for Karin) much face work directed at the lecturer and the two authors present. This last example shows that despite the validity of the descriptors in Beacco's reference description, language users may not necessarily be able to transfer competences acquired and practiced in some conversational contexts to different ones. This certainly calls for additional descriptors (including such that tackle the notoriously complex domain of humour). It also highlights, once again, how context-sensitive intercultural competences are – a fact that needs to be taken into account, for instance, when the descriptors are put into operation for summative testing.

5.   Conclusions

The aim of this chapter was to outline a possible contribution of discursive linguistics to the description of linguistic and communicative competences related to intercultural competences such as presented in Beacco's reference description.

We have demonstrated the relevance of this approach on the basis of the analysis of some examples of a corpus under construction, restricting our analysis to the description of the linguistic/discursive traces of what Beacco calls 'explicitly intercultural communication'. This seems very promising since the more fine-grained analysis of the students' performance in interaction fits very neatly with Beacco's descriptors. In specific, we have singled out the following linguistic phenomena as sensitive in the discursive construction of intercultural competence:

- accurate anaphorisation to avoid ambiguities in cohesion, in order to account for the complexity of multicultural contexts and intercultural settings in an adequate and comprehensible way
- interactive topic development
- richness of conjunctions or discourse markers to present and negotiate different concepts, viewpoints or even ideologies
- complexity of speech acts with 'redressive action' (strategies of linguistic politeness) in the case of (potential) face threats to present or absent persons
- richness of technical (e.g. meta-educational) vocabulary, especially if produced independently of the interlocutor's input
- strategic use of style-shifting/code-switching techniques, e.g. to represent different viewpoints or retell other interactions

At the same time, it remains clear that intercultural competence and linguistic competence cannot be placed in a simple one-to-one relationship. It is obviously possible for people to attain very high levels of communicative competence while remaining, in an extreme case, rather ignorant in one or more domains of intercultural competence. Nonetheless, we argue that the linguistic competence we have described is important in order to be able (a) to express a certain type of intercultural competence in practice, (b) to proceed in intercultural learning with members of another culture and (c) to manage potentially conflictual situations, such as may well arise in situations of student (or other) mobility, especially with less tolerant interlocutors than those represented in this study by the teacher and the researchers. Moreover, we suggest that valid and clear-cut descriptors such as Beacco's, combined with a description of the discursive features to be mastered, can also prove useful for the formulation of competence-based learning objectives, an observation of their development and, eventually, their evaluation. In this way, coming back to our more general question, we claim to have demonstrated that linguistic discourse analysis can indeed contribute to enroot the dimension of intercultural competence in foreign language learning and teaching.

References

Alred, G., Byram, M., & Fleming, M. P. (2003). Introduction. In G. Alred, M. Byram, & M. P. Fleming (Eds.), *Intercultural experience and education* (pp. 1–13). Clevedon: Multilingual Matters.

Beacco, J.-C., Bouquet, S., & Porquier, R. (Eds.) (2004). *Niveau B2 pour le français – un référentiel.* Paris: Didier.

Beacco, J.-C. (2004). Une proposition de réferentiel pour les compétences culturelles dans les enseignements des langues. In J.-C. Beacco, S. Bouquet, & R. Porquier (Eds.), *Niveau B2 pour le français: Textes et références* (pp. 251–287). Paris: Didier.

Beacco, J.-C. & Byram, M. (2007). *Guide for the development of language education policies in Europe (main version).* Strasbourg: Conseil de l'Europe. Retrieved from http://www.coe. int/t/dg4/linguistic/Guide_niveau3_EN.asp#TopOfPage.

Bronckart, J.-P. (1997). *Activité langagière, textes et discours. Pour un interactionnisme socio-discursif.* Paris: Delachaux et Niestlé.

Brown, P. & Levinson, S. C. (1988). *Politeness: Some universals in language usage.* Cambridge: Cambridge University Press.

Byram, M. & Zarate, G. (1994). *Definitions, objectives and assessment of sociocultural competence.* Strasbourg: Council of Europe.

Byram, M. (1997). *Teaching and assessing intercultural communicative competence.* Clevedon: Multilingual Matters.

Byram, M. (2008). *From foreign language education to education for intercultural citizenship.* Clevedon: Multilingual Matters.

Christ, H. (2007). Fremdverstehen in der Praxis interkulturellen Lernens im Fremdsprachen-unterricht. In L. Bredella & H. Christ (Eds.), *Fremdverstehen und interkulturelle Kompetenz* (pp. 51–77). Tübingen: Narr.

Council of Europe (2000). *European Language Portfolio.* Retrieved from http://www.coe.int/t/ dg4/portfolio/default.asp?l=e&m=/main_pages/welcome.html.

Council of Europe (2001). *Common European Framework of Reference for Languages: Learning, Teaching, Assessment (CEFR).* Retrieved from http://www.coe.int/T/DG4/Linguistic/ Source/Framework_EN.pdf.

Council of Europe (2007). *Intergovernmental policy forum: The Common European Framework of Reference for Languages (CEFR) and the development of language policies: Challenges and responsibilities.* Retrieved from http://www.coe.int/t/dg4/linguistic/forum07_web-docs_EN.asp?ecutives.net/.

Hu, A. & Byram, M. (2009). Introduction. In A. Hu & M. Byram (Eds.), *Interkulturelle Kompetenz und fremdsprachliches Lernen. Modelle. Empirie, Evaluation = Intercultural competence and language learning. Models, empiricism and evaluation* (pp. vii–xxv). Tübingen: Narr.

INCA (Intercultural Competence Assessment) Project. *A Leonardo da Vinci Project.* Retrieved from www.incaproject.org.

Kasper, G. & Omori, M. (2010). Language and culture. In N. H. Hornberger & S. Lee MacKay (Eds.), *Sociolinguistics and language education* (pp. 455–491). Bristol: Multilingual Matters.

Kramsch, C. (2009). Third culture and language education. In V. Cook & Li Wei (Eds.), *Contemporary applied linguistics* (Vol. 1, pp. 233–253). London: Continuum.

Lázár, I., Huber-Kriegler, M., Lussier, D., Matei, G. S., & Peck, C. (Eds.). (2007). *Developing and assessing intercultural communicative competence – A guide for language teachers and teacher educators.* Graz: European Centre for Modern Languages Retrieved from http://archive.ecml.at/mtp2/ICCinTE/html/ICC_E_Results.htm.

LOLIPOP, Language On-line Portfolio Project. Retrieved from http://www.lolipop-portfolio.eu/.

Pekarek Doehler, S., de Pietro, J.-F., Fasel Lauzon, V., & Pochon-Berger, E. (2008). *L'organisation du discours dans l'interaction en langue première et seconde: acquisition, enseignement, évaluation (Projet CODI). Rapport final.* Neuchâtel: Université de Neuchâtel. Retrieved from http://www2.unine.ch/webdav/site/codi/shared/documents/Rapportfinal.pdf.

Rampton, B. (1995). *Crossing: Language and ethnicity among adolescents.* London: Longman.

Schneider, G. et. al. (2009). *Konsortium Harmos Fremdsprachen. Wissenschaftlicher Kurzbericht und Kompetenzmodell.* Bern: EDK. Retrieved from http://www.edudoc.ch/static/web/arbeiten/harmos/L2_wissB_25_1_10_d.pdf.

Sercu, L. (2005). Teaching foreign languages in an intercultural world. In L. Sercu et al. (Eds.), *Foreign language teachers and intercultural competence: An international investigation* (pp. 1–18). Clevedon: Multilingual Matters.

Traverso, V. (2004). Grille d'analyse des discours interactifs oraux. In J.-C. Beacco, S. Bouquet, & R. Porquier (Eds.), *Niveau B2 pour le français: Textes et références* (pp. 119–148). Paris: Didier.

A place for pragmatics in intercultural teaching and learning

Troy McConachy
Rikkyo University

This paper describes the way in which a small group of Japanese EFL learners engaged with pragmatics based ideas and texts as a part of a short course designed to raise intercultural awareness through language learning. The data shows how students construct understandings and interpretations of language use in a textbook dialogue, upon which they explore their own cultural assumptions. The paper also pays attention to the teacher's role in supporting intercultural learning, particularly through the use of questions and other scaffolding strategies.

1. Introduction

Despite pragmatics being a discipline concerned with socially constituted meaning, conventional literature on pragmatics instruction in the language classroom has not made clear theoretical or practical links to the intercultural dimension. Literature on pragmatics instruction has often focused on the acquisition of native-like pragmatic norms without due consideration of the fact that many learners will not necessarily want to take on native norms. When this point has been recognized (e.g. Judd 1999) the alternative to taking on pragmatic norms – in other words, developing intercultural positions – has not been adequately discussed. It is almost axiomatic to say that second language learning is intercultural learning – pragmatics is no exception. Thus we are in need of theoretical development regarding the ways in which pragmatics-based tasks and materials can be used to facilitate intercultural learning. This chapter shows how a focus on the meta-pragmatic realm – where language-culture connections are reflected on, discussed and explored – can be useful in developing intercultural awareness.

1.1   Background

Research in pragmatics and the teaching and learning of pragmatics has brought about at least four understandings pertinent to this chapter. The first is that conversational routines, speech acts, and politeness phenomena are intricately tied to a range of cultural assumptions. Everyday interaction not only reflects shared cultural assumptions, but is also instrumental in the intersubjective affirmation and construction of world views (Duranti 1997; Giddens 1984; Bourdieu 1990). The second is that these aspects of interaction vary across languages and even within languages in accordance with differences in social structures, histories, political circumstances and a range of other elements. The third is that as preferred ways of interacting and associated value systems are primarily internalised as a part of the socialization process, users of a particular language tend to remain largely unaware of the complex cultural assumptions underlying language use in context (Ochs & Schieffelin 1986). As a corollary, the implicit nature of L1 pragmatic knowledge can result in second language learners not adequately making use of this knowledge (Kasper & Rose 2001). For example, even learners who may show superior grammatical control, or show great attention to context in their L1, may fail to recognize language-culture connections and the importance of context in the L2 (Tanaka 1988). The fourth is that the intense connection between communicative practices, culture, and identity means that lack of awareness of the culturally contexted nature of language use can lead to communication breakdown or worse. In the context of intercultural communication the potential for misunderstanding and conflict due to differences in pragmatic norms has been well documented in the literature (e.g. Thomas 1983; Scollon & Scollon 1995).

1.2   Beyond accuracy

In recognition of the four points above, a strong case has been made in the pragmatics literature for pedagogical intervention to make learners "aware of what they already know and encourage them to use their universal or transferable L1 pragmatic knowledge in L2 contexts" (Kasper & Rose 2001:07). In much of the conventional discourse on pragmatics instruction however, the impetus for becoming pragmatically aware has been to aid in the acquisition of "native-like" L2 competence. Put another way, there is a distinct lack of theoretical work which explores the possibilities for teaching pragmatics within an intercultural perspective.

There are certainly many language learners who aim to interact in a similar fashion to "native speakers" for integration into a particular society or other purposes. However, interacting in another language is more than just a process where information is exchanged; it is a venue for the enactment and negotiation of so-cial relationships (Liddicoat 2005). In regards to pragmatics, the linguistic forms available to achieve certain speech acts, and the cultural norms concerning the use of speech acts, are highly variable across languages. The language learner is thus required not only to identify the linguistic resources available and their ref-erential meanings, but to come to an understanding of the cultural connotations of particular ways of speaking. When an individual is confronted with pragmatic differences, the individual may experience strong emotional reactions due to the way in which our conventional ways of interacting are deeply associated with our sense of self (Saville-Troike 2003). Therefore the learner is faced with the task of deciding how exactly to interact in the target language in terms of conforming to or diverging from pragmatic norms in view of the consequences for both the individual and the relationship with the interlocutors. As such, depending on the nature of the discourse, the relationship with the interlocutor and a host of other variables, the individual may wish to position oneself in between two cultures – to create intercultural positions (Crozet & Liddicoat 1999).

An intercultural position does not imply that an individual remains static between two cultures; rather it means the individual chooses a way of interacting that is comfortable or beneficial according to the interactional demands of the moment. One pertinent issue here is that the creation of intercultural positions is best done strategically. What this means is that the choice regarding how to position oneself in intercultural interaction should be an informed one based on a heightened awareness of the ways in which interactional practices are informed by culture. From a pedagogical perspective, the issue becomes how opportuni-ties can best be created in the language classroom for learners to develop meta-pragmatic awareness, understood here as a heightened awareness of the cultural assumptions underlying pragmatic phenomena and their relationship to context (Kinginger & Farrell 2004). Such an orientation to the teaching of pragmatics ne-cessitates a reconceptualization of the role of pragmatic norms in instruction – ef-fectively it requires a shift from a focus on "accuracy" to "awareness". The ways in which meta-pragmatic understandings can be developed, and the implications that this has for intercultural learning is the focus of this paper.

2. Methodology

2.1 Teaching context

The data comes from a 12-week course on general communicative English which was taught by the author at a commercial English language institution in Tokyo,

Japan. Each lesson in this course was 110 minutes and designed to increase the oral communicative abilities of the students. Although there were no official guidelines, "culture" was also expected to be taught in this course as it was marketed towards Japanese students hoping to study abroad in the future. The author therefore designed a course around exploring the cultural dimensions of speech acts. The participants in the study are four Japanese students ranging in age from 20–24. All students had studied English in the Japanese school system for 6–10 years and were hoping to study English and other academic subjects at universities outside Japan. All students could be regarded as having intermediate overall English skills.

2.2   Data collection and analysis

The data used in this chapter constitutes a sequence of tasks from week 4 of the course. The lesson was recorded in its entirety by audio-recording equipment, with consent of the students. In accordance with the research focus, three analytical discussions were transcribed. The transcript was subject to content analysis during which the author looked particularly at how the students related to pragmatics-based ideas as expressed through meta-pragmatic commentary, and how these processes were supported by the teacher and the learning task.

2.3   Tasks

In this lesson, a teacher-constructed dialogue was used to focus on the speech act of apologizing. Research on contrastive pragmatics has shown apology formulas to differ across cultures (Cohen 1996), with specific differences between Japanese and English having been identified regarding both the types of language used for apologies and the cultural constraints concerning their use (Sugimoto 1989). Therefore, the author devised a sequence of three analytical discussion tasks to develop the learner's understanding of apologizing as a speech act, the ways in which apologies are structured in discourse, and the types of differences that might exist compared to apologies in Japanese. The focus of each task is described below:

Task 1: Meta-pragmatic focus
The purpose of this task was to aid the learners in making assessments regarding the feelings and intentions of the speakers by making connections between the language used and the communicative context.

Task 2: Discoursal focus
The purpose of this task was to focus on the structure of the speech act itself and how it is negotiated within the dialogue.

Task 3: Intercultural focus
The purpose of this task was to prompt the learners to reflect on the act of apologizing in Japanese and consider how apologizing strategies vis-à-vis this particular dialogue may be different and why.

Tasks were sequenced in this way based on the assumption that an explicit focus on the intercultural dimension would be most beneficial after learners' meta-pragmatic noticings and interpretations of this particular dialogue had been explicated (Liddicoat 2002). The labeling of these tasks does not however imply that "intercultural" processes are absent from tasks one and two. It was assumed from the outset that the ways in which the learners interpreted the L2 pragmatics would be influenced to a certain extent by their L1 cultural frameworks. Hence the labeling of these tasks simply represents what will likely be most salient in terms of pedagogical content within each task.

Dialogue
The dialogue which was used for this teaching was taken from an intermediate English textbook written by this author together with a colleague.

Garry and Kevin are good friends living in a retirement community. Last night there was a dance for residents, and everyone had a good time – except now Garry has something to tell Kevin.

Kevin: *That was a fun dance last night, wasn't it?*
Garry: *It sure was, but listen, I have to tell you something.*
Kevin: *Oh, what is it?*
Garry: *Remember I borrowed your favorite yellow tie for the dance last night? Well, uh, I spilled some red wine on it.*
Kevin: *What? You ruined my favorite tie?!*
Garry: *I'm so sorry that it happened, Kevin. It was my mistake. I was dancing and someone knocked my glass. I should have put it down somewhere.*
Kevin: *But it was my favorite tie!*
Garry: *I know. Please let me buy you a new one.*
Kevin: *Oh, don't worry about it, Garry. It wasn't that expensive. I'm just happy that you were honest about it.*

(Dialogue taken from McConachy & Meldahl 2007)

3. Data

3.1   Task 1: Meta-pragmatic focus

At the beginning of the activity the teacher handed out the dialogue and read out the description of the situation. Students were then asked to act out the dialogue in pairs to become a little more familiar with the situation and the language used within. Once students had finished, the teacher posed questions to the class as a whole to encourage meta-pragmatic exploration. Specifically, learners were asked to draw inferences regarding the feelings of the dialogue characters and justify their ideas. In the ensuing discourse, students make reference to the feelings and communicative intent of the speakers, the likely outcome of the situation, and who should have responsibility for the incident that occurred.

1:T	So, how do you think the speakers are feeling?
2:S1	Kevin might abandon to charge him for the tie. Actually he is thinking Garry is bad, but "**shikata nai**" (It can't be helped).
3:T	So you think he's really angry but he's just forgiving his friend?
4:S1	Yes, because he said twice "My favorite tie". So he really like it.
5:T	Yeah, possibly. Any other comments?
6:S3	"But it was my favorite tie" means he got angry?
7:T	What do you think?
8:S3	Hmm, I don't know.
9:T	Okay, how would you say it in Japanese?
10:S3	"**Boku no suki na tai darou**"? (It was my favorite tie you know)
11:T	"**datta no ni**" (It was unfortunately)
12:S3	Ah, disappointed.
13:T	And so after that Garry says, "I know".
14:S2	So I think if I were Kevin I didn't lend my favorite tie.
15:T	Oh, so you think it is his fault? He was stupid for lending the tie, so it's his responsibility?
16:S2	So, then what happened is possible. I mean anything is possible.
17:T	Oh right? So he has responsibility?
18:S2	Yeah.

The extract of talk above contains a number of issues worthy of discussion in relation to intercultural learning. The first is the way that the framing of the task facilitates meta-pragmatic exploration. In line 1 the teacher makes use of a question which specifically requires students to draw inferences regarding the feelings of the dialogue characters. The word "feelings" itself is general enough for students to interpret in multiple ways, as evidenced by S1's contribution in line 2. Instead of S1 attempting to name an explicit feeling that Kevin is having, he draws an inference regarding the action that Kevin is likely to take in resolving this problem. In other words, S1's comment that even though "[Kevin] is thinking Garry is bad" he is likely to "abandon to charge him for the tie" is a specific example of predicting interactional consequences from consideration of context and the language used in that context. In line 14, S2 takes up the issue of it being unwise to lend one's favorite tie to someone. In line 15 the teacher formulates questions for S1 to confirm that he is assigning responsibility to Kevin for the action, which is confirmed in lines 16-18. In effect, this represents a shift from examination of micro aspects of interaction to a broader meta-pragmatic framework. Within this space, cultural meanings can be assigned to both linguistic and non-linguistic actions. In terms of intercultural learning, these two examples show the potential for meta-pragmatic exploration to create a space in which language can be seen as something which mediates social relationships and has social consequences.

The second is the way in which teacher talk functions to scaffold the development of the learners' contextual understandings. In the discussion, the force behind Kevin's utterance "But it was my favorite tie" was taken up by both S1 and S3 in an attempt to interpret the situation. When it became clear that S3 was unsure of the nuance expressed by the utterance, the teacher asked S3 to create an L1 equivalent (line 9), which she does. The teacher then offers his own L1 equivalent which he perceived to express similar disappointment to the L2 original (line 11). In line 12, S3 reveals immediate understanding of the nuance. In addition, in line 13 in order to show the social function of this particular utterance, the teacher quotes Garry's response to it from the dialogue.

As a teaching phenomenon, what this does is to demonstrate that one way to understand the force of a particular utterance is to look at the way it is taken up by the next speaker in the dialogue. This can provide a clue to the types of social action or speech acts that are achieved by particular utterances. Therefore, in this case we see how the teacher scaffolded student understanding on the one hand by encouraging the use of the L1 as a tool for mediating learning, and on the other hand, scaffolded the contextual understandings of this utterance through drawing students' attention to the way in which the interaction unfolded.

A second important aspect which needs to be considered in relation to teacher talk is its potential for developing the learners' ability to talk about interaction – in other words, to formulate meta-pragmatic commentary. In any instance of language use interpretations are constantly being made and cultural meanings attached to specific ways of speaking (Verschueren 2000). Thus, to facilitate the development of intercultural understandings, it is vital that teachers use comments, questions or reformulations of student utterances which function to bring out student interpretations of language use. This is not a matter of simply "eliciting" some pre-taught information, but rather the use of teacher language that provides a scaffold for the elaboration of increasingly sophisticated interpretations by students. In this task, we can see how S1's interpretation of Kevin's feelings in line 2 is reformulated by the teacher in line 3 in the form of question, which seems to directly elicit a justification for the interpretation in line 4. Here, the teacher question specifically prompts S1 to elaborate on his interpretation of Kevin's feelings, in this case invoking language used from the dialogue. Furthermore, the teacher reformulation introduces the concept of "forgive" as a tool to scaffold S1's explanation. A similar example can be seen in lines 14 where S2 comments on the act of lending one's favorite tie to someone. In lines 15 and 17 the teacher introduces the concept of "responsibility" to assist S2 to articulate the reason for his opinion. Therefore, on the one hand teacher questions act as a scaffold for learning by stimulating students to justify their interpretations. In addition, the questions themselves can contain concepts ("forgive" or "responsibility") which students can make use of when developing their meta-pragmatic explanations or interpretations. In a Vygotskian sense, the building up of students' meta-pragmatic repertoire through the introduction of these concepts can be considered a type of mediation in that the concepts can be used as a framework for talking about language and culture (Gibbons 2003).

In connection to the point above, we can also see that meta-pragmatic commentary itself has the potential to do more than just benefit the individual. Another dimension to consider is the way in which meta-pragmatic commentary can function to make the interpretations of individual students more accessible for collaborative examination and reflection. We can see the way in which S1 quoted from the dialogue in line 4 to explain Kevin's feelings made this language more accessible to S4 in line 6. In other words, the act of verbalization by S1 generated awareness in S4 that she was unsure of the nuance conveyed by the language in this context. In other words, elaborated interpretations of language use in context can scaffold the learning of other learners in that as the commentary becomes more specific, similarities and differences of ideas and opinions can be noticed, and then taken up and developed in the ongoing discussion.

Through this task we see the learners develop their contextual understandings of the dialogue by considering the feelings and intentions of the dialogue characters vis-à-vis the situation and each other as evidenced by the language used. The learners notice the implications of several ways of speaking and begin to develop their ability to formulate meta-pragmatic commentary. Such heightened meta-pragmatic capabilities can be a foundation for intercultural comparison and reflection.

3.2   Task 2: Discoursal focus

Continuing on from the previous task, the teacher now asks the learners to focus on the apology in terms of its internal structure and positioning within the dialogue.

1:T   Okay, let me ask you some more questions. Where does he apologise? Where does it start and where does it finish?

2:S3   "I'm so sorry".

3:S4   "I'm so sorry that it happened"?

4:T   (Writing on the board) Where does it finish?

5:S4   "Please let me buy you a new one".

6:T   Okay, so let's say this is the first step. The saying "I'm sorry". What's the second step?

7:S3   "It was my mistake".

8:T   Right. So what is this? What is he doing here?

9:S3   *Mitomeru.*

10:T   Yeah, but *nani wo mitometeiru?* (What is he admitting?)

11:S3   His fault.

12:T   Okay. So *sekinin*? He's accepting responsibility. Okay, then what happens after that?

13:S2   So he is explaining what happened.

14:T   Yep. Then what's next?

15:S2   So he explains what he should have done.

16:T   Right. So we'll call this the "point of regret". So this is almost like one set, isn't it? It kind of flows. It's all necessary. But what is the next thing that happens?

17:S4   Um, suggesting the solution?

18:T   Good. Good. So basically, offer to do something. But what happened before this?

19:S1   Like introduction?

20:T   Good. So it was the same last week when we studied the requests. We don't just say, "Oh, can I borrow your watch?" or suddenly "I'm sorry I spilled wine on your tie". We need to introduce the topic. So did you notice how he said, "Remember I borrowed your yellow tie for the dance last night? Well, ah, I spilled some red wine on it". Why does he say "Ah"?

21:S1   It's hard to say directly?

22:T   Good. Maybe it is really hard to say. Or maybe he wants to show that it is hard to say.

The first point of interest here is the way in which the initial teacher questions frame the speech act as something which is developed in discourse. In other words, the initial question used by the teacher in this task, "Where does it start and where does it finish?" creates a context in which the students can notice that the act of apologizing is not something achieved by a simple set phrase such as "I'm sorry". Instead, this question requires that the learners focus on the speech act of apologizing as something that is achieved over multiple turns in thematically connected sequences and determined by interactional needs.

A second point of interest is that the teacher does not simply lecture the students on the structure of the speech act, but uses questions to elicit the particular utterances which indicate important social acts in connection to the apology. In lines 8–12, Garry's comment from the dialogue, "It was my mistake" is being focused on. In line 8, the teacher asks, "What is he doing here?" to which S3 responds with *Mitomeru* (admit). The teacher responds in line 10 with the question, *Nani o mitomete iru?* (What is he admitting?). S3 responds in line 11 that he is admitting his "fault". In line 12 the language is finally characterized by the teacher as evidencing "accepting responsibility", which the teacher also conveys in the L1 (*sekinin*). Therefore we see again the way in which the teacher questions scaffold the development of more sophisticated meta-pragmatic commentary. In this case, the teacher and S3 use the L1 as a resource to establish understanding of the nature of the social action achieved by this utterance.

Throughout this task the learners can be seen identifying important stages in the apology sequence and achieve an understanding of the social action that is achieved at each stage. The ability to identify utterances as being connected to particular speech acts, and seeing speech acts themselves as types of social action which are negotiated in discourse provides a framework for more sophisticated understandings of the relationships between language and culture. In addition, the use of the L1 in this extract again demonstrates its usefulness as a resource for analyzing language use and for mediating understanding. In other words, the explication of cultural concepts in both languages which can be used for meta-pragmatic commentary, can be considered an asset for both intracultural and intercultural analysis.

3.3   Task 3: Intercultural focus

In task 1 the learners develop their meta-pragmatic awareness regarding the context of the apology and learn how to talk about the interaction in terms of the feelings and motivations of the speakers. In task 2, the learners notice the specific structure of the apology and come to be able to talk about interactional sequences in terms of social action. In this task, explicit attention is paid to the act of apologizing in Japanese in order to establish a context for reflection and the further development of meta-pragmatic capabilities and intercultural awareness.

1:T   Okay, so do you think anything here would be different to apologizing in Japanese? For example if this situation involved two Japanese people.
2:S4   Point of regret?
3:T   You wouldn't say this bit?
4:S4   Maybe we wouldn't say it. It's obvious.
5:T   Oh yeah? Any other ideas? How about this one? Would you say, "I was dancing and someone knocked my glass".
6:S3   I think I would explain.
7:S1   I think it's not necessary in Japanese because it's kind of excuse.
8:T   It sounds like an excuse?
9:S1   Yes. I feel like that.
10:T   Even though he says, "It was my mistake"?
11:S1   Hmm, this sounds like to show sincerity.
13:T   Which part?
13:S1   Where he says, "It was my mistake".
14:T   Oh yeah? So you think in Japanese it would be best if it didn't have this explanation, and just he says that he takes responsibility for it?
15:S1   Yes, perhaps.
16:S4   I think he shouldn't have to say "someone knocked my glass".
17:T   Yeah, it does sound like a little bit of an excuse. I can understand why you would think that. But I think in English it is usually necessary to explain what happened. This is because you want to show the other person that you didn't intend to do something bad or that you had no control or just made a mistake. It's important to show that you understand your mistake to make the other person feel like you won't do it again. This is so that the other person can trust you again.

The discussion begins with a comparative analysis regarding the specific structure of the speech act. In line 1, the teacher frames the initial question not simply in terms of a generalized comparison between apologies in English and apologies in Japanese, but rather asks the learners to reflect on what some differences might be vis-à-vis this particular situation. This type of question allows intercultural comparisons to be made in a relatively focused way, as students are required to pay attention to the specific dynamics of this context and explore potential differences not only in terms of the language used but the context itself.

In this task we see instances of students appropriating metalanguage from the previous task in order to focus on discourse structure for the purpose of intercultural comparisons. In line 2, S4 comments that a Japanese apology in this situation would not require mention of the "point of regret". Thus, the explicit focus on discourse structure in the previous task has provided an analytical resource which functions to make the language available for further reflection. Furthermore, these categories are applied as a framework for the explication of noticings regarding intercultural phenomena.

In line 4, S4 justifies his comment in line 2 by stating that the point of regret is "obvious", the implication being that in a comparable Japanese interaction stating the obvious would be unfavorable. In other words, the student provides a C1-internal perspective on this aspect of interaction. The teacher does not follow up this particular explanation, but keeps the focus on the types of explanations that might be necessary.

In line 5, the teacher asks whether it would be necessary to explain the context in which the action occurred. Regarding this point, lines 6 and 7 reveal contrasting opinions from S3 and S1 respectively. S1 suggests that explaining the context of the action would be construed as an excuse in Japanese interaction. In lines 8–15, S1's interpretation is slightly clarified. In line 10, the teacher prompts S1 to consider the interactional implication of the use of "It was my mistake" in the context of his current interpretation of explanation as excuse. In line 11, S1 suggests that this language is used by Garry to show "sincerity". The application of the word "excuse" here is most likely a translation of the Japanese equivalent *iiwake*, which has a characteristically negative connotation. The implication in Japanese would be that explaining the circumstances in which a negative action occurred would often be seen as an attempt to alleviate one's responsibility for an action. In this case, we cannot infer whether S1 sees Garry as trying to evade some responsibility for the action, but it is clear that S1 sees such explanatory behavior as likely to be interpreted negatively within the context of L1 interactional norms. In his meta-pragmatic explanation the English word "excuse" is invoked to express a meaning which seems essentially embedded within a C1 cultural framework. However from this extract we do not see whether he realizes the cultural implications of this word. In line 16, S4 also makes metapragmatic comments regarding how mentioning another person's contribution to one's mistake should be left out of a Japanese apology, presumably to prevent the interlocutor from determining a lack of sincerity. Particularly in these kinds of comments it is clear that the students are really going beyond a linguistic analysis. They are exploring the connections between language and culture in terms of cultural norms underlying language use and the specific interactional consequences that might result from failure to adhere to these norms.

In line 17 the teacher for the first time engages in normative metapragmatic commentary regarding this particular situation. He provides the interpretation that explanation of the circumstances surrounding the apology stems from a perceived need to assure the interlocutor that the nature of the mistake is understood and will therefore not be repeated again. It is necessary to mention the pedagogical functions of this type of teacher commentary. Firstly, it has value in that it gives a perspective on the L1/C1 that can be used as a reference point for students to determine their own language use. In this sense, when utilizing pragmatics in intercultural language teaching, it is not necessary for teacher interpretations of L1 norms to have a "coercive" implication. Rather the real usefulness of this kind of talk lies in its potential to provide learners with a perspective on pragmatic phenomena that can be taken into account as they continue to learn about and use the language. The interpretation of the teacher can be reflected on and compared in view of new experiences, which over time may lead to new noticings and the development of more sophisticated intercultural awareness. Additionally, this type of extended meta-pragmatic commentary by the teacher also provides a sophisticated model for students. Of course this does not mean that the students should parrot what the teacher says. What it means is that it shows how interpretations of language and culture can be formulated. In other words, it makes the tools used for intercultural work more salient for the learners.

We see how this task has built on noticings from the previous task and through encouraging reflection on the L1, has assisted the students to compare the speech act across cultures. The students perceive a number of potential differences, which are explained not simply in grammatical or discoursal terms, but in terms of the interactional consequences of particular utterances in view of this specific context. In other words, the students have begun to explore the relationship between language and culture and the implications that it has in regards to this particular speech act.

4. Conclusion

This paper has made an argument and presented one sequence of tasks to illustrate the potential of pragmatics to facilitate the development of intercultural understandings in the language classroom. For intercultural learning it is important for language learners to be able to view language not simply from a grammatical point of view, but from a point of view in which connections can be made between language and the cultural context of use. As was mentioned earlier in this chapter, intercultural positions are taken up by individuals in interaction according to the dynamics of a particular context. As language teachers we cannot predict the specific situations that our learners are going to encounter and the ways in which they are going to want to manage their identities in intercultural interaction. Therefore, what we can do is design classroom experiences to impart the types of awareness and skills that will assist them in developing their understandings of language and culture over time. In this sense, intercultural language teaching could be considered as a type of cognitive apprenticeship (Brown, Collins & Duguid 1989).

In relation to pragmatics, it is essential for teachers to create an environment in which learners notice relevant language use and explore its implications in terms of how language reflects cultural orientations. Analytical tasks which require learners to formulate meta-pragmatic commentary such as verbalizing interpretations regarding language use in context can be considered useful in that they bring out cultural assumptions that may otherwise remain implicit. Additionally important is that teachers scaffold intercultural learning by engaging in collaborative dialogue with learners in a way that understanding is deepened and learners' underlying assumptions and interpretations are formulated in increasingly sophisticated ways. In addition to focusing on the pragmatics of the target language, the strategic incorporation of L1 pragmatic phenomena as an object of comparative analysis and reflection can assist learners to recognize differences in cultural concepts and the limitations of understanding one language within the cultural framework of another. An understanding of relativity at this level can be a valuable tool for generating a broader framework for intercultural exploration (Byram 1991; Kramsch 1993; Crozet & Liddicoat 1999). Furthermore, making these ideas accessible for reflection and further exploration is crucial to intercultural learning (Liddicoat 2002).

References

Bourdieu, P. (1990). *The logic of practice*. Stanford, CA: Stanford University Press.

Brown, J. S., Collins, A., & Duguid, P. (1989). Situated cognition and the culture of learning. *Educational Researcher, 18*(1), 32–42.

Byram, M. (1991). Teaching language and culture: An integrated model. In D. Buttjes & M. Byram (Eds.), *Mediating languages and cultures* (pp. 17–30). Clevedon: Multilingual Matters.

Cohen, A. D. (1996). Developing the ability to perform speech acts. *Studies in Second Language Acquisition, 18*, 253–267.

Crozet, C. & Liddicoat, A. J. (1999). The challenge of intercultural language teaching: Engaging with culture in the classroom. In C. Crozet, A. J. Liddicoat, & J. Lo Bianco (Eds.), *Striving for the third place: Intercultural competence through language education* (pp. 113–126). Melbourne: Language Australia

Duranti, A. (1997). *Linguistic anthropology*. Cambridge: Cambridge University Press.

Gibbons, P. (2003). Mediating language learning: Teacher interactions with ESL students in a content-based classroom. *TESOL Quarterly, 37*(2), 247–273.

Giddens, A. (1984). *The constitution of society.* Cambridge: Polity Press.

Judd, E. L. (1999). Some issues in the teaching of pragmatic competence. In E. Hinkel (Ed.), *Culture in second language teaching and learning* (pp. 152–166). New York, NY: Cambridge University Press.

Kasper, G. & Rose, K. R. (2001). Pragmatics in language teaching. In G. Kasper & K. R. Rose (Eds.), *Pragmatics in language teaching* (pp. 1–9). Cambridge: Cambridge University Press.

Kinginger, C. & Farrell, K. (2004). Assessing development of metapragmatic awareness in study abroad. *Frontiers: The Interdisciplinary Journal of Study Abroad, 10*(2), 19–42.

Kramsch, C. (1993). *Context and culture in language teaching.* Oxford: Oxford University Press.

Liddicoat, A. J. (2002). Static and dynamic views of culture and intercultural language acquisition. *Babel, 36*(3), 5–11.

Liddicoat, A. J. (2005). Teaching languages for intercultural communication. In D. Cunningham & A. Hatoss (Eds.), *An international perspective on language policies, practices and proficiencies* (pp. 201–214). Belgrave: Fédération Internationale des Professeurs de Langues Vivantes (FIPLV).

McConachy, T. & Meldahl, A. (2007). *Learning to communicate in English: A total approach.* Tokyo: Lado International College.

Ochs, E. & Shiefflin, B. B. (1986). Language socialization. *Annual Review of Anthropology, 15,* 163–191.

Saville-Troike, M. (2003). Extending communicative concepts in the second language curriculum: A sociolinguistic perspective. In D. L. Lange & R. M. Paige (Eds.), *Culture as the core: Perspectives on culture in second language learning* (pp. 47–113). Greenwich: Information Age Publishing.

Scollon, R. & Scollon, S. W. (1995). *Intercultural communication.* Malden, MA: Blackwell.

Sugimoto, N. (1989). "Sorry we apologize so much": Linguistic factors affecting Japanese and U.S. American Styles of Apology. *Intercultural Communication Studies, 8*(1), 71–78.

Tanaka, N. (1988). Politeness: Some problems for Japanese speakers of English. *JALT Journal, 9,* 81–102.

Thomas, J. (1983). Cross-cultural pragmatic failure. *Applied Linguistics, 4*(2), 91–112.

Verschueren, J. (2000). Notes on the role of metapragmatic awareness in language use. *Pragmatics, 10*(4), 439–456.

Strategy-based learning of pragmatics for intercultural education

Andrew D. Cohen and Julie M. Sykes
University of Minnesota / University of New Mexico

This chapter deals with an area that has come into its own in research on second language (L2) learning, namely, that of language learner strategies, and, in this specific case, the application of strategies to the learning and performance of L2 pragmatics. Consistent with the theme of this volume, the underlying concern is with the potentially important role of strategies in heightening learners' ability to make informed choices with regard to how they handle intercultural situations. The focus is on assisting learners in developing a more robust repertoire of strategies for their handling of pragmatics within intercultural communication. The aim is to support learners in building a toolkit of common pragmatic options that can be used as they co-construct communication in a variety of intercultural interactions. To begin addressing these issues, a strategic approach to L2 pragmatics was included in the underpinnings of two online spaces – a website and an online virtual space, both intended for the learning of pragmatic behavior appropriate in a variety of Spanish-speaking contexts. A taxonomy of strategies for learning and performing L2 pragmatics was applied to the construction of a website, *Dancing with Words*, aimed at learning the pragmatics appropriate for Spanish-speaking world, with strategy material integrated into the website. Research was conducted by means of two studies, involving both this Spanish pragmatics website and a synthetic immersive environment (SIE), *Croquelandia*, which was designed as a 3-D immersive space for the learning of pragmatic behaviors in Spanish. Results showed some reported differences in strategy use in the two different kinds of digital environments, with the finding of most relevance to the notion of intercultural education discussed in this volume being that in the SIE learners reported an increased use of metapragmatic strategies for dealing with L2 pragmatics. This finding highlighted the role of strategies in making informed choices about pragmatics.

1.   The role of pragmatics in intercultural education

If we take a critical look at efforts to instruct learners in second language (L2)[1] pragmatics, then the aims of such instruction need to be revisited in light of concerns about what intercultural education actually entails. In the foreign language classroom, there may be tension between what is taught about the language and about the associated cultural, societal, political, and interpersonal beliefs that constitute and shape this language (Kramsch 2002). As pointed out in the introductory chapter of this volume, there has been terminological confusion, where terms like *intercultural* and *multicultural* have been treated interchangeably, with neither being adequately defined. In some contexts, there has also been an apparent lack of attention to the dynamic nature of intercultural interactions, with an idealized native speaker model taking precedence in the language classroom. A contrastive approach highlights boundaries between cultures, rather than accentuating the ways in which the cultures may actually overlap and points where individuals within any given culture may vary dramatically, instead, placing primary emphasis on the dynamic, hegemonic, and diverse notion of culture, even within seemingly similar groups. By helping learners develop skills to consider both the internal diversity within a given culture as well as commonalities that might appear in certain communities, an important emphasis is placed on the hegemonic nature of language and intercultural communication. This stands in stark contrast to approaches which view culture as monolithic and idealized. In short, from this perspective, culture is viewed as subjective constructions of lived experience, rather than as compact entities that are convenient for contrastive teaching.

In this chapter, we explore this complex relationship, focusing on learners' control of strategies for developing genuine intercultural awareness so that their pragmatic performance is truly intercultural. The chapter will strive to make a connection between language learner strategies in the domain of intercultural pragmatics, as well as the field of intercultural education as a whole. The challenge is to develop in language learners, through their language learning experiences, the capacity to identify and respond to indications of linguistic differences in encultured behavior. A strategies approach is one way to highlight patterns that emerge while, at the same time, enabling learners to deal with a variety of

---

1.   For the purposes of this chapter, L2 will refer to the learning of either a second or a foreign language, though in reality there can be a marked difference between the two, since a second language is presumably being learned in a context where that language is used by the dominant language group and a foreign language is being learned in a context where the language may have far more limited use.

pragmatic behaviors. For example, in a lesson in L2 pragmatics dealing with requests to professors via email, it is important to highlight email requesting behaviors when writing to a professor in English in the U.S., a pattern which typically involves more indirect discourse with mitigation than the same request of a professor in Mandarin in China. However, stopping at this point does not address the dynamic nature of the requesting behaviors and may send the message that all requesting behavior is the same across speakers. In conjunction with what might be considered prototypical requesting patterns, learners should simultaneously develop strategies to learn, perform, and analyze the immense variation among each of these learning groups, highlighting the need for consistent analysis and adaptation of pragmatic behaviors in the L2. While some will undoubtedly view simultaneous attention to patterns and variation as contradictory, the perspective taken here is that both are essential to the development of intercultural pragmatic competence.

As proposed by Byram (1997) in his model of intercultural competence, L2 learners need to develop the attitudes, knowledge, skills of interpreting and relating, skills of discovery and interaction, critical cultural awareness, and political education to be able to see the relationships among cultures different from their own. Development of intercultural education calls for taking a fresh look at beliefs about language and culture. L2 pragmatics has an important role to play in intercultural communication. Byram (1997:3) points out that "…the efficacy of communication depends upon using language to demonstrate one's willingness to relate, which often involves the indirectness of politeness rather than the direct and 'efficient' choice of language full of information." L2 pragmatics addresses both the learners' willingness to relate, as well as their ability to use language to do so.

More recently, the call has been made to engage in cultural pragmatics as a means for understanding how culture is created in complex situations:

> To the extent that less emphasis is placed on form and culture, and more on the subject that acts and therefore interacts, we find ourselves within the domain of pragmatics… It is not about seeking hypothetical cultural realities, but rather comprehending a form of cultural pragmatics, understanding how the cultural is created in complex situations.   (Abdallah-Pretceille 2006:480)

So this view puts the responsibility on learners to deal with the intercultural complexity of the given situation, and pragmatics happens where language and culture meet (see Ishihara & Cohen 2010). The challenge in L2 pragmatic performance is interpreting intercultural meanings appropriately – which implies that as listeners or readers, learners are able to interpret the intended meanings of what is said or written, the assumptions, purposes or goals, and the kinds of actions that are being performed (Yule 1996: 3–4). For speakers, high intercultural pragmatic ability means that these learners are aware of the norms for politeness, directness, and formality (for instance, in the role of teacher, telling students their work is unacceptable; or in the role of a student, complaining to the teacher about some aspect of a course). They are also aware of what members of a given sociocultural subgroup are likely to refrain from saying and what they are likely to communicate non-verbally.

So, taking a critical approach to interculturality, the onus is on educators to refrain from making claims about right and wrong ways to perform pragmatics, and rather to discuss performance in terms of students' abilities to make informed choices about their communication. This approach allows for language learner strategies to be integrated into a more robust and less closed model of intercultural pragmatics. In this way, intercultural education moves beyond a 'sensitivity to the essentially different behaviours and values of the other and to cultivate individuals who may employ the ability to read culture which derives from underlying universal cultural processes' (Holliday 2011: 2).

For writers, high intercultural pragmatic ability means being fully aware of how locals of a culture write their messages intelligibly, incorporating level of politeness, directness, formality, and appropriateness of the rhetorical structure of the message (for instance, in the role of student, composing an e-mail message to their teacher requesting an extension on a term paper, or writing a message to a neighboring student to borrow a textbook). In each area, learners must be able to balance their own beliefs about culture with those of target-language speakers in each given situation – an endeavor that if performed appropriately, contributes to the quality of intercultural communication (Byram 1997; Kramsch 2002).

Nonnative participants in a speech community may or may not have a sense of norm-based pragmatic behavior for given situations. Coupled with that, they also have a set of beliefs and attitudes which color how they perform, sometimes causing divergent, non-congruent behavior which may impact the interaction. Very often, they are unaware that their behavior is considered divergent. At other times, however, they purposely diverge because to do otherwise would violate their sense of self-identity. In fact, research has been conducted addressing how learners of an L2 may purposely diverge from the pragmatic norms of a given speech community using that L2 (see Ishihara & Tarone 2009 on L2 learner subjectivity). For this reason, then, not only is the sociocultural context in which the interaction is taking place a crucial variable, but also how the interlocutors respond to it.

A critical approach to intercultural pragmatics would be to eschew the notion of mastery of a fixed body of knowledge, and rather to support the development in learners of the capacity to negotiate practices and conventions. Language learner strategies play an important role in equipping learners with the necessary skills to engage interlocutors in negotiating interactions in intercultural situations. Learners need strategies for learning about L2 pragmatics expeditiously, strategies for performing according to pragmatic norms or for opting out, and strategies for coping with gaps when they do not know what to do (e.g., what to say at a funeral) and strategies for negotiating in the face of impending pragmatic failure.

There is at present a robust research literature on speech acts (see, for instance, Kasper & Rose 2002; Márquez Reiter & Placencia 2005; Alcón Soler & Martínez-Flor 2008). There is also a growing literature on the teaching of speech acts (e.g., Rose & Kasper 2001; Tatsuki 2005; Ishihara & Cohen 2010; Tatsuki & Houck 2010), as well as the use of computer-mediated technologies to facilitate L2 pragmatic development and intercultural competence (Belz 2007; Sykes 2005, 2009; Belz & Thorne 2005; González-Lloret 2010). What has been lacking, for the most part, in both theoretical and practical work, is any systematic attention to the strategies learners use to deal with L2 pragmatic behaviors, especially strategies for how to be differentially appropriate according to the subjective criteria of the given learners.

This chapter reports on beginning efforts to apply language learner strategies to the development of intercultural competence and, in particular, to the learning of speech acts, through a taxonomy which included strategies for learning speech acts, for performing them, and for monitoring the results (Cohen 2005). This taxonomy was included in the instructional content for two online environments for learning Spanish L2 speech acts: a website and an experimental online, 3D, immersive space. Each of the spaces was designed from the perspective that learners need support in identifying prototypical NS pragmatic behaviors as well as deciding how these norms should, or should not, apply to their own intercultural interactions. Findings from research with the online spaces are discussed in terms of insights gained with regard to the reported strategies for learning, performing, and analyzing L2 pragmatics. In this chapter, we focus on how these findings relate to promoting intercultural education.

2. Language learner strategies

It would be an understatement to say that *language learner strategies* have been defined in numerous ways over the years. Our own working definition would be as follows: "Thoughts and actions, consciously chosen and operationalized by language learners, to assist them in carrying out a multiplicity of tasks from the very onset of learning to the most advanced levels of target-language performance" (Cohen 2011:7). They can be very important for enabling learners to observe the world around them and make conscious choices about their language use and behavior (see Cohen & Weaver 2006; Cohen 2007). Such strategies have been classified in different ways – for example, strategies for learning and use, strategies according to skill area, and strategies according to function (i.e. metacognitive, cognitive, affective, or social). Language learner strategies can be categorized as *language learning* strategies (i.e. strategies for the learning of language material for the first time) and *language use* strategies (i.e. strategies for using the material that has already been learned to some degree). *Communication strategies* are viewed as a type of language use strategy:

1. to steer the conversation away from problematic areas by expressing meaning through paraphrase or gestures,
2. to compensate for gaps by using literal translation from the L1, or
3. to keep the conversation going by asking for help, seeking clarification or confirmation, or using fillers (such as *uh* and *uhm*) for pauses, along with other hesitation devices such as repeating key words.

With regard to the function of strategies, *metacognitive strategies* are seen as highly valuable because they allow learners to control their language learning by planning what they will do, checking on progress, and then evaluating their performance on a given task (Chamot 1987; Oxford 1990, 2011). While the research literature suggests there is a positive relationship between learners' reports that they use the metacognitive strategies and higher levels of language proficiency (Anderson 2008), there is at present little research evidence regarding the role of metacognitive strategies in the performance of L2 pragmatics, strategies which are referred to as *metapragmatic*. In the context of intercultural education, metapragmatic strategies would serve the crucial function of monitoring pragmatic performance so that it conforms to the intentions of the learner as well as the context of the specific intercultural encounter.

Cognitive strategies involve the processes, or mental manipulations, learners go through in both learning the L2 and in using it. *Social strategies* encompass the means employed by learners for interacting with other learners and native speakers (NSs). *Affective strategies* help learners to regulate their emotions and motivation, and to reduce anxiety while providing self-encouragement.

The field of language learner strategies has always had its detractors over the years. Dörnyei (2009: 183) minimized the value of looking at language learner strategies altogether since what learners do is better viewed as "idiosyncratic self-regulated behavior, and a particular learning behavior can be strategic for one learner and non-strategic for another." Similarly, Oxford (2011) embraces a self-regulation model for L2 learning, but unlike Dörnyei's approach, in Oxford's model, learners actively and constructively use strategies to manage their own learning. So, a compromise position might be to include self-regulation as perhaps an umbrella notion when referring to language learners and to also include the strategies that they use for both learning and performing in an L2. A recent article by Rose (2012), however, argues that Dörnyei's reconceptualization might be a matter of throwing the baby out with the bathwater, in that it throws out a problematic taxonomy and replaces it with another one, which is also problematic – including the same 'definitional fuzziness' for which previous taxonomies have been criticized. So, for the purposes of this chapter, we will stick to the more "traditional" approach to viewing language learner strategies, without involving the concept of self-regulation.

In response to the claim that the language learner strategy theory is weak, there has appeared a volume replete with reviews highlighting the theoretical underpinnings of the strategy field (Cohen & Macaro 2007), and new volumes on language learner strategies – including a focus on strategy instruction – have also appeared (Oxford 2011; Cohen 2011). At the practical level, available teachers' guides for strategy instruction (Cohen & Weaver 2006; Chamot 2009) would attest to the fact that strategy instruction for language learners is an ongoing and productive field. One of the more recent and explicit examples of strategy instruction in action would be found in the Spanish Grammar Strategies Website.[2] There has also been an effort to embed strategies into L2 pragmatics instruction through websites for both Japanese[3] and Spanish L2 pragmatics.[4]

While the application of strategies to the performance of L2 pragmatics is still in need of additional empirical investigation, we would assert that having facility with a repertoire of strategies for dealing with L2 pragmatics can assist learners in analyzing complex interactional situations – both in order to interpret the behavior of others and to perform in a desired way pragmatically in a variety of contextual and dialectal situations. Ultimately, it is left to learners to determine the appropriate pragmatic behavior for any given situation and to determine the extent to which they wish to conform to perceived idealized norms for how the members behave in terms of language and culture. In the best-case scenario, the pragmatics materials that are used for instructional purposes are empirically-based, rather than being generated by textbook writers on the basis of intuition.

---

2. http://www.carla.umn.edu/strategies/sp_grammar/index.html (accessed December 28, 2010).

3. http://www.carla.umn.edu/speechacts/japanese/introtospeechacts/index.htm (accessed December 28, 2010).

4. http://www.carla.umn.edu/speechacts/sp_pragmatics/home.html (accessed December 28, 2010).

This helps to establish pragmatic patterns that might be helpful to learners in a variety of contexts. Critical to the use of these materials is the recognition they are a guide and not an idealized absolute. Adherence to these materials is not the goal, but rather interpretation of the materials for use in a variety of intercultural interactions.

3. A strategic approach to the learning and performance of speech acts

The studies to be described here represented an effort to provide explicit strategy instruction to enhance the learning and use of appropriate pragmatic behaviors in Spanish. In doing so, we were careful not to assume a homogeneous set of pragmatic behaviors used by all speakers of Spanish. Rather, in referring to Spanish pragmatics, we addressed tendencies and empirically-based findings intended to aid learners when interacting with speakers of different varieties of Spanish. A strategic approach to L2 pragmatics enables learners to deal with both common patterns and variety simultaneously through observation, explicit inquiry, and experimentation.

While strategy instruction can take a number of different forms, it is likely to have the following features (from Rubin, Chamot, Harris, & Anderson 2007; see also Chamot 2008):

1.   raising awareness of the strategies that the learners are already using,
2.   presenting and modeling strategies so learners become increasingly aware of their own thinking and learning processes,
3.   providing multiple practice opportunities to help learners move towards autonomous use of the strategies, and
4.   getting learners to evaluate the effectiveness of the strategies used, as well as their efforts to transfer these strategies to new tasks.

The effectiveness of strategy instruction with given learners depends on the specific learning context, the tasks at hand, and the characteristics of the learners (i.e. the learners' background knowledge, their goals for learning the particular language, their style preferences, and their language strategy repertoire). While there is a growing literature on the impact of instruction in the use of speech acts (see, for example, Rose 2005), the literature on the impact of strategy use on the learning and performance of L2 pragmatic behavior was still in a fledgling state when our two studies were conducted.

3.1   A website for learning Spanish pragmatics

In an effort to make strategy instruction for pragmatics more concrete, a taxonomy was generated of strategies for *learning* L2 speech acts (e.g., observing what various NSs do by noting what they say, how they say it, and their non-verbal behavior), strategies for *performing* speech acts (e.g., using communication strategies to get the message across, like "I'm not sure how to say this right"), and metapragmatic strategies for *evaluating strategy use* (e.g., monitoring various elements of the communicative act, such as level of directness, terms of address, timing, organization, and sociocultural factors) (Cohen 2005). As pointed out above, metapragmatic strategies can serve an important role in the interpretation and performance of interculturality.

In order to validate this taxonomy empirically, a website was constructed for learning Spanish speech acts, *Dancing with Words: Strategies for Learning Pragmatics in Spanish*.[5] The website consists of an introductory module as well as eight additional modules: (1) compliments, (2) gratitude and leave taking, (3) requests, (4) apologies, (5) invitations, (6) service encounters, (7) advice, suggestions, disagreements, complaints, and reprimands, and (8) considerations for pragmatic performance. Content and learning tasks on the website are similar in each of the modules and include examples from numerous varieties of Spanish (e.g., Venezuelan and Peninsular Spanish). By utilizing both general tendencies, as well as examples of specific dialect differences, our aim was to provide basic guidelines from which learners can choose, as well as specific differences that they will find across dialects.[6] This approach was intended to provide learners the skills and content necessary to build a repertoire of both specific pragmatic behaviors, as well as the strategies for fine-tuning in a given context in a given speech community. Ideally, learners will come away with greater confidence about moving between different speech communities and adapting their behavior accordingly. Tasks include short-answer, multiple-choice, and listening activities. The activities are targeted at developing strategies for learning and performing L2 pragmatics both in general and with specific speech acts, and for evaluating their performance.

---

5.   Cf. Note 4 above.

6.   All the examples were taken from empirical work available at the time. This empirical work is still somewhat limited, making it impossible to give examples from all possible varieties of Spanish.

3.2   A synthetic immersive environment for practicing Spanish pragmatics

A second L2 pragmatics environment was also constructed by co-author Sykes and a team of programmers at the University of Minnesota. In order to help validate the strategy taxonomy, an experimental online L2 Spanish pragmatics environment, *Croquelandia*, was constructed, constituting what is referred to as a *synthetic immersive environment* (SIE) (Cohen 2008; Sykes 2008, 2009; Sykes & Cohen 2008, 2009). SIEs are online, multi-user virtual environments with an educational purpose. Their aim is to integrate the many benefits of multiuser on-line gaming spaces targeted at specific learning objectives (for a more detailed discussion see, for example, Sykes 2009; Sykes, Oskoz, & Thorne 2008; Thorne, Black, & Sykes 2009). Utilizing much of the content from the Spanish pragmatics instructional materials found in the first website,[7] the SIE gave participants a chance to further explore their L2 pragmatic performance and to put into practice the skills and strategies targeted in the taxonomy. This space gave the learners an opportunity to hone the skills which would allow them to move beyond a learned system of prescriptive behaviors towards a repertoire of possible ways to approximate appropriate models for pragmatic behavior. In the context of intercultural education, there would now be an emphasis on making informed communicative choices, regardless of whether they approximate native-speaker norms.

This new virtual space allowed for assessment of both speech act performance, as well as students' abilities to use the resources within the SIE environment in their efforts to interact successfully. Learners could move through the space and select various clues and tips, and then use what they had learned to interact with a native-speaker-controlled avatar[8] in the virtual world. The interactions with NSs (a female from Colombia and a male from Spain) were targeted at specific language functions and allowed the learners to utilize the content and skills they had learned based on their experience with the interlocutor and the context. Although not explicitly taught a set of behaviors for the specific SIE interactions, the experience afforded the learners an opportunity to utilize the skills that they had learned for observing and adapting to different situations, which involved choosing from

---

7.   As noted previously, the website materials include examples from numerous varieties of Spanish and different contextual situations, all which come from empirical data. The intention is to provide learners with concrete tendencies and potential patterns without assuming a homogenous set of behaviors that can be used in any variety of Spanish. Learning to discern language variety is an important component of L2 pragmatic competence, as well as intercultural competence.

8.   An avatar is the virtual representation of one's character in the online virtual space. One's avatar is controlled by the user and can interact with features of the digital space.

pragmatic behaviors with which they were familiar. For example, learners needed to adjust their pragmatic behavior so that it was appropriate for interacting both with the Colombian female (e.g., more deference and indirect requests) and with the male Spaniard (e.g., more direct requests).[9] It should be noted that although clearly a possibility in the real world, participants in Croquelandia were not given the communicative choice of opting out from performing these speech acts.

The research reported in this chapter represents a comparison of perceived strategies learners used in the two digital spaces, one involving the Spanish pragmatics website, *Dancing with Words*, and the other involving the virtual world, *Croquelandia*. The research question addressed was: How do learners perceive their strategy development for L2 Spanish pragmatics through the use of two different CALL environments, a self-access website and a synthetic immersive environment?

4. The research design

4.1   The design for Study 1

Study 1 involved a group of ten student participants (N = 5 females, N = 5 males). The results reported here are a subset of the findings from a larger study. For a description of the complete study see Sykes and Cohen (2008: 147–150). Due to space constraints, we describe in detail only the procedures relevant to this specific analysis. The participants had an average age of 23 and came from a variety of language learning contexts. All were enrolled in advanced level Spanish courses (i.e. beyond the introductory and intermediate levels), were NSs of English, and had an average reported grade-point average in Spanish of 3.63. The instructional website, *Dancing with Words*, played a major role in content delivery and was the only means of *explicit* pragmatic instruction available to the learners.

First, all subjects attended a general descriptive session about the project and completed the entrance survey. The survey section analyzed here consisted of one section specifically addressing strategies for L2 pragmatics based on the Cohen (2005) taxonomy. This survey is included as Appendix A. This session lasted 30 minutes. The subjects then completed a before-measure, a one-hour instructional session, three content modules, and an immediate and delayed after-measure. Each of the three online modules were from the *Dancing with Words* website (i.e.

---

9. While the current study did not address this issue of regional variation in norms for pragmatic performance, the ability to adapt to regional differences is a desired outcome in a strategic approach to L2 pragmatic development.

requests, apologies, and service encounters). Each was completed in a laboratory setting within a two-week period in an order selected by the participants who completed one module per session at a self-selected time. The requests and apologies modules each took approximately 90 minutes to complete and the service encounter module took the participants 1 hour.

Note that in Study 1, the before- and after-measures were conducted in what was then a rudimentary version of the SIE, used only to assess the students' pragmatic ability, not as a learning environment for pragmatics which it evolved into. After completing both after-measures, the subjects engaged in retrospective, one-on-one interviews with the researcher. Each interview was audio-recorded and entailed questions addressing the learners' evaluation of the experience, reported behavior, and suggestions for improvement of each of the website modules. The interviews were especially useful for gaining insights from learners regarding their experience with the online spaces and their perceptions of them. The interviews helped to provide a better understanding of the learners' interactions in the digitally mediated spaces. They then completed an exit survey similar to the measure completed at the beginning of the project (see a sample in Appendix A). The survey data is most relevant to the current analysis.

4.2   The design for Study 2

Study 2 involved the use of Croquelandia, the space for delivery of the pragmatic materials (see Sykes 2008, 2009 for more details on this SIE).

In the SIE itself, learners could collaborate and interact in three primary areas – their host family's house, a central plaza and market place, and the university (see Figure 1 for a view of the marketplace). Learners could move seamlessly among the three spaces using an interactive map in which they could click on the area to which they wanted to travel. In this SIE, learners were able to move an avatar throughout the environment and talk with other learners via avatar interaction. While the interlocutors (i.e. the learners) only saw each other virtually, they were able to interact with one another via voice chat and written chat.

As was the case with Study 1, the results reported here are a subset of the findings from the study as a whole. For a description of the complete study see Sykes (2008:87–90). In Study 2, 25 participants reported their perceptions of the impact the materials had on their strategizing about pragmatics. Much as with Study 1, an entrance survey in this study was designed to collect demographic and experiential information from each of the learners prior to the start of the instructional activities. The purpose was to obtain self-report from students as to

Figure 1. Sample virtual setting – the marketplace in the SIE *Croquelandia*

the speech-act learning and performance strategies that they were already using (see the Appendix).

Upon completion of the entrance survey, the participants completed a before-measure, two class sessions dedicated to pragmatics, two modules in the SIE (i.e. one targeted at requests and the other at apologies), a one-on-one midpoint interview with the researcher, a group presentation, an after-measure, an exit interview, and an exit survey. The participants' exit survey was used to obtain an after-measure of perceived strategy use. In both studies, the measure of strategy use was based on perception, rather than on actual use.

4.3   Procedures for data analysis

The data from learners' reported strategy use in the three categories of pragmatic strategies from the before- and after-measures for both Study 1 and 2 (strategies for learning L2 pragmatics, strategies for using pragmatics, and metapragmatic strategies) were submitted to analysis. In each survey, the respondents evaluated their own strategy use on an ordinal scale as follows: seldom/never = 1, somewhat likely/sometimes = 2, likely/often = 3, very likely/very often = 4, almost always = 5, and don't know = 0. For the purposes of this analysis, a change rate of less than .5 was considered as no change. A change rate between .5 and 1 in either direction was considered a minor increase or decrease. A change rate greater than 1 in either direction was considered a moderate change. In the case of a strategy dealing with learning style preference (U-6), the subjects in Study 1 were queried using one survey item whereas in Study 2, two items were used to examine individual style (i.e. cognitive style and personality). In this case, the two items in

Study 2 were averaged for the purpose of comparison to the item in Study 1. Due to the small sample size and different groups of learners in each study, the results could not be verified through calculation of statistical significance. Hence, these findings have to be taken as merely suggestive of possible trends in the data. They should be interpreted as an initial starting point for analysis.

5.   The findings

First, with regard to reported frequency of strategies aimed at learning L2 pragmatics, strategies exhibiting a minor increase in reported use in both studies were *gathering information on how the speech acts were performed* (L-4) and *paying attention to what native speakers did by noting what they said, how they said it, and their non-verbal behavior* (L-6). In Study 1 of the research, there was also a moderate change in *asking NSs to model how they performed the speech acts* (L-2) and *identifying the speech acts to focus on* (L-3), and a minor change in strategy *referring to published sources* (L-1). Overall, results for the learning strategies category suggested a greater reported frequency of use of learning strategies from participation in the online website activities in Study 1 than in the SIE experience in Study 2 (see Table 1).

In terms of reported frequency of strategies for using L2 pragmatics, a similar picture emerged, with a greater increase in reported frequency of use for strategies in Study 1 than in Study 2. There was a minor reported increase in *remaining true to own cultural identity and personal values* (U-1) in both studies. In Study 1 alone, there was a moderate reported increase for *asking for feedback on pragmatic abilities from natives* (U-3), and a minor reported increase for *practicing in order to improve pragmatic skills* (U-4) and *attending to own learning style preferences* (U-6). So overall, there was some reported increase in language use strategies after having participated in the online website activities in Study 1, and virtually no reported change after participation in the SIE in Study 2 (see Table 2).

In terms of reported frequency of strategies for supervision of strategy use, there appeared to be a minor increase of use in both studies for *paying attention to pre-planning* (M-1), and just for Study 2 in *deciding whether to focus on comprehension, performance, or both* (M-2) (see Table 3).

Table 1. Reported frequency of strategies for learning pragmatics (adopted from Sykes & Cohen 2009)

Strategy	Study 1					Study 2				
	Before measure		After measure		Change	Before measure		After measure		Change
	M	SD	M	SD		M	SD	M	SD	
L-1: I will refer to published material (e.g., articles, websites) dealing with communicative acts.	2.0	0.94	2.60	0.84	0.60	1.45	0.71	1.75	0.98	0.30
L-2: I will ask natives to model how they perform the communicative act.	2.4	1.17	3.50	0.87	1.10	1.62	0.71	1.58	0.92	−0.04
L-3: I will identify the communicative acts (i.e., requests, apologies, compliments) that I want/need to focus on.	2.2	1.54	3.83	1.06	1.63	2.58	1.43	2.88	1.07	0.30
L-4: I will gather information (through observation, interviews, written materials, movies, radio) on how the communicative acts are performed.	2.9	1.28	3.55	1.30	0.65	2.62	1.36	3.16	1.34	0.54
L-5: I will conduct my own cross-cultural analysis (e.g., identify norms and strategies specific to a given communicative act like "requesting," determine the similarities and differences between my first language and Spanish).	3.2	0.91	3.30	1.05	0.10	2.62	1.51	3.00	1.25	0.38
L-6: I will pay attention to what native speakers do by noting what they say, how they say it, and their non-verbal behaviour.	3.4	1.26	4.10	0.87	0.70	3.12	1.65	3.62	1.01	0.50

Table 2. Reported frequency of strategies for using pragmatics (adopted from Sykes & Cohen 2009)

Strategy	Study 1					Study 2				
	Before measure		After measure		Change	Before measure		After measure		Change
	M	SD	M	SD		M	SD	M	SD	
U-1: I will remain true to my own cultural identity and personal values while still being aware of the cultural expectations of native speakers.	3.50	0.97	4.10	0.87	0.60	3.29	1.60	3.91	1.10	0.62
U-2: I use communication strategies to get the message across (e.g., "I'm not sure how to say this right," repair when necessary, attempt to follow native speaker examples).	3.60	0.84	3.80	0.91	0.20	3.16	1.20	3.16	1.23	0
U-3: I ask native speakers for feedback on my pragmatic abilities.	2.75	0.92	3.80	1.03	1.05	1.54	1.11	1.58	0.82	0.04
U-4: I practice (e.g., role-plays, imaginary situations, conversations with native speakers) in order to improve my pragmatic skills.	2.75	1.31	3.60	1.17	0.85	1.88	1.30	1.91	0.97	0.04
U-5: I will devise and utilize memory strategies for retrieving the communicative act materials that has already been learned.	2.60	0.69	3.05	1.30	0.45	2.29	1.28	2.79	1.25	0.50
U-6: I will determine my style preference as a learner and try approaches that are consistent with my individual style.	3.10	0.99	3.60	1.07	0.50	3.40	1.38	3.29	1.55	-0.10

Table 3. Reported frequency of metapragmatic strategies (adopted from Sykes & Cohen 2009)

Strategy	Study 1						Study 2					
	Before measure		After measure		Change		Before measure		After measure		Change	
	M	SD	M	SD			M	SD	M	SD		
M-1: I will be conscious of the necessity for pre-planning.	3.0	0.81	3.50	1.35	0.50		2.91	1.22	3.70	1.08	0.79	
M-2: I will decide what my focus is. Performance? Comprehension? Both?	3.3	1.15	3.10	1.19	−0.20		2.25	1.40	2.91	1.24	0.66	
M-3: I will monitor my performance of communicative acts (e.g., level of directness, terms of address, timing, organization, sociocultural factors).	2.6	1.07	3.05	1.21	0.45		2.33	1.41	2.79	1.25	0.46	

6.   Discussion and conclusions

6.1   Discussion

This chapter has looked at strategizing about pragmatic performance in two different kinds of environments. Study 1 looked primarily at the reported strategies used by learners to access information about how to perform L2 pragmatics from a website ("Dancing with Words") where they appeared in various formats. Study 2 had the learners in an experimental environment where learners were able to interact with avatars and add pragmatic knowledge more experientially. The argument we are making is that learning about pragmatics does not just happen by osmosis for the most part. Learners need their awareness heightened, and furnishing them with specific strategies for making more informed choices in their pragmatic performance seems to us to be of keen value in our increasingly global world where insularity no longer works. This study would seem to suggest that orienting learners to strategies for performance of L2 pragmatics in an interactive and self-selective way can make a difference for interculturality.

These findings would suggest that participation in the two distinct types of mediated contexts – the self-access website and the SIE – may have had a slightly different impact on the reported use of the three types of strategies. With regard to strategies for learning and performing pragmatics, two learning strategies (L-2: *Ask native speakers to model how they perform the communicative act*, and L-3: *Identify the second language speech acts learners want/need to focus on*) and a use strategy (U-3: *Ask native speakers for feedback on your pragmatic abilities*) are especially noteworthy because there was a moderate increase in perceived use from the participants in Study 1 and no change in Study 2. One feasible explanation for this difference across the two studies may be the emphasis on the use of an NS as a resource for pragmatic learning in the website itself. While caution needs to be taken in suggesting an ideal NS model,[10] the use of NSs as a starting point helps provide some benchmark for the development of L2 pragmatics. In the activities on the website, learners utilized a variety of models and examples to improve their awareness of pragmatic choices. However, for additional information they would need to talk with many NSs in the real world and, as a result, were instructed to do so. In the SIE, learners were not explicitly encouraged to talk with NSs outside of the virtual space. Therefore, participants in Study 2 may

---

10.   We do not intend to imply that learners should try to emulate NS behavior, especially given that the notion of the *native speaker* can be problematic and given the learners' need to maintain their own identity. See, for example, Kramsch and McConnell-Ginet (1992), Thorne (2005), and Ishihara & Tarone (2009) with regard to learner subjectivity.

not have viewed explicitly asking for help from NSs as a necessary resource for pragmatic development. While some may argue against the value of a NS as the expert in determining appropriate pragmatic behavior, learning to utilizing NSs as resources can, in all reality, be very helpful for learners. Furthermore, dialogue about pragmatic aspects of language (e.g., what actually counts as an apology), can help spark introspection and discussion about cultural assumptions and beliefs and the ways these vary among members of the same community, an aspect of intercultural education that is vital for understanding the dynamic nature of culture in general.

With regard to metapragmatic strategies, in the *Dancing with Words* website, explicit identification and exploration of each of the strategies was included as part of the instructional activities. In the SIE, the strategies-based approach entailed experiential learning. That is, instead of explaining to the learners how they might use a specific strategy to improve their pragmatic abilities (the case of the website), the SIE quests and activities required that learners implement each of the strategies through practice and use. The distinct delivery method of instruction may explain the slight differences found in the learning and use strategies categories, especially with regard to greater increase in strategy M-1 in Study 2. It would appear that the Study 2 subjects employed and practiced metapragmatic strategies more as they worked in the immersive space and while participating in their in-class group activities. This is a noteworthy advantage of SIEs for the development of strategies for gaining greater intercultural awareness. Learners are able to experiment with different points of view and implement different strategies to explore potential outcomes, thereby developing two areas viewed as critical in Byram's (1997) approach – the skills of interpreting and relating and the skills of discovery and interaction.

6.2 Limitations

The first limitation of this research is that since it was not possible to use measures of statistical significance, the findings are simply suggestive. Secondly, in considering these results, it is important to remember that the findings are based on learner report, and not on actual use. Learners reported the strategies they would use for improving their pragmatic abilities based on their experience in each of the environments. Retrospective, self-observational data may not be completely accurate, depending on the amount of elapsed time from the events themselves, and so the verbal report data are not necessarily indicative of how the strategies were actually used (Cohen 2011). An additional consideration was the use of two distinct sets of students to compare the perceived strategy use of each of the mediated contexts.

6.3   Suggestions for future research

Future research should utilize other measures for confirming actual strategy use to complement the self-reported perception data used in this analysis, as well as its impact on intercultural awareness. Such measures could include, for example, think-aloud protocols, observation of user behavior,[11] targeted measures for examining language variety distinctions, recording in the digitally-mediated spaces, and scenarios targeted at assessing the use of specific types of strategies. Future studies should also consider perceived strategy development in each of the mediated contexts by the *same* learners. Additionally, it would be beneficial to investigate both whether the use of these strategies does indeed enhance pragmatic abilities and whether learners are actually using the strategies they say they are using. Since there is increasing evidence that the conscious use of strategies in other skill areas can have a significant impact on both the learning and performance of language (see for example, Cohen & Macaro 2007; Griffiths 2008; Hurd & Lewis 2008), there is every reason to believe that this would be the case for L2 pragmatics as well.

6.4   Pedagogical implications

Although the results from this research are by no means definitive, they still would suggest the value of including strategies for the learning and performance of speech acts, as well as for metapragmatic evaluation of their impact on intercultural awareness and the making of informed choices. For too long, the field of language learner strategies has lacked the fine-tuning necessary for tackling the more complex and challenging aspects of language learning, such as L2 pragmatics and intercultural competence. The results of this study speak to the benefits of making accessible to learners through digitally-mediated spaces the strategies that may help learners engage in pragmatically informed interactions. In addition, with the emergence of new technologies such as SIEs, we now have the opportunity to create learning spaces specifically for addressing challenging complexities associated with L2 pragmatics (Sykes 2009; Sykes, Oskoz, & Thorne 2008) and to assess the impact of such spaces on intercultural education.

---

11. Although not reported here, screen capture through the software *Camtasia* was used in both the website and SIE to observe learner behaviors.

6.5 Conclusions

The purpose of this chapter has been to highlight the potential role of language learner strategies in the development of L2 pragmatic awareness within the domain of intercultural education. Strategies for performing pragmatics can contribute to a learner's repertoire for dealing with performance at the intersection of language and culture. This includes enabling them to deal with prototypical pragmatic patterns from a dynamic perspective and making informed choices about their own behavior. Hence, we see the value of strategy instruction in L2 pragmatics, as well as research focused on its impact. Strategy instruction enables learners to move beyond language to culture – supporting them in developing interpretative capabilities so that they can make truly informed choices about just how pragmatically appropriate they wish to be.

This chapter also serves to highlight the critical role L2 pragmatic abilities play in the larger arena of intercultural education. By integrating L2 pragmatic instruction with other elements of intercultural education, bridges can be built to emphasize the fact that at times language and cultural elements are inseparably bound together. Pragmatic assumptions must be informed through intercultural experiences. By giving learners the skills to perform communicative acts as intended, we enable access to a wealth of opportunities that might not otherwise be possible.

References

Abdallah-Pretceille, M. (2006). Interculturalism as a paradigm for thinking about diversity. *Intercultural Education, 17*(5), 475–483.

Alcón, E. S. & Martínez-Flor, A. (Eds.). (2008). *Investigating pragmatics in foreign language learning, teaching, and testing.* Clevedon: Multilingual Matters.

Anderson, N. (2008). Metacognition and good language learners. In C. Griffiths (Ed.), *Lessons from good language learners* (pp. 99–109). Cambridge: Cambridge University Press.

Belz, J. (2007). The role of computer mediation in the instruction and development of L2 pragmatic competence. *Annual Review of Applied Linguistics, 27*, 45–75.

Belz, J. & Thorne, S. (2005). *Internet-mediated intercultural foreign language education.* Boston, MA: Thomson Heinle.

Byram, M. (1997). *Teaching and assessing intercultural communicative competence.* Clevedon: Multilingual Matters.

Chamot, A. U. (1987). The learning strategies of ESL students. In A. Wenden & J. Rubin (Eds.), *Learner strategies in language learning* (pp. 71–84). Englewood Cliffs, NJ: Prentice-Hall.

Chamot, A. U. (2008). Strategy instruction and good language learners. In C. Griffiths (Ed.), *Lessons from good language learners* (pp. 266–281). Cambridge: Cambridge University Press.

Chamot, A. U. (2009). *The CALLA handbook: Implementing the cognitive academic language learning approach* (second edn). White Plains, NY: Longman.

Cohen, A. D. (2005). Strategies for learning and performing L2 speech acts. *Intercultural Pragmatics, 2*(3), 275–301.

Cohen, A. D. (2007). Coming to terms with language learner strategies: Surveying the experts. In A. D. Cohen & E. Macaro (Eds.), *Language learner strategies: 30 years of research and practice* (pp. 29–45). Oxford: Oxford University Press.

Cohen, A. D. (2008). Teaching and assessing L2 pragmatics: What can we expect from learners? *Language Teaching, 41*(2), 215–237.

Cohen, A. D. (2011). *Strategies in learning and using a second language* (second edn.) Harlow: Longman/Pearson Education.

Cohen, A. D. & Macaro, E. (Eds.). (2007). *Language learner strategies: 30 years of research and practice.* Oxford: Oxford University Press.

Cohen, A. D. & Weaver, S. J. (2006). *Styles and strategies-based instruction: A teachers' guide.* Minneapolis, MN: Center for Advanced Research on Language Acquisition, University of Minnesota.

Dörnyei, Z. (2009). *The psychology of second language acquisition.* Oxford: Oxford University Press.

González-Lloret, M. (2010). Conversation analysis and speech act performance. In A. Martínez-Flor & E. Usó-Juan (Eds.), *Speech act performance: Theoretical, empirical and methodological issues* (pp. 57–74). Amsterdam/Philadelphia: John Benjamins.

Griffiths, C. (Ed.). (2008). *Lessons from good language learners.* Cambridge: Cambridge University Press.

Holliday, A. (2011). *Intercultural communication and ideology.* London: Sage.

Hurd, S. & Lewis, T. (2008). *Language learning strategies in independent settings.* Bristol: Multilingual Matters.

Ishihara, N. & Cohen, A. D. (2010). *Teaching and learning pragmatics: Where language and culture meet.* Harlow: Pearson Education.

Ishihara, N. & Tarone, E. (2009). Emulating and resisting pragmatic norms: Learner subjectivity and foreign language pragmatic use. In N. Noguchi (Ed.), *Pragmatic competence in Japanese as a second language* (pp. 101–128). Berlin: Mouton de Gruyter.

Kasper, G. & Rose, K. R. (2002). *Pragmatic development in a second language.* Malden, MA: Blackwell Publishing.

Kramsch, C. & McConnell-Ginet, S. (1992). *Text and context: Cross-disciplinary perspectives on language study.* Lexington, MA: DC Heath.

Kramsch, C. (Ed.). (2002). *Language acquisition and language socialization: Ecological perspectives.* London: Continuum.

Márquez Reiter, R. & Placencia, M. E. (2005). *Spanish pragmatics.* Houndmills: Palgrave Macmillan.

Oxford, R. L. (1990). *Language learning strategies: What every teacher should know.* New York, NY: Newbury House/Harper Collins.

Oxford, R. L. (2011). *Teaching and researching language learning strategies.* Harlow: Longman/Pearson Education.

Rose, H. (2012). Reconceptualizing strategic learning in the face of self-regulation: Throwing language learning strategies out with the bathwater. *Applied Linguistics, 33*(1), 92–98.

Rose, K. R. (2005). On the effects of instruction in second language pragmatics. *System, 33*(3), 385–399.

Rose, K. R. & Kasper, G. (2001). *Pragmatics in language teaching.* New York, NY: Cambridge University Press.

Rubin, J., Chamot, A. U., Harris, V., & Anderson, N. J. (2007). Intervening in the use of strategies. In A. D. Cohen & E. Macaro (Eds.), *Language learner strategies: 30 years of research and practice* (pp. 141–160). Oxford: Oxford University Press.

Sykes, J. M. (2005). Synchronous CMC and pragmatic development: Effects of oral and written chat. *CALICO Journal, 22*(3), 399–431.

Sykes, J. M. (2008). *A dynamic approach to social interaction: Synthetic immersive environments and Spanish pragmatics.* Doctoral dissertation, University of Minnesota, Minneapolis.

Sykes, J. M. (2009). Learner requests in Spanish: Examining the potential of multiuser virtual environments for L2 pragmatic acquisition. In L. Lomika & G. Lord (Eds.), *The next generation: Social networking and online collaboration. 8th CALICO Monograph Series* (pp. 199–234). San Marcos, TX: Texas State University.

Sykes, J. M. & Cohen, A. D. (2008). Observed learner behavior, reported use, and evaluation of a website for learning Spanish pragmatics. In M. Bowles, R. Foote, & S. Perpiñán (Eds.), *Second language acquisition and research: Focus on form and function. Selected Proceedings of the 2007 Second Language Research Forum* (pp. 144–157). Somerville, MA: Cascadilla Press.

Sykes, J. M. & Cohen, A. D. (2009). Learner perception and strategies for pragmatic acquisition: A glimpse into online learning materials. In C. R. Dreyer (Ed.), *Language and linguistics: Emerging trends* (pp. 99–135). Hauppauge, NY: Nova Science.

Sykes, J. M., Oskoz, A., & Thorne, S. L. (2008). Web 2.0, synthetic immersive environments, and mobile resources for language education. *CALICO Journal, 25*(3), 528–546.

Tatsuki, D. (Ed.). (2005). *Pragmatics in language learning, theory, and practice.* Tokyo: The Japan Association for Language Teaching Pragmatics Special Interest Group.

Tatsuki, D. & Houck, N. (Eds.). (2010). *Pragmatics from research to practice: Teaching speech acts.* Alexandria, VA: Teachers of English to Speakers of Other Languages.

Thorne, S. (2005). Pedagogical and praxiological lessons from internet-mediated intercultural foreign language education research. In J. Belz & S. Thorne (Eds.), *Internet-mediated intercultural foreign language education* (pp. 2–30). Boston MA: Thomson and Heinle.

Thorne, S. L., Black, R. W., & Sykes, J. M. (2009). Second language use, socialization, and learning in internet interest communities and online gaming. *Modern Language Journal, 93*(1), 802–821.

Yule, G. (1996). *Pragmatics.* Oxford: Oxford University Press.

Appendix: Survey of strategies for L2 pragmatics (from Sykes 2008)

C. Evaluating your strategies for learning Spanish pragmatics

Rate your use of each of the strategies below to improve your own pragmatic ability in Spanish. If you are not sure what the strategy is, please mark the "Don't know" option.

Strategy	Seldom / never	Sometimes	Often	Very often	Almost always	Don't know
I determine my style preferences as a learner and try approaches that are consistent with my individual perceptual style (visual, auditory, or hands on).						
I try approaches that are consistent with my individual cognitive style preferences (e.g., global or detail-oriented, abstract or concrete, summarizer or analytic).						
I try approaches that are consistent with my individual personality (extrovert/introvert, reflective/impulsive, open/closure-oriented).						
I identify the language functions (i.e., requests, apologies, compliments) that I want/need to focus on.						
I gather information (through observation, interviews, written materials, movies, radio) on how the communicative acts are performed.						
I devise and utilize memory strategies for retrieving the communicative act material that has already been learned.						
I conduct my own "cross-cultural" analysis (e.g., identify norms & strategies specific to a given communicative act like "requesting," determine similarities and differences between my first language and Spanish).						
I pay attention to what native speakers do by noting what they say, how they say it, and their non-verbal behavior.						
I ask native speakers to model how they perform the communicative act.						
I refer to published material (e.g., articles, websites) dealing with communicative acts.						

I monitor my performance of communicative acts (e.g., level of directness, terms of address, timing, organization, sociocultural factors).						
I practice with pragmatics (e.g., role-plays, imaginary situations, conversations with native speakers) in order to improve my pragmatic skills.						
I ask native speakers for feedback on my pragmatic abilities.						
I use communication strategies to get the message across (e.g., "I'm not sure how to say this right," repair when necessary, attempt to follow native speaker examples).						
I remain true to my own cultural identity and personal values while still being aware of the cultural expectations of native speakers.						
I decide what my focus is. Production? Comprehension? Both?						
I am conscious of the necessity for pre-planning.						

Making the 'invisible' visible

A conversation analytic approach to intercultural teaching and learning in the Chinese Mandarin language classroom

Yanyan Wang and Johanna Rendle-Short
Australian National University

This chapter demonstrates how conversation analysis or talk-in-interaction can be utilized in the language classroom in order to promote intercultural language learning. It shows how tertiary Mandarin language students can be given the techniques and opportunities to reflectively examine their own culture and its intersection with other cultures. It uses intercultural pragmatics and conversation analysis to examine the Chinese Mandarin *ni hao ma* ('how are you') in an oral Chinese language test. The chapter contrasts two groups of Chinese Mandarin learners, one of which received intercultural training in the use of *ni hao ma* during telephone openings and the other group who didn't receive any intercultural language teaching. The chapter illustrates how language learners can reflexively examine their language use and demonstrates ways of encouraging language learners to think about hidden cultural assumptions within their own talk and language.

1. Introduction

In spite of an increased emphasis on intercultural language education (Byram 1989; Kramsch 1993; Dervin 2007; Liddicoat 2009), very little research has focused on how culture and intercultural pragmatics can be incorporated into the language classroom (Liddicoat et al. 2003; cf. McConachy in this volume). Of particular interest in this chapter is how tertiary language learners develop their intercultural capabilities in order to achieve 'intercultural communicative competence' (Byram et al. 2001). We will show how one way of developing intercultural awareness is through close linguistic analysis of people (whether they be students, language learners, language educators or conversational participants) interacting both within their own culture and across cultures. Using the framework of conversation analysis (CA) or talk-in-interaction with its emphasis on close and detailed analysis of naturally occurring everyday interaction, we will show how language learners and educators can be given the tools to examine their own talk and the talk of others in order to explicate and understand hidden cultural assumptions. The specific interactional moment under consideration in this chapter is the telephone opening, a site where participants are most likely to display cultural norms (Bowles 2006). In particular, the chapter will examine language learners' use of *ni hao ma* (generally translated as 'how are you') in the tertiary Chinese Mandarin[1] language classroom.

Contrastive analyses of (landline) telephone openings across a number of languages and cultures have made frequent reference to the 'how are you' expression that generally occurs during English conversational openings (e.g. Sun 2004 on Chinese Mandarin; Hopper & Chen 1996 on Taiwanese Mandarin; House 1982 on German).[2] Whereas English speaking (landline) telephone callers tend to ask 'how are you' prior to moving to the first topic of the conversation, called the anchor position (Schegloff 1986), no such expectation has been shown to exist in, for example, Mandarin (landline) telephone conversations (Sun 2004). One of the difficulties, however, for Chinese Mandarin language teachers is that scripts containing *ni hao ma* ('how are you') tend to occur in the first or second lesson of some Chinese language textbooks.[3] The occurrence of the *ni hao ma* expression in text books together with the tendency for language learners to unreflectively transfer their cultural understanding of their own language to the target language means that beginner Chinese language learners are very likely to use *ni hao ma* in telephone openings, even though this expression is generally considered to be culturally inappropriate within an everyday setting and is seldom used by native Mandarin speakers from Mainland China.

The first aim of this chapter is to use the methodology of conversation analysis to examine telephone openings by two groups of language learners of Chinese Mandarin. It will show how one group of language learners who did not receive

---

1.   The Chinese language referred to in this paper is Mandarin from mainland China.

2.   More recently, analysts have begun the process of analysing mobile telephone conversations (e.g. Hutchby 2005; Hutchby & Barnett 2005; Arminen & Leinonen 2006; Arminen & Weilenmann 2009). One of the differences that seems to be emerging between mobile and landline phone conversations relates to the more personalised nature of the mobile call due to call recognition. In this paper, we analyse landline phone conversations between students and their teacher. None of these were carried out on the mobile.

3.   Chinese text books that use *ni hao ma* within Chinese conversational openings tend to be published for learners of Chinese as a second language (see, for example, Liu 2004).

intercultural teaching and learning incorrectly used the *ni hao ma* expression. This group demonstrated a lack of cultural understanding of how telephone conversations should be opened in Chinese. In contrast, the analysis will show how a second group of students who were given the tools to reflectively examine their own cultural assumptions as well as the cultural assumptions of the target language were, on the whole, able to appropriately open a Chinese telephone conversation. The second aim of this chapter is to show how a methodology such as conversation analysis or talk-in-interaction can be utilized in the language classroom in order to promote intercultural language learning. It shows how it is possible to give tertiary Mandarin language students (as exemplified by the second group) a conversation analytic tool that provides them with the techniques and opportunities to reflectively examine their own culture(s) and its intersection with other cultures.

2.   Overview of intercultural language learning

Dervin (2011) argues that culture is not a static or fixed thing; it is not something that is supplementary to language teaching, focusing on facts or stereotypes about the Other. Liddicoat et al. (2003:7) further argue, "culture is not about information and things, it is about actions and understanding" with the task of the language educator being to teach language learners about differences and similarities between diverse cultures, different ways of interacting, and the diversities of Self and Other (Dervin 2009). Teaching interculturality within the language classroom requires language teachers to move beyond the teaching of a 'grammar of culture' (Dervin 2010), to understanding the idea that "knowledge, society and subjectivity are all dynamic and contextual phenomena which can be theorized in terms of dialogues between different (real and imagined) perspectives" (Gillespie & Cornish 2010:33).

Dervin (2010) argues that the notion of interculturality has to be distinguished from cultural, transcultural or multicultural approaches. It has to be thought of as a fluid concept, encapsulating the idea that individuals are constantly constructing and co-constructing themselves through their talk. This is particularly relevant for language learners or as Byram & Zarate (1997:11) call them, 'intercultural speakers' who are developing their 'intercultural communicative competence' (Byram et al. 2001). Through their language learning, they are developing their understanding of their own language(s) and culture(s) in relation to additional language(s) and culture(s). They are engaged in the process of facilitating negotiation of meaning, involving recognition, mediation and acceptance of different and similar perspectives (Crozet, Liddicoat & Lo Bianco 1999). They learn to make choices about what is appropriate as they engage in meaningful intercultural communication (Crozet & Liddicoat 2000: 1); they learn to create culture and to show their understanding of Others (Dervin 2010).

The Intercultural Language Teaching (ILT) and Learning (ILL) paradigm enables learners "to develop the ability to create multiple 'third places' as they learn to interact with 'otherness'" (Crozet & Liddicoat 2000: 1). Intercultural language teaching and learning is different from traditional pedagogies for teaching languages – it requires teachers to make a pedagogical shift in order to fuse language and the sometimes invisible cultures, together with learning, into a single educative approach (Liddicoat et al. 2003: 43). Through the development of language learners' intercultural awareness, teachers encourage language learners to acknowledge the need to interact with people from other cultures while maintaining their own identity. As Liddicoat et al. (2003: 6) argue interactions between people are context-sensitive, negotiated, mediated and variable. This means that students should engage in developing intercultural competence from the beginning of their language learning, even from lesson one or two where they learn how to greet each other in the target language. Through raised awareness of their own culture and language contexts in which they live, they are able to position their already familiar language(s) and culture(s) alongside target cultures and language contexts. They are then in a position to develop an intercultural perspective to their language learning.

However, intercultural language learning is easier to talk about than to put into practice. The aim of this chapter is to show (a) how a methodology such as conversation analysis can be used in the language classroom not only for detailed analysis of the conversations or snippets of interaction between language learners and language educators as they talk to each other in the target language, but also to show (b) how conversation analysis can be used as an analytic tool by the language learners themselves – a tool that enables them, through fine-grained intercultural analysis, to unpack some of the hidden cultural assumptions in their own language, to reflectively discuss intercultural communication, and to anticipate additional hidden cultural assumptions that might also exist in the target language.

3.   Making the 'invisible' visible through talk-in-interaction

One of the challenges for intercultural language teaching is how to display the range of hidden or invisible aspects of interaction that underlie effective communication. Although we might have an intuitive sense of how language is used and how conversations work, such intuitions rely on our cultural understanding of language within particular contexts. As Liddicoat et al. (2003: 8) argue "language is always used to communicate something beyond itself and is at the same time affected by the context in which it is found". So any attempt to teach intercultural awareness as a way of increasing language learners' cultural knowledge has to do more than just focus on how different cultures operate, it has to provide an explanation of how language(s) and culture(s) affect our everyday talk and communication.

Conversation analysis (CA) or talk-in-interaction is particularly suited to displaying the hidden linguistic features of interaction, and by extension, to displaying the cultural underpinnings of communication. CA, a framework for displaying "the technology of conversation" (Sacks 1984:411), shows the micro-detail of language in naturally occurring talk, as people communicate in real time to accomplish activities and to create and understand ordinary social life. CA examines the practices and competencies by which people organize social interaction and discovers how interaction is locally ordered by participants, moment by moment. It is for these reasons that CA is particularly well-suited to intercultural language teaching and learning as it gives both educators and students a tool for examining their talk, their conversations, their interaction, and for also assessing whether their intercultural communication is effective or not.

A fundamental notion of conversation analysis is that people exhibit, in the design and timing of their own talk and conduct, their understanding and treatment of other's prior talk and conduct. Conversation analysts therefore focus on the sequential development of interaction, on seeing what happens and what happens next. Conversation analytic concepts fundamental to understanding the organization of talk-in-interaction are the 'turn construction unit' (TCU) as the basic unit of talk; the transition relevance place (TRP) as the point in interaction where speaker change becomes interactionally 'relevant'; and the rules by which speakers organise turn-taking in everyday conversation (Sacks, Schegloff & Jefferson 1974). (For introductions to CA see: Drew 2005; Drew & Heritage 2006; Hutchby & Wooffitt 1998; Liddicoat 2007; Schegloff 2007; Sidnell 2010; ten Have 2007).

The basic organising sequence of conversation is the adjacency pair, made up of an action initiating first pair part (FPP), sometimes simply called a 'first', and a second pair part (SPP), or 'second', that completes the action initiated by the first (Sacks et al. 1974). Classic adjacency pair sequences are question and answer sequences, in which there is a clear expectation of 'conditional relevance', such that given a first, the second is expected. As argued by Schegloff (1968:1083), the strength of the conditional relevance is such that if the second doesn't occur it can be heard as being 'officially absent'. The adjacency pair under discussion in this paper consists of the *ni hao ma* ('how are you') question and its possible type-appropriate response. Of interest in the current analysis is (a) whether it is culturally appropriate to initiate a *ni hao ma* type adjacency pair in Chinese Mandarin telephone openings and (b) given such a question or FPP, what would be a type-appropriate response or SPP. In English telephone openings, the most likely position for a 'how are you' sequence is just before the first topic (anchor position); and in response to the 'how are you' FPP, there is a limited range of possible responses with the neutral 'fine' or 'not bad' being very common (Schegloff 1986). In Chinese Mandarin telephone openings, as the analysis will show, *ni hao ma* is less likely to occur in this sequential environment and if it is asked, the set of possible responses is less restricted.

Utilising CA as a framework within applied linguistics for analysing language learners' interaction is not new. CA has already been used to examine language learners' naturally occurring interaction in order to understand research questions, such as, what do language learners do interactionally when they talk to other people (Schegloff et al. 2002); how does language learning actually take place (e.g. Gardner & Wagner 2004); what are the advantages and disadvantages of assessment formats and how can CA be used to inform the design of assessment tasks (Seedhouse 1998). However, although Huth & Taleghani-Nikazm (2006) argue that L2 learners may benefit from instruction using CA-based materials to enable them to anticipate, interpret and produce socio-pragmatically appropriate verbal behaviour in the target language, there are very few discussions of what CA-based teaching materials might look like.

One CA-based teaching approach that has been developed by Barraja-Rohan (1999, 2000; Barraja-Rohan & Pritchard 1997) for teaching conversation to adult learners of English shows how CA can be a rich resource for language teachers. Barraja-Rohan's approach, consisting of five phases, emphasises the links between the discourse structure of conversation and sociocultural aspects of talk. Learners are initially introduced to the concepts of CA through unscripted authentic interactions. They then discuss the concepts within their own first language in order to develop an intercultural perspective on the communication systems of languages. They are given a chance to use the language learnt in role-plays in order to discover new things about the phenomenon. They then reflect on and discuss their performance in order to evaluate their conversational behaviours. Emphasis is given to 'noticings' of pragmatic transfers from the first language in order to explore the different cultural features between the systems of the first and second language.

The aim of this chapter is to show how CA can be integrated into the language classroom, not just for the language teachers but also for the language learners themselves. CA provides both teachers and learners with a tool for explicating features of naturally occurring interaction in order to make salient the social and cultural aspects of interaction. As Seedhouse (1998: 93) points out, cultural and social features are potentially related to the production and understanding of interaction. Thus through engagement with the cultural norms of interaction, L2 learners need to have the linguistic understanding and interactional tools to be able to communicate successfully and effectively. The following analysis will provide an example of how CA can be used as a tool for teaching intercultural awareness (with respect to the use of the Chinese Mandarin expression *ni hao ma*). Section 4 will provide an overview of how the expression *ni hao ma* is used in Chinese Mandarin telephone conversations. Section 5 will analyse the telephone openings of two groups of Chinese Mandarin language learners in order to contrast those who were not taught using ILL with those who were taught using ILL. Finally, Section 6 will show the applicability of a tool such as CA for explicating the social and cultural norms of expressions such as *ni hao ma*.

4.   Chinese Mandarin telephone openings and the use of *ni hao ma*

The following example shows a typical telephone opening in Chinese Mandarin. Y has rung to speak to her mother (M).[4]

Example 1
1.   ((ring))
2. M: wei
        hello
3. Y: wei Ma wo shi yingying
        hello Mum I am Yingying
        hello Mum this is Yingying
4.   (0.2)
5. M: ei ni hao=
        hi you good
        hi hello
6. Y: =nihao gan ma ne
        =you good do what ne(particle)
        =hello what are you doing
7.   (.)
8. M: kan dianshi ne
        watch TV ne (particle)
        I am watching TV
9. Y: xianzai kan dianshi
        now watch TV
        watching TV now

---

4.   Transcription conventions are found in Appendix 1.

10. M: women zher gan wudian
         we here only half past five
         here is only half past five

English (landline) telephone openings are most likely to follow a four-part sequence, comprising a summons-answer sequence, identification sequence,
greeting sequence and a 'how are you' sequence (Schegloff 1986). As shown in Example 1, this telephone opening is very similar to the English paradigm, although
there is no 'how are you' sequence. The summons-answer sequence takes place
in line 1 and line 2. Identification is provided in the caller's first turn to talk in
line 3 *wei Ma wo shi yingying* ('hello Mum this is Yingying'). Following a pause of
0.2 seconds, M says *ei ni hao* in line 5. The *ni hao* expression, generally translated
as 'hello', is the first pair part of the greeting sequence. Y responds with a paired *ni
hao* ('hello') greeting, before saying *gan ma ne* ('what are you doing').

Although the above example displays similarities with Schegloff's paradigm,
there are two clear differences. The first difference relates to the *ni hao* expression.
In order to understand this difference, it is necessary to understand the difference
between *ni hao* and *ni hao ma*. Although, *ni hao* literally means 'you good', it is
generally considered to be a greeting (Sun 2004), similar to the English greeting
'hi'. As a result, *ni hao* is generally translated as 'hello'; in contrast, *ni hao ma* is
more likely to be translated as 'how are you'. In Chinese Mandarin the response to
ni hao is usually *ni hao*; the response to *ni hao ma* is something like 'I am well' or
some other description of a person's state like 'not very well' or 'not too bad'.

This leads onto the second difference – typically in Chinese Mandarin telephone openings, there is no *ni hao ma* or 'how are you' question. As can be seen
in Example 1, after the paired greeting response in line 6, Y asks *gan ma ne* ('what
are you doing'). M responds by telling her daughter that she is watching television.
In Sun's (2004) analysis of informal Chinese Mandarin (landline) telephone conversations between female participants,[5] Sun also found that participants asked
questions such as 'have you eaten', 'are you busy', 'how are things going' and 'what
are you doing', rather than the ubiquitous 'how are you' question that tends to
occur at the beginning of English (landline) telephone conversations. She called
these types of questions, 'questions-after-you'.

Although 'questions-after-you' are similar to the 'how are you' question in
that they are a pathway to the first topic or reason for the call (Sun 2004), they differ from the 'how are you' question in two main ways. First, such personal enqui-
ries are relationship-oriented and context-driven. For example, 'have you eaten
yet' would be appropriate around mealtime and in informal contexts; 'how is your

---

5.   The participants in Sun's (2004) analysis were Chinese speakers living in America.

health' is used among family members or close familiars. As in Example 1, 'what are you doing' is used between close friends or relatives. Second, as indicated in Example 1, such 'questions-after-you' tend to be treated as a 'real' question that leads to further talk and sequence expansion, rather than being responded to by a neutral 'fine' or 'okay' (Sun 2004). In English, neutral responses to 'how are you' questions typically result in sequence closure, demonstrating that the question is not being treated as a request for information (such as finding out how the other person is); rather it is functioning as a transition between the greeting sequence and the first topic. Less commonly, if the 'how are you' question *is* treated as a request for information as evidenced by a positive response (such as 'fantastic' or 'really good') or a negative response (such as 'terrible' or 'awful'), it will result in sequence expansion (Jefferson 1980; Schegloff 1986). Similarly in Chinese Mandarin telephone openings, Y's question about what her mother is doing does not close down the sequence; instead it leads to further talk about television and appropriate or possible times to watch television.

Although potentially *ni hao ma* could be asked as a 'question-after-you', in reality it seldom occurs in Chinese conversational openings. However, given the tendency to translate *ni hao ma* as 'how are you', and given the occurrence of *ni hao ma* as a way of opening Chinese conversations in some Chinese Mandarin language textbooks, it is not surprising that English speaking language learners of Chinese might find it difficult to know whether they should use *ni hao ma* or not when opening a conversation in Chinese.

5.   Analysis of language learners' use of *ni hao ma*

A group of tertiary learners of Chinese Mandarin were required to ring their teachers in order to test their Chinese oral proficiency. Students were told to prepare questions, using language points covered in the textbook prior to ringing their teacher. The aim of the phone call was for students to be assessed on their ability to carry out a naturally occurring telephone conversation in Chinese Mandarin. Seven out of ten students used *ni hao ma* inappropriately at the beginning of the conversations. The following examples show different students (S) initiating a sequence through the use of *ni hao ma* as a FPP. Through examination of the teacher's SPP response, the next turn, we can see how the teacher (T) treated this intercultural use of *ni hao ma*.

Example 2 [student (S) rings teacher (T) in her office]
1.   ((ring))
2. T: wei ni hao
         wei you good
         hi hello

3. S: o:h Laoshi zhe shi wo Tim=
         Teacher this is me Tim
         o:h teacher, this is me Tim=
4. T: =oh Tim ni hao
         Tim you good
         =oh Tim, hello
5. S: mm > ni hao ma↑<
         you good ma
         mm >how are you↑<
6. T: wo hen hao=ni you shenme shi
         I very good you have what thing
         I am fine=what can I do for you

In this example, S uses *ni hao ma* in accordance with an English telephone opening sequence, following the greeting sequence. However, it is not clear if the student is aware of the interculturality of using such an expression in Chinese openings, although he does preface the *ni hao ma* with 'mm', which could indicate uncertainty in using *ni hao ma* to transition to the anchor position – the first question or topic. Additionally, the student uses a rising tone (as would be appropriate when asking 'how are you' in English), marked with ↑ on the transcript at the end of line 5, whereas *ma* should be said with in neutral tone in correct Chinese.

The next turn shows the teacher responding with a neutral *wo hen hao* ('I am fine') response, as would be appropriate in the L1 English culture in which the student and teacher were living. After closing the adjacency pair sequence (line 6), T immediately moves to ask the student what she can do for him (as demonstrated by the = sign to show that the following talk is latched to the prior talk), with *ni you shenme shi* ('what can I do for you'), in keeping with her institutional role and the oral test task requirement (Drew & Heritage 1992). The main thing is to get the student to talk and to ask questions and not to query their interlanguage use of *ni hao ma*.

In the following example (Example 3), the teacher again responds to the *ni hao ma* question with a neutral *wo ting hao de* ('I am well'). But this time she adds *ni ne* ('and you'), following the script (Figure 1) given in the students' text book (Liu 2004: 4).[6]

---

6. Unfortunately Chinese language text books written for English speaking students encourage students to think of the Chinese 'question-after-you' as a 'how are you' type question. As can be testified by native Chinese speakers, this is incorrect. An examination of 30 interviews on the Chinese Central TV showed no use of the expression *ni hao ma* in any of the interviews. In addition, in none of Sun's (2004) 39 telephone conversation openings does *ni hao ma* occur. This is not to say, however, that *ni hao ma* cannot occur as part of a conversational opening;

English version of script:
Libo: Lina, how are you?
Lina: I am fine, and you?
Libo: I am fine too.

Figure 1. Script from Liu (2004: 4) text book

Example 3 [student rings teacher in her office]
1.   ((ring))
2. T: ni hao::
          you good
          hello::
3. S: ni hao Wang Laoshi zhe shi Sammy=
          you good Wang Teacher this is Sammy
          hello Teacher Wang this is Sammy=
4. T: =o:h Sa:mmy>niaho nihao<
          Sammy you good you good
          =o:h Sammy >hello hello<
5. S: oh >ni hao ma↑<
          you good ma
          oh >how are you?<
6. T: wo ting hao de(.) ni ne
          I very good de you ne
          I am well (.) and you

rather it is just only one of the possible ways of asking a question-after-you, and so although it can occur, it frequently does not occur.

```
7. S:    u:m u:m hai keyi
         u:m u:m still ok
         u:m u:m not too bad
8. T:    hai ke [yi
         still ok
         not too bad
9. S:          [keshi tianqi hen leng
               but weather very cold
               [but it is very cold
```

In response to the teacher's *ni ne* ('and you'), the student says *hai keyi* ('not too bad') in line 7. However, although such a response could be considered a neutral response in Australian English, it is treated as a downgraded negative response in Chinese Mandarin. As a result, it is topicalised by the teacher, leading to talk about the weather. The downgraded response in line 7 is preceded by two 'uhms' which might indicate that the student is uncertain as to whether the *ni ne* ('and you') should be treated as a topic question or part of the greeting exchange.

Both Examples 2 and 3 show the way in which the teacher scaffolds the interaction so that any inappropriate use of *ni hao ma* is smoothed over and not shown to be problematic or misplaced. As Hosoda (2006) states, when non-native speakers have problems in producing correct language within a cross-cultural communication context, the native speaker frequently offers a solution. In the above examples, the teacher scaffolds the interaction, offering a solution to the *ni hao ma* 'problem' by encouraging the student to talk more (in accordance with the task of the oral test).

There are times, however, when the inappropriate use of *ni hao ma* makes the conversation difficult to carry on, as shown in Example 4.

Example 4 [student rings teacher in her office]

```
1.       ((ring))
2. T:    wei ni hao
         Wei you good
         hi, hello
3.       (0.3)
4. S:    laoshi hao
         teacher good
         hello Teacher
5. T:    o:h shui ya
         who ya
         o:h who is calling
6.       (.)
```

7. S: oh wo shi Jenny
        I am Jenny
        oh it's Jenny
8. T: oh Jenny ni hao you shenme shi ma
        Jenny you good have what thing ma
        oh Jenny hello, what can I do for you
9.   (0.5)
10. S: em wo you (.) jingtian kaoshi
        I have today exam
        em I have (.) today is exam
11. T: o:::h
12. S: ni ni hao ma↑
        you you good ma
        how how are you
13. T: wo ting hao de ni ne
        I very good de you ne
        I am fine, and you
14. S: wo hen hao
        I very good
        I am well
15. T: em=
16. S: =nide baba mama zenmeyang
        your father mother how
        =how are your parents
17. T: oh (.) wo baba ma:::ma:: hai hao
        my father mother   still good
        oh (.) my Dad and Mu::::m not too bad

In Example 4, following an overt request for identification, the teacher asks *oh Jenny ni hao you shenme shi ma* ('Jenny hello, what can I do for you?') in line 8. The student pauses for 0.5 seconds before saying *em wo you (.) jingtian kaoshi* ('we have the exam today'). The student's delayed answer that overtly mentions the exam, plus the teacher's prolonged 'oh' response to the mention (line 11), demonstrates the student's lack of understanding of the oral test task (to carry out an ordinary telephone conversation). Although following the teacher's 'oh' response a first topic would be the next relevant action, the student goes on to ask a misplaced self-repaired *ni ni hao ma* with rising intonation (as shown by the upward arrow ↑) in line 12.

For this student, there are a number of difficulties. First, the student demonstrates her lack of understanding of where to sequentially place *ni hao ma* when opening a conversation. Even though the teacher and student have already moved onto the first topic (the exam), the student asks *ni hao ma* in line 12, demonstrating a misunderstanding of the role and function of *ni hao ma*. In effect, the student is restarting the conversation. Second, the *ni hao ma* is said with rising intonation, even though such a question would be said with neutral tone in Chinese. The rising intonation provides evidence that the student is transferring her understanding of the English 'how are you' question onto the *ni hao ma* question.

In line 16, the student goes on to ask *nide baba mama zenmeyang* ('how are your parents') following the script in the text book in which questions about family members follow the greeting exchange. At this point, the teacher displays her intercultural competence by adapting to the student's question, even though such a question is sequentially misplaced, following the already completed opening sequence. The only hint that there is some sort of hitch is evident in the teacher's 'oh' at the beginning of her turn.

The three examples above show how students who were not taught using intercultural language teaching found it difficult to appropriately use *ni hao ma* at the beginning of a conversation. They were basing their understanding of *ni hao ma* on the text book and their own cultural norms around the English 'how are you' expression. This contrasts strongly with a second group of students (a total of 44 students) who were taught how to use *ni hao ma* from an intercultural base.

This second group of students were given the tools to reflectively examine their own cultural assumptions as well as the cultural assumptions of the target language. Subsequent analysis of their oral test phone calls showed an increased awareness of the different ways of opening a conversation in Mandarin Chinese. Of the 44 students, 23 students initiated a first topic without saying *ni hao ma*; 16 students used a question-after-you (including expressions such as 'how are things', 'busy or not', 'how is your health') before initiating the first topic; with only five students using *ni hao ma* in the opening exchange, as would be expected when opening an English conversation.

Using a conversation analytic framework, this second group of students were explicitly encouraged to reflect on their own language practices with special emphasis on identifying similarities and differences between their own language and the target language prior to undertaking the oral test. They were provided with a structured framework that enabled them to examine specific language phenomena, in this case telephone openings, from an intercultural perspective. The focus of this intercultural language learning (ILL) classroom was based on five principles developed by Liddicoat et al. (2003: 45–51). Their principles of intercultural language learning address (1) how to purposefully and actively construct knowledge within a sociocultural context in order to explore language and culture through active engagement, and to develop a personal, intercultural space with multiple dimensions (*active construction*); (2) how to make connections or bridges between the home language and the target language (*making connections*); (3) how to communicate across linguistic and cultural boundaries, including the identification of such boundaries (*social interaction*); (4) how to become aware of the processes underlying thinking, knowing, and learning through conscious awareness and reflection and to articulate the multiple dimensions of their own intercultural space and identity (*reflection*); and (5) how to encourage learners to accept responsibility for contributing to successful communication across languages and cultures, and for developing intercultural perspectives (*responsibility*).

For example, using an extract such as Example 1, students in this second group were introduced to the concepts of conversation analysis, including turn-taking, adjacency pairs, FPPs, SPPs, turn design, repair, overlapping talk (*active construction*). They were encouraged to look at the extract and identify, for example, that the *ni hao* in line 5 is a FPP and the *ni hao* in line 6 is a SPP. They learned how to call these paired turns an adjacency pair. They were given the opportunity to discuss the relationship between the speakers, place and timing of the opening, as well as meanings of some words and phrases. Such preparation meant that they were given the space to reflexively examine the role of telephone openings across cultures.

Example 5 (Example 1 is repeated here for the reader's convenience)
1.   ((ring))
2. M: wei
     hello
3. Y: wei Ma wo shi yingying
     hello Mum I am Yingying
     hello Mum this is Yingying
4.   (0.2)
5. M: ei ni hao=
     hi you good
     hi hello
6. Y: =nihao gan ma ne
     =you good do what ne(particle)
     =hello what are you doing
7.   (.)
8. M: kan dianshi ne
     watch TV ne (particle)
     I am watching TV
9. Y: xianzai kan dianshi
     now watch TV
     watching TV now

10. M: women zher gan wudian
         we here only half past five
         here is only half past five

Students in this second group were encouraged to notice things about the sequences of talk. For example, what are the possible ways of answering a phone in Chinese Mandarin (summons-answer sequence in lines 1 and 2); how is identification carried out (identification sequence in line 3); is there a preference for self-identification or other identification; how is the greeting achieved (greeting sequence in lines 5 and 6); should interlocutors have to say a paired *ni hao* as in this example (lines 5 and 6); where do 'questions-after-you' normally occur; must they follow the greeting sequence. They examined the detail of the extract and identified, for example, the features of the 'question-after-you' sequence. They were encouraged to notice that Y asks *gan ma ne* ('what are you doing') after greeting her mother (line 6) and that this leads onto more talk about watching television. The discussion opened up opportunities for the teacher to talk about the range of 'questions-after-you', and which sorts of questions are possible within different types of contexts or between different speakers with different relationships. These early analytic discussions were situated within CA, using terminology and principles, thus giving teachers and students a way of talking about the data in a clear and precise manner.

The students were then asked to role play a short phone call in their own language so that they could write down a typical conversational opening (*making connections*). This encouraged students to compare the differences between the English 'how are you' (or openings in other languages) and the Chinese Mandarin 'questions-after-you' and to discuss other ways of opening conversations in Chinese. Students were asked to role play a short phone call in Chinese Mandarin so that they could write down a typical Chinese Mandarin conversational opening and compare their own production with video recordings of Chinese L1 speakers opening a conversation (*social interaction*). This opened up a space for further discussion of address terms, response tokens, interjections, laughter, greetings in Chinese Mandarin.

Students were finally given an opportunity to put into practice their own understanding of language use by ringing their teacher as part of an oral test. As presented above, this group of 44 students demonstrated an increased awareness of the *ni hao ma* expression. They had been encouraged to reflect on their own cultural identity and how it is expressed through language and intercultural behaviour (*reflection*). The telephone conversation was recorded and students had the opportunity to listen to this recording of their own language use in order to understand and take responsibility for their own intercultural contribution to successful communication (*responsibility*). This final step provided teachers with an opportunity to further develop students' understanding of conversation analysis as a tool for analyzing future intercultural interaction. Appendix 2 provides more details of how teachers could use conversation analysis as a tool for Intercultural Language Learning (ILL) (Steps for teaching *ni hao ma* in the beginner Chinese language classroom).

Encouraging students to learn using ILL is crucially important if we are to equip them with the skills and intercultural understanding of their own language and the target language. The above analysis showed how 89% of the second group of students who were taught using ILL were able to open a conversation without hitches and uncertainties and without the use of *ni hao ma*. The ILL method used with this group of students gave students the tools to analyse and reflect on their own language use and the target language use. Based on the methodology of CA, and utilizing ideas from Barraja-Rohan's (1999, 2000; Barraja-Rohan & Pritchard 1997) five stages and Liddicoat et al.'s (2003) five principles of ILL, students in the second group were taught how to analyse interaction in order to unpack hidden cultural assumptions within both their own home language and the target language. As the results show, CA-based ILL was very effective in ensuring that the second group of students developed intercultural awareness with respect to telephone conversation openings in Chinese Mandarin.

6.   Using CA as an effective tool in ILT and ILL

One of the difficulties for intercultural language teaching and learning is how to reconcile the expectation that we need to teach students about cultural expectations and language norms while at the same time, allowing for, and encouraging, interculturality within their interaction. As Abdallah-Pretceille states:

> If educational effectiveness becomes defined in terms of focusing on learning profiles according to cultural membership, there is a risk that education and training will become culturalized by highlighting inter-group differences to the detriment of intra-group and inter-individual differences. Between the 'cultural zero', meaning the ignorance or negation of the cultural dimension of education, and the 'cultural all', meaning an overemphasis on culture as the determining factor of behaviour and learning, the margin for manoeuvring is narrow. The fairly recent emphasis on culture pushes us in the direction of a 'dictatorship' of the cultural by reducing the individual to his/her cultural membership.
>
> (Abdallah-Pretceille 2006: 476)

The intercultural difficulty for the first group of students occurred as a result of their L1 transference of 'how are you' onto the Chinese Mandarin expression *ni hao ma*. For this first group of students there are three reasons for such transference. First, intercultural teaching and learning did not take place. For this group of students, the expression *ni hao ma* was not discussed in classes, nor were students given any opportunity to examine the similar English 'how are you' expression in order to compare conversational openings in their own language with the target language. Second, there was no discussion of the fact that the scripts given in the text book were not appropriate. Based on the text book, it is not surprising that students might have thought it was culturally appropriate to ask *ni hao ma* at the beginning of a conversation, and that the most likely translation of *ni hao ma* was 'how are you' because *ni hao ma* occurred in a similar sequential environment. They would also have understood from the text book that a neutral response, such as 'I'm fine', was appropriate (as in English) and that a follow up 'and you' question was also expected. Third, they did not receive any negative evidence from the teacher. She responded to their use of *ni hao ma* without any indication of the fact that *ni hao ma* seldom occurs at the beginning of Chinese conversations. Thus, although in the oral test she demonstrated her own ability to respond to the interculturality of the students' talk, students were not able to use her response as a learning tool concerning the use of *ni hao ma*. In contrast, the second group of language learners, who were given the opportunity to explore the cultural ramifications of using (or not using) expressions such as *ni hao ma* at the beginning of a conversation, demonstrated (for the most part) their ability to transfer their intercultural learning to an actual conversation when phoning their teacher as part of an oral test.

The analysis of the two groups of language learners above demonstrates the importance of giving students the tools to reflectively examine their own cultural assumptions as well as the cultural expectations and language norms of the target language. CA, as a methodology that focuses on the way in which interaction is constructed, provides them with the skills to examine the different ways in which they construct culture, their identity, and their own intercultural competence(s). CA gives them a framework for examining how they can respond to different contexts and different people in terms of what they say and do.

If we don't explicitly teach students how to understand particular expressions in the target language and to compare them with similar expressions in their own language, then it is highly likely that they will simply transfer their own L1 cultural norms and assumptions to the target language. The question for language educators is how to develop the most effective methods for enabling learners to understand hidden cultural assumptions within their language use. As Liddicoat (2002: 5) says "culture shapes what we say, when we say it, and how we say it from the simplest language we use to the most complex. It is fundamental to the way we speak, write, listen and read."

7. Conclusion

The strength of ILL lies in providing knowledge, skills and values for language learners that will enable them to use language in culturally aware and sensitive ways. This paper has shown how the framework of conversation analysis is particularly useful for developing a linguistic model of ILL. CA encourages people to make 'noticings' about how conversations develop and evolve and how social interaction is co-constructed moment by moment. One of the advantages of CA is that it provides students and educators with the tools and techniques for making visible what might initially seem hidden or invisible. Through a CA-based model of ILL, students are able to:

-   use the framework of conversation analysis as a tool for displaying hidden aspects of social interaction;
-   make 'noticings' concerning their home language(s) and the target language(s);
-   explore the idea of co-constructed discourse and the multi-faceted nature of intercultural interaction;
-   make connections and identify linguistic and cultural boundaries between their home language(s) and culture and target language(s) and culture(s);
-   recognize and reflect the intersection between language and culture and their own intercultural competence;
-   take responsibility for their own contribution to successful communication.

References

Abdallah-Pretceille, M. (2006). Interculturalism as a paradigm for thinking about diversity. *Intercultural Education, 17*(5), 475–483.

Arminen, I. & Leinonen, M. (2006). Mobile phone call openings: Tailoring answers to personalized summonses. *Discourse Studies, 8*(3), 339–368.

Arminen, I. & Weilenmann, A. (2009). Mobile presence and intimacy – Reshaping social actions in mobile contextual configuration. *Journal of Pragmatics, 41*(10), 1905–1923.

Atkinson, J. M. & Heritage, J. (Eds.). (1984). *Structures of social action: Studies in Conversation Analysis*. Cambridge: Cambridge University Press.

Barraja-Rohan, A. M. (1999). Teaching conversation for intercultural competence. In J. Lo Bianco, C. Crozet, & A. J. Liddicoat (Eds.), *Striving for the third place: Intercultural competence through language education* (pp. 143–154). Canberra: Language Australia.

Barraja-Rohan, A. M. (2000). Teaching conversation and socio-cultural norms with conversation analysis. In A. J. Liddicoat & C. Crozet (Eds.), *Teaching languages, teaching cultures* (pp. 65–78). Melbourne: Language Australia.

Barraja-Rohan, A. M. & Pritchard, C. R. (1997). *Beyond talk: A course in communication and conversation for intermediate adult learners of English*. Melbourne: Western Melbourne Institute of TAFE.

Bennett, J. M., Bennett, M. J., & Allen, W. (1999). Developing intercultural competence in the language classroom. In R. M. Paige, D. L. Lange, & Y. A. Yershova (Eds.), *Culture as the core: Integrating culture into the language curriculum* (pp. 13–46). Minneapolis, MN: CARLA, University of Minnesota.

Bowles, H. (2006). Bridging the gap between conversation analysis and ESP – an applied study of the opening sequences of NS and NNS service telephone calls. *English for Specific Purposes, 25*(3), 332–357.

Byram, M. (1989). *Cultural studies in foreign language education*. Clevedon: Multilingual Matters.

Byram, M. & Zarate, G. (1997). *The sociocultural and intercultural dimension of language learning and teaching*. Strasbourg: Council of Europe.

Byram, M., Nichols, A., & Stevens, D. (Eds.). (2001). *Developing intercultural competence in practice*. Clevedon: Multilingual Matters.

Crozet, C. & Liddicoat, A. J. (2000). Teaching culture as an integrated part of language: Implications for the aims, approaches and pedagogies of language teaching. In A. J. Liddicoat & C. Crozet (Eds.), *Teaching languages, teaching cultures* (pp. 1–18). Melbourne: Language Australia.

Crozet, C., Liddicoat, A. J., & Lo Bianco, J. (1999). Intercultural competence: From language policy to language education. In J. Lo Bianco, C. Crozet, & A. J. Liddicoat (Eds.), *Striving for the third place intercultural competence through language education* (pp. 1–20). Canberra: Language Australia.

Dervin, F. (2007). Dissociation and "complex" interculturality. In *Innovations in language teaching and learning in the multicultural context (Research Papers, International NordicBaltic conference of the World Federation of Language Teacher Associations)* (pp. 59–64). Riga: SIA.

Dervin, F. (2009). Transcending the culturalist impasse in stays abroad: Helping mobile students to appreciate diverse diversities. *Frontiers: The Interdisciplinary Journal of Study Abroad, 18*, 119–141.

Dervin, F. (2010). Assessing intercultural competence in language learning and teaching: a critical review of current efforts in higher education. In F. Dervin & E. Suomela (Eds.), *New approaches to assessing language and (inter-) cultural competences in higher education.* (pp. 157–173). Frankfurt: Peter Lang.

Dervin, F. (2011). A plea for change in research on intercultural discourses: A 'liquid' approach to the study of the acculturation of Chinese students. *Journal of Multicultural Discourses, 6*(1), 37–52.

Drew, P. (2005). Conversation analysis. In K. L. Fitch & R. Saunders (Eds.), *Handbook of language and social interaction* (pp. 71–102). Mahwah, NJ: Lawrence Erlbaum Associates.

Drew, P. & Heritage, J. (Eds.). (1992). *Talk at work: Introduction in institutional settings*. Cambridge: Cambridge University Press.

Drew, P. & Heritage, J. (Eds.). (2006). *Conversation analysis. Benchmarks in social research methods* (4 Vols). London: Sage.

Gardner, R. & Wagner, J. (Eds.). (2004). *Second language conversations*. London: Continuum.

Gillespie, A. & Cornish, F. (2010). Intersubjectivity: Towards a dialogical analysis. *Journal for the Theory of Social Behaviour, 40*(1), 19–46.

Hopper, R. & Chen, C. (1996). Language, culture, relationships: Telephone openings in Taiwan. *Research on Language and Social Interaction, 29*, 291–313.

House, J. (1982). Opening and closing phases in German and English dialogues. *Grazer Linguistische Studien, 16*, 52–82.

Hosoda, Y. (2006). Repair and relevance of differential language expertise in second language conversations. *Applied Linguistics, 27*(1), 25–50.

Hutchby, I. & Wooffitt, R. (1998). *Conversation analysis*. Cambridge: Polity Press.

Hutchby, I. (2005). "Incommensurable" studies of mobile phone conversation: A reply to Ilkka Arminen. *Discourse Studies, 7*, 663–670.

Hutchby, I. & Barnett, S. (2005). Aspects of the sequential organisation of mobile phone conversation. *Discourse Studies 7*, 147–171.

Huth, T. & Taleghani-Nikazm, C. (2006). How can insights from conversation analysis be directly applied to teaching L2 pragmatics? *Language Teaching Research, 10*(1), 53–79.

Jefferson, G. (1980). On "trouble-premonitory" response to inquiry. *Sociological Inquiry, 50*, 153–185.

Kramsch, C. (1993). *Context and culture in language teaching*. Oxford: Oxford University Press.

Liddicoat, A. J. (2002). Static and dynamic views of culture and intercultural language acquisition. *Babel, 36*(3), 4–11.

Liddicoat, A. J. (2007). *Introduction to conversation analysis*. Continuum: London.

Liddicoat, A. J. (2009). Communication as culturally contexted practice: A view from intercultural communication. *Australian Journal of Linguistics, 29*(1), 115–133.

Liddicoat, A. J., Scarino, A., Papademetre, L., & Kohler, M. (2003). *Report on intercultural language learning*. Canberra: Commonwealth Department of Education, Science and Training.

Liu, X. (2004). *New practical Chinese reader*. Beijing: Beijing Language University.

Sacks, H. (1984). On doing "being ordinary". In J. M. Atkinson & J. Heritage (Eds.), *Structures of social action: Studies in conversation analysis* (pp. 413–429). Cambridge: Cambridge University Press.

Sacks, H., Schegloff, E. A., & Jefferson, G. (1974). A simplest systematics for the organization of turn-taking for conversation. *Language, 50*, 696–735.

Schegloff, E. (1968). Sequencing in conversational openings. *The American Anthropologist, 70*(6): 1075–1095.

Schegloff, E. A. (1986). The routine as achievement. *Human Studies, 9*, 111–151.

Schegloff, E. A. (2007). *Sequence organization in interaction: A primer in conversation analysis*. Cambridge: Cambridge University Press.

Schegloff, E. A., Koshik, I., Jacoby, S., & Olsher, D. (2002). Conversation analysis and applied linguistics. *American Review of Applied Linguistics, 22*, 3–31.

Seedhouse, P. (1998). CA and the analysis of foreign language interaction: A reply to Wagner. *Journal of Pragmatics, 30*, 85–102.

Sidnell, J. (2010). *Conversation analysis: An introduction*. London: Wiley-Blackwell.

Sun, H. (2004). Opening moves in informal Chinese telephone conversation. *Journal of Pragmatics, 36*(8), 1429–1465.

ten Have, P. (2007). *Doing conversation analysis: A practical guide*. Thousand Oaks, CA: Sage.

Appendix 1. Transcription conventions

A full discussion of CA transcription notation is available in Atkinson & Heritage (1984). Punctuation marks are used to capture characteristics of speech delivery, not to mark grammatical units.

hello.	falling intonation
hello,	slight rising intonation
hello¿	rising intonation, weaker than that indicated by a question mark
hello?	strongly rising intonation
hel-	talk is cut off
>hello<	talk is faster than surrounding talk
<hello>	talk is slower than surrounding talk
HELLO	talk is louder than surrounding talk
°hello°	talk is quieter than surrounding talk
↑ or ↓	marked rising or falling shifts in pitch
he::llo	lengthening of a sound or syllable
he̲llo	emphasis
(1.0), (0.3)	timed intervals (silence), in seconds and tenths of seconds
(.)	short untimed pause, less than 0.2 of a second
.hh	audible inhalations
hh	audible exhalations
=	latched talk – talk following previous talk with no gap
[ ]	simultaneous/overlapping talk
(ook)	transcriber uncertainty

Appendix 2. Using Conversation Analysis as a tool for ILL: Steps for teaching *ni hao ma* in the beginner Chinese language classroom

Principles	Activity	Teaching focus	Outcomes
1. Active construction	Watch a range of videos of people greeting each other. Listen to how some Chinese language learners open a conversation (first group of students).	1. Introduce students to CA concepts, including turn-taking, adjacency pairs, FPPs, SPPs, turn design, repair, overlapping talk. 2. Encourage students to notice things about the openings, using CA as a tool for showing different aspects of the data. 3. Encourage discussion of relationship between the speakers, place and timing of the opening, as well as meanings of some words and phrases.	1. Develop students' ability to notice things in conversational openings. 2. Develop students' intercultural understanding of their own language and the target language. 3. Encourage students to explore the idea of a multi-faceted intercultural space.
2. Making connections	Role play opening a conversation with each other in students' L1.	1. Ask students to role play a short phone call in their own language so that they can write down a typical conversational opening. 2. Encourage students to compare the differences between English 'how are you' (or openings in other languages) and Chinese *ni hao, ni hao ma* and other ways of opening conversations in Chinese.	1. Develop students' ability to make connections between their home language and culture and target language and culture. 2. Students are expected to work out the sequential organisation of Chinese telephone openings, including the different placement of 'how are you' and *ni hao ma*.
3. Social interaction	Role play opening a conversation with each other in the target language, Chinese.	1. Ask students to role play a short phone call in Chinese so that they can write down a typical Chinese conversational opening. 2. Encourage students to make their communication practice more culturally focused. 3. Open up a space for discussion of address terms, response tokens, interjections, laughter, greetings. 4. Compare their own production with video recordings of Chinese L1 speakers opening a conversation.	1. Develop students' ability to identify the linguistic and cultural boundaries between openings in their home language and the target language. 2. Continue to develop students' ability to make 'noticings' about their language and the target language.

(*continued*)

Principles	Activity	Teaching focus	Outcomes
4. Reflection	Students ring their teacher to have a conversation (oral test).	1. Test the students' ability to open a conversation in the target language (oral test). 2. Using CA, the teacher individually analyses the openings in order to find out how students carried out the task. 3. Encourage students to critically and constructively reflect on opening telephone conversations in Chinese. 4. Encourage students to discuss and name their own 'identity' and intercultural behaviours.	1. Develop students' ability to recognize and reflect on their own cultural identity and their intercultural behavior.
5. Responsibility	Students listen to a recording of their own telephone conversation.	1. Students analyse their own conversations, using the framework of CA, in order to focus on cultural similarities and differences. 2. Encourage students to see how they can use their intercultural understanding when communicating with others.	1. Develop students' ability to take responsibility for their own contribution to successful communication. 2. Develop students' intercultural perspective. 3. Develop students' ability to use the framework of CA as a tool for analyzing future intercultural interaction.

PART II

Linguistics for studying interculturality in education

Language teachers and learners interpreting the world

Identifying intercultural development in language classroom discourse

Lesley Harbon and Robyn Moloney
The University of Sydney / Macquarie University

For better or for worse, neither linguistics nor applied linguistics are mandatory in the pre- or in-service education of Australia's language teachers. It may therefore be serendipitous that a teacher of languages and cultures in an Australian school can access techniques from the domain of applied linguistics to apply to issues arising in the languages classroom. The invitation in this volume to examine the nexus between intercultural education and applied linguistics has challenged us to examine what may be possible when a simple strategy is employed. In this paper we examine classroom data from a junior secondary school Spanish classroom and superimpose a linguistic frame – the linguistic turn in the linguistic exchange – to examine teacher talk and turn-taking and its relationship with construction of intercultural understanding in students. Building on the work undertaken on the evaluative exchange and turn-taking (Edwards & Westgate 1994), we analyse existing data from one of our studies in the past three years (Moloney & Harbon 2010a). We posit that teacher awareness of the linguistic aspects of classroom discourse can highlight the intercultural negotiation of meaning-making in a foreign language classroom.

1. Introduction

When the term 'multiculturalism' merged into what was developing as the area of intercultural education two decades ago (Coulby 2006: 245), education systems realised they could encourage dialogue between students of different cultures, beliefs and religions to make "an important and meaningful contribution to sustainable and tolerant societies" (UNESCO 2006: 8). Intercultural education became "the process of responding to the adaptive demands that result from interacting with a new cultural environment" (Shaules 2007:20) and has been considered "a major theme, which needs to inform the teaching and learning of all subjects" (Coulby 2006:246). Intercultural educational programs develop students' abilities to think, act, discriminate and experience cultural difference in appropriate ways (DeJaeghere & Zhang 2008:255). It is logical that intercultural education has rightly found its place in language teaching (UNESCO 2006:27). In fact, Lin (2010:433) maintains that the foreign language curriculum can now essentially be "for the common good (e.g., intercultural understanding and acceptance, respect for ethnic, linguistic and cultural diversity)".

Research directions and methodologies in the intercultural arena are reconnecting with the methodological resources of new approaches in linguistics which give emphasis to language in active use, role of context, and the culturally embedded nature of language. According to Kramsch (2010) we need to turn to discourse to explain communication across cultures. Discourse embedded in language is at the heart of intercultural communication, and yet the intercultural communication literature has paid limited attention to the role of linguistics in understanding language, culture and intercultural aspects of language learning. The early development of intercultural work focused on the nature of intercultural interaction, as found in the literature of interlanguage pragmatics (see for example Kasper & Rose 2002; Kinginger & Belz 2005; Liddicoat 2006). However, in the field of language education, the focus became more urgently the development of pedagogical solutions for classroom practitioners (Lo Bianco & Crozet 2003; Scarino & Papademetre 2000), rather than how a linguistically-oriented focus on classroom interactions could shed light on intercultural processes.

In a number of our research projects on intercultural language education in Australian school contexts over the past five years (Harbon & Browett 2006; Moloney 2008; Moloney & Harbon 2008; Moloney & Harbon 2010a) we have focused on 'the intercultural stance' where language learners come to "know how, know why, know about and know themselves" (Moran 2001) through teachers' pedagogical interventions. We have made little space to explore the linguistic aspects of interculturality. To address this issue, in this chapter we have examined some classroom data by superimposing a linguistic frame over our existing understandings of talk and turn-taking in the languages classroom. We explore the linguistic aspects of classroom intercultural negotiation. Building on the work undertaken on the evaluative exchange and turn-taking (Edwards & Westgate 1994), we analyse existing data from one of our studies in the past three years (Moloney & Harbon 2010a). With the aim of our research impacting classroom practice, we heed Boxer's comments:

> By studying how language users employ their language(s) in a variety of contexts, with a variety of types of interlocution, and on a variety of topical issues, teachers and other experts are enabled to create curriculum, materials, and assessment instruments based on natural, spontaneous data from mother tongue users, bilinguals, and language learners.
>
> (Boxer 2006:677)

Boxer is referring to how research on language teaching and learning in the classroom can include naturalistic data and can be subject to linguistic and intercultural analysis, an argument very important to what we present here.

There are two key sections in this chapter. The first is an examination of how a linguistics focus may underpin studies of intercultural learning in languages classrooms. We posit that an examination of the linguistic turn (Edwards & Westgate 1994) may provide the tools for language teachers to do this. We take a close look at the definition of intercultural language education. There we make the link as to how the linguistic turn literature, especially work on the I-R-E exchange (Sinclair & Coulthard 1975, 1992), may scaffold teachers and learners to develop their interculturality. The second section is our presentation of our classroom data, indicating that a language teacher moves in and out of different patterns of exchange through the different rhythms of communicative interchanges, and that variations on the I-R-E exchange, and a teacher's explicit reflection and awareness of that, may impact on intercultural learning.

2. Linguistics and its possibilities for understanding intercultural learning

The field of pragmatics tells us that linguistic representations relate to the language of thought and that through language we *"interpret the world and the people in it"* (Smith 2006:354). The pragmatic aspect of linguistics is important and may impact on language learners' attempts to master the second language. Important too, is that linguistics affords attention to more than just surface structures involved in language interactions. We also know from the work of Bakhtin on dialogism (noted in Morson 2006:561), that so many variables impact on humans producing language – "we think in terms of dialogues. We address each other silently... we make ourselves by gradually choosing among the meaning-laden ways of speaking given by our culture." These aspects of linguistics confirm for us that language learning is therefore an inherently complex activity. What language teachers may require, it seems, in their endeavour to understand their language choices and discourse strategies, is an awareness of their discourse strategies, and a pedagogy for them to guide learners in language and culture learning.

2.1   The linguistic 'turn': A useful branch of linguistics for the teacher of languages and cultures

Sacks, Schegloff and Jefferson (1974) was one of the first studies to examine turn-taking in conversation. According to Clyne (1994: 8), it was around the same time that Sinclair and Coulthard (1975, 1992) isolated the "three-part exchanges: Initiation–Response–Follow on" as a linguistic focus to further understand interaction. Edwards and Westgate (1994) cite Johnson's (1979) work from observations in sixty classrooms in three southern American states where the 'discussion cycle' of Initiation–Response–Evaluation was "so frequent and persistent" that it was seemingly linked to power and race issues. Hall states:

> … the teacher-led, three-part-sequence of Initiation – Response – Evaluation
> (IRE), typifies the discourse of Western schooling from Kindergarten to univer-
> sity. Commonly referred to as 'recitation script', the pattern involves the teacher
> asking a question to which the teacher already knows the answer. The purpose of
> such questioning is to elicit information from the students so that the teacher can
> ascertain whether they know the material.   (Hall 2002: 80)

However, the I-R-E exchange may not be such a productive pedagogy (Dashwood 2004) as it discourages students from investigating or exploring language and culture because of the teacher's tight control of the linguistic exchange. Tsui (1995) and Dashwood (2004) are two scholars who have more recently examined language teaching and learning in classroom interaction from a linguistics orientation. Tsui's work in 1995 concluded that "studies conducted on classroom interaction have shown that student talk accounts for an average of less than 30 per cent of talk in "teacher-fronted" classrooms" (Tsui 1995: 81). Dashwood's (2004: 20) Australian research found how the language teacher "invariably reclaims the 'turn', thus reducing student opportunities to talk on task".

2.2   The challenge to create intercultural learners in differing classroom contexts

Intercultural language teaching and learning is much encouraged in contemporary foreign and second language learning classroom contexts (Board of Studies New South Wales 2003; Corbett 2003; Kramsch 2006; Lazar, Huber-Kriegler, Lussier, Matei & Peck 2007; Scarino & Liddicoat 2009). When applied to languages education, intercultural practice in classrooms asks students to think and act appropriately within a growing knowledge of the culture in language. No longer is linguistic proficiency the sole aim of teaching and learning, rather a set of intercultural understandings allows students to develop understandings of why language is as it is, and how processes of language impact on meaning. As noted by Liddicoat, Papademetre, Scarino and Kohler (2003: 58) "within the framework for intercultural language learning, meaning-making is a linguistic and sociocultural act". The literature of intercultural language learning (and cited in Liddicoat et al. 2003: 6) acknowledges its debt to anthropologist Geertz, who saw culture as sets of practices, that is, as lived experience of individuals (Geertz 1973). Byram (1989) and Kramsch (1993) describe a process of the individual developing intercultural competence through de-centering from their own first culture. Intercultural behaviour is seen as the individual's ability to negotiate meaning across cultural boundaries as he/she establishes his/her own identity as a user of another language. Kramsch (1993) has suggested the notion of the learner developing a "third place" from which he/she can make reflective observations of both the home culture and the target culture.

Liddicoat et al. (2003) trace and synthesise developments in language, culture, intercultural learning, models of intercultural sensitivity, and how to measure it. Earlier Liddicoat (2002) had argued for a non-linear, cyclical process of intercultural competence which draws attention to the student's internal processes of 'noticing' similarities, differences, features of the language, and teacher behaviours. Such notions focus on the production of learners' speaking/writing output. This process continues as the student evaluates or reflects on their language output, compares current knowledge with prior knowledge, and adjusts and modifies language output as a result. The essential link we see between a linguistically-oriented examination of discourse in the language classroom, and the aims of intercultural language learning, is outlined by Kramsch (2006), where she traces the work of Edmondson and House (1998) who examined how communication could be investigated by interrogating turns-at-talk. Kramsch says (2006: 324) that "language teachers should teach non-native speakers how to recognize and adopt the discursive behaviour of the native speakers... in order to find out ultimately how they think, what they value, and how they see the world". Communicative competence requires the explicit linguistic analysis of the cultural dimension. Kramsch also cites Hu's work from 1999 that notes:

> an intercultural pedagogy takes into account the students' culturally diverse representations, interpretations, expectations, memories, and identifications, that are, in turn, made thematic, brought into the open through personal narratives and multilingual writings, and discussed openly in class.   (Kramsch 2006: 324)

It is the role of the language teacher to mediate these pedagogical and linguistic processes. Intercultural scholars have suggested this pedagogical sequence (listed below) as integral to an intercultural stance to teaching and learning foreign languages (Liddicoat et al. 2003; Moran 2001):

- a concrete experience and an active construction of language;
- reflective observation by making connections between the languages in play;
- social interaction referring to the communication intended;
- reflection by abstract conceptualization of the language notions;
- active experimentation representing the teachers affording the learners an opportunity to trial their language knowledge; and
- responsibility, where the language learner must take the knowledge of the new culture seriously and process it responsibly.

A language teacher, planning for learners to become communicatively competent (and to also achieve an intercultural awareness), can build on these intercultural pedagogies listed above, adding to those strategies a focus on the linguistic notions inherent in them. There is a good chance that if the linguistic exchange becomes a pedagogical strategy in terms of questioning technique (Dashwood 2004), then the resulting language learning may have a wider scope of the intercultural reflectivity embodied within it.

A simple linguistic orientation taken by teachers on their interculturally focused pedagogies, may enrich both teachers' and learners' knowledge of both content (subject matter being learned) and processes in the language classroom. Intercultural language learning involves risk-taking by teachers (Byram, Gribkova & Starkey 2002), in asking questions to which learners may not know the answer, to which there may not be one single truth/answer, or may not be able to predict from prior experience. Jokikokko (2005:76) describes the importance of teachers' ability to engage in dialogical relationship with their language students as part of teacher intercultural competence, and describes teacher intercultural competence as the "courage to think and act interculturally" in the broader school environment.

We acknowledge the line of argument that even in teachers trying to take what they understand to be an intercultural approach, a 'solid' rather than a 'fluid' approach to culture may result (Dervin 2011). Teachers' enthusiasm for imparting cultural knowledge and a focus on artefacts and practices can still lead to static, reductive essentialisation of the culture (Dervin 2011; Moloney & Harbon 2010b) and a failure to allow students to construct their own interpretations and subjectivities in relation to their peers in the other language. We accept this important emerging critique of intercultural learning. Where intercultural learning exists only at the level of simplistic comparisons, it may continue inadvertently to promote fixed, essentialised notions of cultures (Holliday 2010; Young & Sercombe 2010:182). Current languages education pedagogy importantly challenges teachers and learners to consider what culture may be, and how they understand the place of culture within language learning. The examples below offer what we believe is possible, through working on the linguistic aspects (the I-R-E exchange and its variations) of intercultural language learning.

2.3   A variation to the I-R-E turn to assist intercultural language learning

We are challenged by the discoveries which teachers may make, if they have the opportunity to examine and reflect on their own classroom discourse and turn-taking. They may discover the extent to which they have the capability to allow more construction of intercultural learning in their students. The traditional I-R-E exchange may look something like the following:

Initiation:	What do Italians do when greeting others, John?
Response:	A hand shake, Miss?
Evaluation:	No.
Initiation:	Someone else? Maddie?
Response:	A big hug and a pat on the back, Miss.
Evaluation:	Yes, that's correct.

With the option for teachers to change classroom discourse and interaction with a simple focus on adapting their questioning strategies from the usual I-R-E pattern, and thereby allowing a more open and potentially intercultural learning, our thesis is that (i) an examination of the linguistics aspects of the language notions assists in teachers and their learners knowing more about the language classroom practices, and (ii) this 'knowing about' language, allows a deeper critical intercultural stance to be taken, resulting possibly in learners achieving intercultural learning outcomes.

An alternative to the above I-R-E interchange might have been:

Initiation:	What have you noticed about the ways the Italian people might greet each other?
Response:	Shaking hands, Miss?
	(Teacher consciously silent.)
Reponse:	A big hug and a pat on the back, Miss?
Evaluation:	Possibly.
	(Teacher consciously silent again.)
Follow up:	How can we find out? What ideas do you have?

The continued intercultural exploration can result for the teacher and the learners together, and the variation to the I-R-E, is the exchange pattern linguistic orientation that encouraged more learning and discovering to occur. The usefulness of this approach lies in its ability to go beyond the so-called "solid" model of culture (Dervin 2011), where questioning and teaching have promoted "truths" and knowledge or stereotypes about the Other. It clearly also offers the opportunity to develop hypothesising skills in students. We are aware that the I-R-E exchange is a useful one in certain contexts, especially for checking comprehension, checking recall, and for behaviour management purposes. Yet we are also mindful that there are questioning techniques that allow teachers to offer I-R-R-R-F and I-R-R-E-F exchanges which become fruitful for them to create a learning culture, elicit learner interpretations, build on learner contributions, negotiate meaning, provide feedback and promote reflection (Hall 2002: 90). In an attempt to understand this supposition further, we have applied a discourse analysis technique, an examination of the linguistic turn, in order to ascertain how language teachers in one case in a secondary school in Sydney, Australia, vary their exchange patterns. We hypothesise how a language teacher's pedagogical choice to vary the linguistic exchange may impact on learners' developing their intercultural knowings (Moran 2001).

2.4   The linguistic exchange in the intercultural language learning classroom

We move now to an examination of turn-taking in the linguistic exchange patterns of communicative interchange in our classroom data. We consider how a teacher's explicit awareness of the I-R-E exchange can function as a tool in constructing intercultural understanding within language learning. This section examines our classroom data. It covers the method of data collection and the research site, a description of the activities of the focus lesson as a whole, and a close analysis of four selected extracts of teacher/student exchange. It concludes with a discussion of the data in relation to the research literature.

The data presented here are taken from a larger study. The researchers originally collected a body of data in six different language classrooms in the case study school, in order to capture illustrative examples of intercultural language learning in practice, in the secondary school setting. The University of Sydney Human Research Ethics Committee granted permission for the researchers to undertake this project in the nominated school. The school's principal approved the researcher's approach to the language teacher. The findings of this larger study have been reported elsewhere (Moloney & Harbon 2010a). For the purposes of this chapter however, in order to focus on the linguistic aspects of the construction of learning, we have elected to examine one lesson – in depth – from that data. We have selected one lower secondary school Spanish lesson, to look for evidence of student intercultural learning and how it may be constructed.

The methods selected to collect data were classroom observation field notes and an audio recording of the lesson. A transcript of the audio-recording was made. As neither of the researchers spoke Spanish, a translation was also made of all Spanish language content. The analysis of the lesson transcript was the principal source of data, while analysis of classroom field notes afforded some extra notation of evidence of students and teacher behaviour in the interactions. Informed consent was given by the participating teacher, the students and their parents.

The school where the data collection took place is a co-educational independent school in Sydney, Australia. It features language programs across the span of its primary and secondary school. The school has been described as culturally and linguistically diverse, with teachers and students having local, European or Asian heritage, and with languages other than English spoken in some teachers' and students' homes. The teacher of the class featured below is Anita (not her real name), who speaks Romanian, Spanish, English, German and French. The class was made up of 25 students, aged 14. Most had studied an additional (non-English) language in primary school. The students were in their second year of learning Spanish.

We present below an analysis of one Spanish lesson with a Year 8 class. Year 8 is the second year of secondary school in Australia. The purpose of the lesson was to examine the language and behaviour represented in a dialogue about visiting friends for a dinner party in a Spanish home.[1] We first look at the lesson as a whole, to observe the range of rich language activities which made up the lesson. Anita can be considered an "accomplished" language teacher (AFMLTA 2005), with a lively personality, an engaging classroom manner, and in separate discussions with her (Anita, pers. comm.), she indicates she is committed to maximising her use of the target language in the lesson, resembling as close as possible to an immersion approach. She moves fluidly between Spanish and a minor amount of English. With an understanding of her commitment to using target language, we can appreciate that in the segments where she uses or allows English to be used, it is because she attaches value to the learning which is happening in English.

---

1. Both researchers are Australian of Anglo background, and speak English as their first language. We have both been classroom language teachers of various languages but our repertoires have not included the Spanish language and culture as represented in the chosen classroom data sample. As neither researcher possess skills in Spanish, the translations noted in the tables below were provided by a translator external to the project. We acknowledge meaning and intent that may be 'lost in translation'.

3.   The language lesson

The timeline of the complete lesson featured a range of language activities. The timeline of the lesson is represented in Table 1. The Year 8 Spanish teaching programme focuses on one topic for an eight week term. This lesson examined below was scheduled towards the end of the teaching term, part of the topic "Food". Other aspects of the topic had included identifying and buying food, recipes and cooking, restaurants and menus.

Table 1. Timeline of complete lesson, Year 8 Spanish class

Mins	Lesson activity	Language used
1–9	Activity 1. To raise language issues in formal/informal forms of greeting, teacher requests students to move around an imaginary Plaza Mayor, and use different greetings in Spanish for nominated people.	Fully explained and conducted in Spanish.
9–22	Activity 2. Pair-work activity. Students sequence pictures and dialogue segments of Spanish dinner party.	Teacher explanation of task in Spanish, students confer in English. During negotiation of correct sequence, teacher explains in Spanish, students ask questions in English, teacher replies in Spanish.
23–30	Activity 3. Teacher constructs an overview of the context, in a series of short discussions of behaviours. For example, greetings, gift giving, house, late hour, punctuality. Comparisons with Australian behaviour in similar situation. Students offer unsolicited comments in English re their family practice, which contributes to their understanding of Spanish behaviour.	Use of both Spanish and English by both teacher and students.
31–34	Activity 4. Students listen to recording of dialogue text, match text segments against the picture sequence.	
35–44	Activity 5. Detailed examination of text, language details, check comprehension, spot translations. Notice differences in Spanish language practice, vs Australian English language used. *¿Que mas no hay?* what's missing? (e.g thankyou, its delicious, goodbye). Discussion of behaviour.	Use of both Spanish and English by both teacher and students.
44–58	Activity 6. In groups of four, students construct their own dinner party dialogue. Teacher circulates and gives help.	Teacher gives help in Spanish, students confer in English, write in Spanish.
59–75	Activity 7. Performance of group dialogues in Spanish.	Spanish

3.1   The student/teacher interactions

The four extracts from the lesson data below represent only very short segments of this rich language lesson, which as noted was conducted principally in Spanish. The analysis of the sequences, following the model used by Doherty and Singh (2008: 12), uses the notion of 'framing' to examine the function of each utterance. Doherty and Singh (2008) have used the phrase – what's going on here? – to suggest an interpretation of the purpose and intent of the exchange. This framing, or interpretation, is influenced by the particular reading of the two researchers. Following Doherty and Singh (2008), the "framing" column in our tables is also referred to as the "what's going on here?" column.

The first extract, a short segment occurring during Activity 3 above, has been chosen to illustrate the first strategy of this teacher, that is, the Inclusive Enquiry Question (IEQ) designed to elicit reference to the students' own experience (as distinct from other strategies adopted in other of the lesson activities such as Responding to Student Enquiry (RSE) in Activity 5, or Requesting Mediation (RM) as in Activity 3). As noted in Table 1 above, the students had arranged the sequence of pictures and sections of the dialogue in correct order. This had occasioned discussion of the time frame of the dinner party, and elicited many comparisons, both guided and spontaneous, with Australian behaviour and expectations in a similar context. Activity 3 consisted of a series of five very short discussions where the teacher asked questions which focused attention on five aspects of Spanish behaviour in this context. Extract 1 covers greetings upon arrival and departure from the host's home (see Table 2).

Although the I-R-E pattern is still evident, we note in Extract 1 that the pattern may be constructed as I-R-E-F-I-R-R-F. The I-R-E pattern is extended to allow for follow-up, multiple student personal responses to the problem, and exploration. The key to the intercultural dialogue is not only the teacher's questioning technique, but also the value she attaches to the students' responses and further questions. The teacher is acknowledging and affirming student hypothesizing skills. Although she offers her reading, or explanation, of Spanish behaviour (lines 13, 14), she has also encouraged some diverse student interpretation and negotiation.

Extract 2, also from Activity 3, explores issues surrounding punctuality in Spain. It has been chosen to illustrate the movement between languages, and a surprising reversal of teacher–student roles in Initiation and Response (see Table 3).

In Extract 2, the pattern may be seen to be I-R-F-I-R-F-I-R-I-R-F. The lack of teacher evaluation is evident. However, from the first student utterance in Table 3, we note a reversal of the typical pattern of I-R-E where the teacher initiates and evaluates, and the student responds. Here it is the student who initiates three times,

Table 2. Extract 1 from lesson transcript data

	Line	Text	Framing (what's going on here?)
T	1	What do they do here? Do they kiss, or what do they do?	Initiation (I) Question to class re their observation of photo text.
S	2	They shake hands	Response (R)
T	3 4 5 6 7 8 9	*Le dan la mano.* Because they don't know each other, what they do is they shake hands. And what do you do, when you want to leave? You say oh its getting kind of late I think I should be going… and then what do you reckon the host do – "No no no, oh you should stay longer!" How much longer would *you* stay?	Evaluation (E) Teacher confirms student answer in Spanish. Teacher offers explanation. Follow-up (F) Teacher sets up next scenario, supplies information about Spanish host behaviour. Initiation (I) Teacher offers problem: Asks students for their imagined personal response, as guest, to the scenario. Elicits learner interpretation.
S	10	Like 20 minutes, half an hour, but that's like…	Response (R) Student personal response to problem solving. Further illustration from his life experience.
S2	11 12	My mum 'd stay three hours, because it takes her like two hours to say goodbye [various students join in to discuss how long their parents take]…	Response (R) Further unsolicited student response.
T	13 14	In Spain, it's not that the guest wants to go home, it's that they want to hear that the host wants to have them there.	Follow-up (F) Teacher supplies underlying explanation of Spanish guest behaviour.

and the teacher who responds. The student is empowered to pursue his/her enquiry and determination to know exactly how late someone (or he himself) could be. The student has assumed the role of initiator not merely to recall facts, but to investigate, to be motivated by a personal sense of needing to know how to act in the situation. We could describe this second teaching strategy as Encouraging Student Enquiry (ESE). There is an observable difference in the power structure involved. The teacher sets up the scenario (a problem to solve, regarding behaviour, asking for student imagined personal response), with students offering their response in reference to local expectations, but generating further questions, out of curiosity, in order to get more information about how they might respond to the Spanish conditions. As they reach their conclusions, intercultural knowledge is being co-constructed in and through social interaction (Liddicoat et al. 2003).

Table 3. Extract 2 from lesson transcript data

	Line	Text	Framing (what's going on here?)
T	1	*Pero tambien en Espana* we talked about that	In Spanish, recalls prior discussion
	2	punctuality, *la puntualidad en Espana. Cuando*	re Spanish behaviour in regard to
	3	*te invitan y te dicen que tienes que venir a las*	punctuality. Sets up context.
	4	*nueve a que hora llegas? Llegas a las nueve y*	Initiation (I) Gives own Response
	5	*quince. Llegas tarde. Te invitan a tomar una*	(R) Follow-up (F). Elicits learner
	6	*copa o unas tapas, puedes llegar hasta una hora*	interpretation.
	7	*mas tarde.*	
		(Translation: But also, in Spain, we talked about that punctuality. When they invite you over and tell you to come at nine, what time do you arrive? You come at nine fifteen. You arrive late. They invite you for a drink or some tapas, you can arrive up to an hour late.)	
S	8	If you're like meeting with friends for like, at	Initiation (I) Checking his com-
	9	a café or whatever, ... Oh! But wouldn't	prehension of the Spanish context,
	10	you find it annoying?	unsolicited student question in English, in reference to his Australian expectations – curiosity.
T	11	*You* would find it annoying. *We* would find it	Response (R) Teacher draws com-
	12	annoying. You might get there at quarter past	parison behaviour expectation in
	13	six and for us that is late! But you sit there and	2 places. Follow-up (F) Explains.
	14	an hour later people turn up and nobody will	*Note inclusive use of pronouns (you,*
	15	be offended!	*us, we)*. Builds her explanation on student contributions.
S	16	How late would you have to be for them to like	Initiation (I) Student unsolicited
	17	actually be offended? Just not go?	question to get further information – curiosity
T	18	Well if you don't go, you would send a mes-	Response (R) Teacher responds.
	19	sage.	
S	20	But like how late?	Initiation (I) Student unsolicited Question.
T	21	I think 2 hours is kind of the limit. Or patience	Response (R) Teacher responds.
	22	for people to say ok I've just had enough.	
S	23	Its not like a rude kind of ... and then you're	Follow-up (F) Student comment,
	24	really relaxed if you turn up late and then	evaluation. *Note: student/teacher*
	25	they're like "oh that's fine".	*roles reversed.*

Extracts 1 and 2 have presented the short segments of intercultural enquiry being conducted moving between English and Spanish with some code-switching. Our third extract from Activity 3 (see Table 4) has been chosen to illustrate

Table 4. Extract 3 from lesson transcript data

	Line	Text	Framing (what's going on here?)
T	1	*OK A que hora cenais en Australia?* (Trans. Ok. So what time do you have dinner in Australia?)	Initiation (I)
S	2	*A las seis y media.* (Six-thirty).	Response (R)
T	3	*Que es la hora tipica en Espana?* (Trans. What's the typical dinner time in Spain?)	Initiation (I)
S	4	*Nueve..* (Nine..)	Response (R)
T	5 6 7 8 9	*A las nueve. Se invita a la gente a las nueve. . (..) a los nueve (..)* *porque os sabeis que en Espana se come muy tarde no? Ahora aqui* *ponen dos horas tambien. Muy bien. Y Cuando piensas que...* *James por favor, arriba con la cabeza. Cuando pensais que.. When* do you reckon they leave? (Trans. Nine. You invite people over for nine. And you know that in Spain they have dinner very late, right? And hear you can see they have drawn two hours later also. Very good and when do you think that... James please, put your head up. When do you think that..)	Evaluation (E) Initiation (I)
S	10	*Once. Diez y media.* (Eleven. Ten thirty).	Response (R)
T	11 12	*Doce.* Twelve ... James, you did an interesting gesture before, when you said "closer". What is this gesture?	Evaluation (E) Follow-up (F)
S	13	For introducing someone.	
T	14 15	Do you do that here too, do you? When you introduce some- body?	Initiation (I)
S2	16	... Same thing.	Response (R)

the intercultural dialogue being conducted largely in the target language. An English translation has been provided for the reader, but was not part of the lesson.

The pattern may be represented as I-R-I-R-E-I-R-E-F-I-R, with the first seven interactions conducted in Spanish. The authors are engaged in teacher professional development and can anecdotally report that there has been in the wider Australian language teacher community, some perception that intercultural enquiry is complex and thus can only be conducted in English. The teacher here however is using her strategy of the Inclusive Enquiry Question, in Spanish, simply by asking what time students eat dinner in Australia, which elicits a simple answer in Spanish. In this extract, Anita also notices that a student has made a particular interesting gesture in class when he answered an earlier question, and enquires as to its meaning. Anita emigrated to Australia eight years ago and so can assume the stance of 'outsider', that is, to express an apparent need for the student's explanation of meaning. Through her question, however, she makes visible to the students the culture inherent in the Australian gesture. We could describe this third teaching strategy as Requesting Mediation.

Our final extract is taken from Activity 5, to illustrate a particular use of I-R-E exchange with a questioning technique that elicits critical noticing of language in reference to students' prior knowledge and expectations. In Activity 5 students are paying close attention to the language of the dinner party scene. A 'solid' approach to examining language and culture may still perhaps be reflected in some of the discourse data here, with the teacher's recourse to some explanations of "Spanish behaviour" (for example, arriving late). Our interpretation however is that the teacher is not wishing to "museify" (Cheng 2009) Spain, that is, to impart fixed notions of the culture. Our interpretation is that the teacher in this study is engaged in constructing the students' deeper understanding of both themselves and their own framework, their reading of the particular language behaviours evident in the dinner party dialogue being studied. As stated by Scarino and Liddicoat:

> It is not just a question of learners developing knowledge about another culture, but of learners coming to understand themselves in relation to some other culture... learning to understand how one's own culture shapes perceptions of oneself, of the world, and of our relationship with others.
>
> (Scarino & Liddicoat 2009: 21)

Students are developing a "fluid" vision of themselves, and of their understanding of how their perceptions shape their relationship with their Spanish peers (Dervin 2011).

It is interesting to note in Table 5, Extract 4, that the teacher uses the simple and repeated I-R-E pattern no less than six times. We may view this teacher's reliance on the I-R-E pattern as a strategy not to check factual recall, but as a strategy here to elicit original Critical Comparison. The teacher has probably identified for herself, in preparation, the linguistic differences she hopes will be discovered. However, when she asks the question "what's missing?" she is taking a risk that students will successfully make the discoveries by themselves. She is implying a confidence in the intercultural skills which students have developed over time in her class.

The extracts demonstrate what Hall has described as the "creation of community of learners" (Hall 2002) in their patterns of linguistic interchange. The teacher initiates a process, by posing a problem. This elicits enquiry, in which students respond and offer further unsolicited contributions. The teacher then follows up, incorporating students' responses into her explanations. The community of students and teacher together are co-constructing intercultural dialogue,

Table 5. Extract 4 from lesson transcript data

ST	Line	Text	Framing (what's going on here?)
T	1	And then this is a very interesting sentence. *"Bueno sabeis donde*	
	2	*teneis vuestra casa."* If you translate it literally it says "Well you	
	3	know where you are living, don't you?" Kind of sort of saying,	
	4	"OK… it's time for you to go. You know where you're living." And	
	5	they say *"A ver cuando venis a nosotros –* let's see when you guys	
	6	come to our house." *"Vale. Nos llamamos y citamos –* we'll ring	
	7	you… and we'll fix a date." So, what's not in here? What's missing?	Initiation (I)
S1	8	Bye!	Response (R)
T	9	*Adios,* yep. What else is missing?	Evaluation (E) Initiation (I)
S2	10	Thank you.	Response (R)
T	11	Thank you. There is no way of thanking. *No hay palabra que dice*	Evaluation (E)
	12	*'muchas gracias'. Hay 'mucho gusto' y 'encantado' que son muy*	Initiation (I)
	13	*respetuosos. Pero en ningun momento se dice 'gracias'. Que mas no*	
	14	*hay?* What else is not there?	
		(Trans. There isn't a word in this dialogue about thank you or please. There is 'mucho gusto', and 'very pleased to meet' which are very respectful. But at no point do they say 'thanks'. What else is not there?)	
S3	15	*Por favor.*	Response (R)
T	16	*Si. 'Por favor.' No hay 'por favor', no hay 'gracias'. Pero os pregunto,*	Evaluation (E)
	17	*pensais que esta gente esta amable o que no tiene educacion?* Do	Initiation (I)
	18	you think they are like polite or impolite?	
		(Trans. Yes, please. There is no 'please' and no 'thanks'. But I ask you, do you think these people are friendly or that they are impolite? Do you think they are like polite or impolite?)	
S	19	Polite.	Response (R)
T	20	*Ya.* Polite. But they don't say thank you and they don't say please.	Evaluation (E)
	21	So, how do they express the politeness and the respect?	Initiation (I)
S	22	Compliments.	Response (R)
T	23	Compliments. *Hacen complimentos. Que mas?*	Evaluation (E) Initiation (I)
S	24	They invite them to their house?	Response (R)
T	25	Yeah. So they invite them over. That's very typical in Spain. Before	Evaluation (E)
	26	you leave you say "Oh how about you come to our house in two	Follow-up (F)
	27	weeks? *Nos vemos en dos semanas."* No?	

through their collective negotiation of meaning. The evidence from this study demonstrates that the teacher is conducting a dialogical relationship (Jokikokko 2005) with students here.

3.2   The value of using the I-R-E exchange and its variations

Our aim in conducting this study has been to examine the linguistic exchanges within a communicative set of teacher and student interchanges in a relatively typical language classroom. We aimed to determine whether a linguistic approach to examining the interchange illuminates what current scholars are advocating should be occurring in contemporary languages education: that is, teachers and students taking an intercultural stance towards all teaching and learning processes. After examining the transcript of the Spanish lesson, listing the teachers' and students' 'turns' by 'framing' (Doherty & Singh 2008: 12) and annotating the function of each utterance (essentially, examining what is going on in each of the turns), we now make a number of statements about our findings. As language teachers we had little experience in examining the linguistic notions within our language classroom discourse. We believe that the language education community has come a long way in being able to help us to recognize intercultural pedagogy (Liddicoat et al. 2003; Moran 2001). However it is clear to us now that with the linguistic tools to deconstruct the classroom discourse, we are able to see exactly what strategies in the classroom communicative interactions allow a deeper examination of an 'intercultural' orientation.

The 'framing' (Doherty & Singh 2008) that was made possible after the transcribing of the lesson allowed us to break down the linguistic exchanges into 'turns'. Thereafter the classification of these turns allowed us to label the turns as either one of, I (initiation), R (response), E (evaluation), and F (follow-up). From that point we could clearly see how the teacher's questioning techniques caused students to become the intercultural 'investigators' intended in the new vision for languages learning (Liddicoat et al. 2003). At one point, in Extract 2, we maintain we can observe in the transcript the teacher empowering (Johnstone 2002) the students to be questioning, thereby conducting their own intercultural enquiry. What is happening between students and teacher is not just a "Spain encounter", but also the fluid development of student inter-subjectivity. This entails diversity of response, potential manipulation, emotions, indeed going well beyond the cultural.

The 'intercultural' is not just about culture. We believe we have seen how to track the language teachers' strategies to get their students to understand the personal nature of the 'intercultural': the culturally diverse representations, interpretations, expectations, memories, and identifications brought alive in language classrooms through the questioning of the teacher and, what is new to us, the enquiry undertaken by the students. There is no fixed "truth" about Spain. Students are constructing an awareness of the complex phenomenon of intercultural communication, and the skills they need to become critical towards knowledge and facts they are given about Spanish people.

The teaching strategy we observed using the framing (Doherty & Singh 2008) of the linguistic turns showed us how to label culture learning through offering concrete experiences, opportunities to reflectively observe, invitations to abstractly conceptualise, and to actively experiment (Moran 2001: 18). The Liddicoat et al. (2003) principles of intercultural pedagogy were observable when the linguistic framing allowed us to label teachers and students actively constructing new understandings, making connections, socially interacting when using the language, reflecting, and taking responsibility for answering and questioning. We posit that the exchanges are inherently intercultural in nature and reflect the principles of intercultural pedagogy. We believe that a close examination of the transcript of this lesson shows a language teacher involved in linguistic risk-taking (Byram, Gribkova & Starkey 2002). The teacher takes a risk in asking students questions without fixed answers. We believe that by examining the linguistic turn, we have seen what Jokikokko (2005: 76) alluded to when she talked about the teacher engaging in a dialogical relationship with language students, with the ultimate aim of intercultural learning (Morson 2006: 561).

4.   Language teachers and learners interpreting their worlds

It is clear to us that by adopting a strategy of being aware of the linguistic turn, the teacher can adopt intercultural pedagogies and students can engage deeply with the kind of intercultural understandings suggested in the literature. In the learning space created by the teacher's awareness of the linguistic exchange, the students are able to construct, rather than essentialised understandings of the culture, their own meanings and interpretations of the world and the people in it. As researchers we have been empowered to engage in a process of detailed examination of classroom data. The current study shows we have been involved in a process which we believe could be easily adopted and adapted by teachers. By being aware of the turn patterns, the teacher can guide the student to intercultural learning with a conscious choice of questioning technique. The teacher can learn to choose variations of the I-R-E pattern to achieve different goals for student learning.

References

AFMLTA. (2005). Professional standards for accomplished teaching of languages and cultures. Australian Federation of Modern Languages Teachers Associations. Retrieved from pspl. afmlta.asn.au/doclib/AFMLTA_standards_for_teaching.pdf.

Board of Studies NSW. (2003). *K-10 language syllabus: Japanese.* Sydney: Board of Studies NSW.

Boxer, D. (2006). Discourse studies: Second language. In K. Brown (Ed.), *Encyclopedia of language and linguistics* (pp. 677–680). New York, NY: Elsevier.

Byram, M. (1989). *Cultural studies in foreign language education.* Clevedon: Multilingual Matters.

Byram, M., Gribkova, B., & Starkey, H. (2002). *Developing the intercultural dimension in language teaching. A practical introduction for teachers.* Strasbourg: Council of Europe.

Cheng, A. (2009). *Histoire intellectuelle de la Chine.* Paris: College de France/Fayard.

Clyne, M. (1994). *Inter-cultural communication at work: Cultural values in discourse.* Cambridge: Cambridge University Press.

Corbett, J. (2003). *An intercultural approach to English language teaching.* Clevedon: Multilingual Matters.

Coulby, D. (2006). Intercultural education: Theory and practice. *Intercultural Education, 17*(3), 245–257.

Dashwood, A. (2004). Talk and productive pedagogies in languages education. *Babel, 39*(1), 20–25, 38.

DeJaeghere, J. G. & Zhang, Y. (2008). Development of intercultural competence among US American teachers: Professional development factors that enhance competence. *Intercultural Education, 19*(3), 255–268.

Dervin, F. (2011). A plea for change in research on intercultural discourses: A 'liquid' approach to the study of the acculturation of Chinese students. *Journal of Multicultural Discourses, 6*(1), 37–57.

Doherty, C. & Singh, P. (2008). Native speaker TESOL teacher's talk: Examining the unexamined. *English Teaching and Learning, 32*(2), 39–75.

Edwards, A. D. & Westgate, D. P. G. (1994). *Investigating classroom talk* (second edn.). London: Falmer Press.

Geertz, C. (1973). *The interpretation of cultures.* New York, NY: Basic Books.

Hall, J. K. (2002). *Methods for teaching foreign languages: Creating a community of learners in the classroom.* Upper Saddle River, NJ: Merrill Prentice Hall.

Harbon, L. & Browett, J. (2006). Intercultural languages education: Challenges for Australian teacher educators. *Babel, 41*(1), 28–33, 38.

Holliday, A. (2010). Cultural descriptions as political cultural acts: An exploration. *Language and Intercultural Communication, 10*(3), 259–272.

Hu, A. (1999). Interkulturelles Lernen. Eine Auseinandersetzung mit der Kritik an einem umstrittenen Konzept. *Zeitschrift für Fremdsprachenforschung, 10*(2), 277–303.

Johnson, M. (1979). *Discussion dynamics: An analysis of classroom teaching.* Rowley, MA: Newbury House Publishers.

Johnstone, B. (2002). *Discourse analysis.* Oxford: Blackwell.

Jokikokko, K. (2005). Interculturally trained Finnish teachers' conceptions of diversity and intercultural competence. *Intercultural Education, 16*(1), 69–83.

Kasper, G. & Rose, K. (2002). *Pragmatic development in a second language.* Oxford: Blackwell.

Kinginger, C. & Belz, J. A. (2005). Sociocultural perspectives on pragmatic development in foreign language learning: Microgenetic case studies from telecollaboration and residence abroad. *Intercultural Pragmatics, 2*(4), 369–421.

Kramsch, C. (2010). The symbolic dimension of intercultural competence. Keynote Presentation at the Second International Conference on the Development and Assessment of Intercultural Competence. CERCLL, Tucson, A, 29–31 January.

Kramsch, C. (2006). Culture in language teaching. In K. Brown (Ed.), *Encyclopedia of language and linguistics* (pp. 322–329). New York, NY: Elsevier.

Kramsch, C. (1993). *Context and culture in language teaching.* Oxford: Oxford University Press.

Lazar, I., Huber-Kriegler, M., Lussier, D., Matei, G. S., & Peck, C. (2007). *Developing and assessing intercultural communicative competence – A guide for language teachers and teacher educators.* Strasbourg/Graz: Conseil de l'Europe/Centre européen pour les langues vivantes.

Liddicoat, A. J. (2002). Static and dynamic views of culture and intercultural language acquisition. *Babel, 36*(3), 4–11, 37.

Liddicoat, A. J. (2006). Learning the culture of interpersonal relationships: Students' understandings of personal reference in French. *Intercultural Pragmatics, 6*(1), 55–80.

Liddicoat, A. J., Papademetre, L., Scarino, A., & Kohler, M. (2003). *Report on Intercultural Language Learning.* Australian Government: Department of Education Science and Training.

Lin, A. M. Y. (2010). Curriculum: Foreign language learning. In P. Peterson, E. Baker & B. McGaw (Eds.), *International Encyclopedia of Education* (third edn.) (pp. 428–434). London: Elsevier.

Lo Bianco, J. & Crozet, C. (2003). *Teaching invisible culture: Classroom practice and theory.* Melbourne: Language Australia.

Moloney, R. (2008). *Young language learners and their intercultural competence.* Saarbrucken: HDM, Verlag Dr Mueller.

Moloney, R. & Harbon, L. (2008). I speak therefore I am: Self-perceptions of identity in immersion program language learners as an expression of intercultural competence. *University of Sydney Papers in TESOL, 3,* 111–129.

Moloney, R. & Harbon, L. (2010a). Making intercultural language learning visible and assessable. *Proceedings of the Second International Conference on the Development and Assessment of Intercultural Competence* (pp. 281–303). CERCLL, Tucson, Arizona, USA, 29–31 January.

Moloney, R. & Harbon, L. (2010b). Student performance of intercultural language learning. *Electronic Journal of Foreign Language Teaching, 7*(2), 177–192.

Moran, P. R. (2001). *Teaching culture: Perspectives in practice.* Boston, MA: Heinle & Heinle.

Morson, G. S. (2006). Dialogism, Bakhtinian. In K. Brown (Ed.), *Encyclopedia of language and linguistics* (pp. 561–563). New York, NY: Elsevier.

Sacks, H., Schegloff, E. A., & Jefferson, G. (1974). A simplest systematics for the organization of turn-taking for conversation. *Language, 50*(4), 696–735.

Scarino, A. & Liddicoat, A. J. (2009). *Teaching and learning languages: A guide.* Canberra: Commonwealth of Australia.

Scarino, A. & Papademetre, L. (2000). *Integrating culture learning in the languages classroom.* Melbourne: National Language and Literacy Institute of Australia.

Shaules, J. (2007). *Deep culture: The hidden challenges of global living.* Clevedon: Multilingual Matters.

Sinclair, J. & Coulthard, M. (1975). *Toward an analysis of discourse: The English used by teachers and pupils.* Oxford: Oxford University Press.

Sinclair, J. & Coulthard, M. (1992). Toward an analysis of discourse. In M. Coulthard (Ed.), *Advances in spoken discourse analysis* (pp. 1–34). London: Routledge.

Smith, N. (2006). History of linguistics: Discipline of linguistics. In K. Brown (Ed.), *Encyclopedia of language and linguistics* (pp. 341–355). New York, NY: Elsevier.

Tsui, A. (1995). *Introducing classroom interaction.* London: Penguin.

UNESCO. (2006). *UNESCO guidelines on intercultural education.* Paris, France: UNESCO.

Young, T. & Sercombe, P. (2010). Communication, discourses and interculturality. *Language and Intercultural Communication, 10*(3), 181–188.

Constructing a relationship to otherness in web-based exchanges for language and culture learning

Virginie Trémion
Université de Lille 3

This study aims at demonstrating the relevance of linguistics for studying learning in online intercultural education. Adopting a critical approach to the 'intercultural', the chapter is based on the perceptions of French and American students who participated in Cultura, an online exchange program with a cultural objective. The program was created at the MIT and has been replicated and adapted in many international institutions. During the exchanges, the students were asked to explore the links between culture and communication using a comparative approach. This article examines how linguistic theories (French Discourse Analysis) can reveal the construction of *alterity* – the link between self and other – in the students' discourses while they negotiate and co-construct French and American cultures.

> The digital is not a separate realm, it is a conceptual suit we put on, a house we enter, an arcade we visit for a while, a poem we recite in our play at culture. To argue a new model of the self that is a break with the past passes judgment that is unnecessary and falls into a reductive will to erase. Digitopia can never completely erase the past – our activities 'carry over' traces of where we have been, what we have done, and who we have been, to enrich the present and to serve as material with which to actively build the future. (Downes 2005: 143)

1. Introduction

This article introduces the relevance of linguistics for intercultural education. It considers some of the discursive events that are specific to an online exchange program with a cultural objective. These programs have become increasingly common in education due to the advent of the Internet, the development of online communication tools and the presence of "digital natives" (Prensky 2001) in schools. At first glance, using Information and Communication Technologies (ICT) can be seen as a godsend for facilitating interpersonal exchanges. Nonetheless, research has shown that their use in education implies shifts that are yet to be defined (*What does one need to know in order to learn to communicate online? Which skills are called upon?*).

As far as the field of Foreign Language Teaching and Learning is concerned, studies have looked at the potential of computer-mediated communication (CMC) for the development of communicative skills. While syllabi and curricula stress the importance of *plurilinguism* (Council of Europe 2001), online exchanges are often related to the study of "*intercultural competence*" (Belz 2002). For instance, all the chapters in "Online intercultural exchanges. An introduction for teachers" (O'Dowd 2007) look at how online collaboration can be used for the development of students' intercultural communicative competence. However, the meaning the authors give to the term *intercultural* varies. In education, the word *intercultural* often has many interpretations that can lead to "differentialist, culturalist even functionalist" discourses, which Dervin (2009) condemns as *impostures de l'interculturel* ("intercultural impostures").[1] For Abdallah-Pretceille (2004), intercultural education refers to the learning of the ability to "objectivise one's own reference system, to distance oneself from it and thus to admit the existence of other perspectives without sinking into the drift of absolute relativism, but by leaning on the learning of relativity from a series of successive *decentrations*" (p. 111). What is at stake is a better understanding of the complexity and dynamism of the world. In this interpretation, the notion of *alterity* – the link between Self and Other – can serve as a useful starting point to observe the diverse and instable phenomena linked to communication between individuals. Following Dervin's (2009) suggestion of pairing linguistic theories with dialogism (Bakhtin 1970) for the analysis of the construction of Self and the Other, this paper will examine parts of this process in an online exchange program. It addresses the following questions: What relation to alterity is constructed during an online exchange which lays the emphasis on culture? Are there signs of the students' ability to step back and reflect critically on the 'intercultural'?

The chapter will attempt to show how the construction of alterity is linked to the context of discourse production in online exchange. In the data I analyse below, the students report their exchange activities. The corpus consists of written texts extracted from the student's logbook – *Discovery pad* – and semi-structured interviews. In both cases, the students reflect on salient episodes in their

1.   All translations are mine.

participation in the program. The chapter begins by presenting the theoretical framework, before delving into the background of the online program chosen for this study: Cultura. It will then present the corpus and the methodology adopted to study it before discussing the results.

2.   Discourse analysis of the 'intercultural'

As specified in the introduction, adopting an intercultural approach means thinking of humankind in terms of *variation* and not in terms of dichotomies, borders and categories (Abdallah-Pretceille 2006). A priority in this approach is the question of *interactions, evolutions,* and *tensions between self and other* rather than the mere learning of declarative knowledge. As Abdallah-Pretceille (1986) points out, attention must not be centred on culture as culture does not exist by itself: "Cultures exist, indeed, only by and in the mediation of individuals and groups. They cannot, as such, be reduced to observable realities, susceptible to normative and analytical approaches" (p. 77). Abdallah-Pretceille criticizes the use of generalizations and stereotypes to describe unstable, multiple realities in evolution.

Linguistic Discourse Analysis has a number of advantages for intercultural research. Dervin (2009) states that Discourse Analysis offers an operating frame, I follow his work in this chapter. First, as opposed to Content Analysis, there are no fixed categories preceding data analysis in Discourse Analysis (Mangenot 2006). This should free the analysis from the researcher's *a priori* constructs and facilitate the hermeneutic dimension of the interpretation of data. Furthermore, as Dervin (2009) points out, Discourse Analysis can allow the researcher "to renew the intercultural in language education so as to avoid the dominant approach, that of *differentialism-culturalism*". The particularity of the French School of Discourse Analysis (Maingueneau 2002a) is that it can reveal the subjectivity of discourse bringing together the *intersubjective relations* between texts, speakers and environments. So the French School of Discourse Analysis seems useful for intercultural research in an online learning environment as it underlines the influences of the tools of communication through positioning in discourse. Positioning consists of "the operations by which the enunciative identity is established and remains in a discursive field" (Maingueneau 2002b: 453). The usefulness of the analysis of enunciation in revealing the speaker's attitudes through linguistic forms of his subjectivity (i.e. through the use of such or such personal pronouns, possessive adjectives, etc.) has been demonstrated by Kerbrat-Orecchioni (2002). Accordingly, this study considers that the analysis of positioning can be a relevant tool for an intercultural analysis of discourse. The challenge of this study, as Moirand (2004) has emphasized, is to be able to identify linguistic regularities and, at the same time, to be able to contextualize them (i.e. to link them to a specific place, at a particular time, with unique speakers) which seem to be contradictory. Thus, the subjectivity of discourse and of data should be kept in mind during its interpretation.

3. Cultura

Created in 1997, Cultura is a web-based program of exchanges whose aim is "to develop foreign language students' understanding of foreign cultural attitudes, concepts, beliefs, and ways of interacting and looking at the world."[2] Its authors, Gilberte Furstenberg, Shoggy Waryn and Sabine Levet (2001), wanted to make visible "The Hidden Dimension" (Hall 1966) of culture. The activities in the Cultura program are based on the comparison and analysis of materials produced by the students before participating in the online exchange. In the first stages of Cultura, the students must fill in three questionnaires (word associations, sentence completions and reactions to hypothetical situations) and then log into the forums to analyze their responses, make hypotheses and formulate queries in collaboration with other participants. As stipulated in their online guidelines, the creators of Cultura explain the importance of gathering groups of students "in relatively similar contexts (two high schools, two universities, etc.)" and having them work on the same online documents through which the students observe, analyze and compare the constitutive elements of the culture.

Another striking point is the language used in the forums. Discussions should be written in "the student's native language" to facilitate in-depth cultural understanding. According to Furstenberg, three benefits can be highlighted for the use of the students' first language: "(1) it puts all students on an equal linguistic footing; (2) students, not being bound by limited linguistic abilities, can express their views fully and in detail, formulate questions and hypotheses clearly, and provide complex, nuanced information; (3) the student generated texts provide the foreign partners with rich sources of authentic reading, and, in turn, become new objects of linguistic and cultural analysis, highlighting the different ways in which cultures can be expressed" (Furstenberg 2004).

---

2. Introduction to Cultura and teacher's guidelines available at http://cultura.mit.edu/community/index/cid/1.

4.   A methodology for understanding the "*inter*"

Data collection was spread out over a period of 10 weeks from February to May 2006. The Cultura program set up between the Massachusetts Institute of Technology (MIT), Boston-USA, and L'Ecole Polytechnique (X), Paris-France was at the center of my analysis. The MIT group was composed of 17 student learners of French as a Foreign Language. Of this group, 40% were international students.

To analyze the learners' interpretations, I chose to work on the discursive materials from a personal diary where the learner does not need "to put up a good show" (Goffman 1974:9) as would be the case in a public and collective tool (like a forum). I postulate that in this environment the students would be more likely to express their personal points of view. In an effort to make them put into words the changes in their representations of culture, I invited them to write their discoveries and their surprises in a logbook. The instructions I gave were: to note each time they participated (by reading and/or writing) in the forums, their discoveries, their surprises. The methodology was inspired by the "*Surprise diary*" – (*Journal d'étonnement*) created and implemented by Barbot (2005, 2010) in a course for mobile students. Barbot explains that the expression and the analysis of his own moment of astonishment enables the writer "to become aware" of his own "expectations" which act "as a distorting glass" (Barbot 2005:9).

Individual interviews were also carried out with the students. They were designed to capture on the one hand, the intentions and purposes hidden behind the visible online interactions, and on the other hand, the contextual elements that could play a role in discourse production. During the 45–60 minutes of the interview, I focused on the student's descriptions of the aims of the program, their uses of the forums, and their communication practices in the forums (*what did you … when you did…?*). The method used for the Discourse Analysis was to establish networks based on meaning by focusing on the regularities of the corpus. I first subjected the data to Lexico3, a tool for statistical analysis, to obtain an initial map of the patterns of linguistic regularities. Lexico3 allows for the identification of graphical markers as well as their distribution in a text. The corpus was separated by source and by student and further analysed to identify features of text types and particular students.

5.   Positioning of the students: Some linguistic markers

In this section, I will discuss the linguistic expressions in the chosen corpus which reflect the points of view of the students. In the analysis I have divided the regularities found into two discursive events: *associations* and *modalisation*.

5.1   Associations and subjectivity

An association can be defined as a relation between two mental representations. The observation of associations expressed through pronouns, nouns, adjectives and adverbs can reveal the points of view of the learners (e.g. "French students are ..."). They are places where subjectivity expressed itself. In the extracts chosen, the students report their discoveries following their exchanges. To identify positioning, at this point I focus on students' representations of the exchange partners. In the following extract from the forum "Etudiant/Student", the student draws a conclusion after his participation in the following terms:

> I was surprised that **a student in France** would know about the intelligent design/evolution debate going on in the United States.

In this extract, the student develops a sociocultural category: *a student in France.* From this particular exchange he draws a conclusion encompassing all the French students; the indefinite article *a* allows him to make reference to students in France in general. He develops a stereotypical account of all students based on experiences of one.

Very often associations are made by means of nationalities, as stated in the instructions of the exchange. The next excerpt is drawn from an MIT-Polytechnique exchange and the remarks of the student tend to reproduce a bipolar view: "France/America":

> I felt like **French students** were more politically active than **US Students**. When looking at the issue of 'Europe', the French students exhibited a greater deal of political and economic understanding than the American students which **I think** is characteristic of the fact that French society is focused on foreign affairs while in the US, the emphasis is on internal affairs.

The student describes his discoveries opposing *French students* and *US students.* Moreover, he tries to connect his observations of the forum with his knowledge of the politico-economic systems of both countries using a narrative strategy with *I think*, which is employed to underline his hypotheses. This division of reality places imaginary borders between the groups of students. The challenge faced in a comparative exchange using an intercultural approach is to manage going beyond such "culturalist" borders. The danger is that they may seem to be unbridgeable even to the students themselves, as illustrated by this quote from one of the interviews:

> Some of the differences between the responses really surprised me, especially those between the responses for individualism. We **just** saw the word in **two**

completely different ways and reconciling those differences is proving to be somewhat difficult.

The use of *just* is final; there is no further discussion. The use of the expression *two completely different ways*, excludes the possibility of another alternative to "French" or "American".

The expression of a dichotomy France/America can even be strengthened when it is coupled with other linguistic processes as illustrated in the following example:

> **When comparing the French and US views on the traits possessed by a good student**, the French place greater emphasis on the importance of passion and making an effort to understand and play a proactive role in your education.

The disappearance of the enunciator in the use of the gerundive *when comparing* instead of the personal pronoun "I + verb" – "when I compare", depersonalises the conclusion. This effect is strengthened by the location to the left of the clause *when comparing the French and US views on the traits possessed by a good student*. In this excerpt, the use of *the* + plural (*the French*) and the possessive pronoun *your* can be underlined. This process distances the student from seeing the multiple and diverse reality that is encapsulated in the intercultural approach discussed above. The study of associations, from a linguistic point of view, identifies the representations of others produced by the students. It reveals their view of alterity. In an intercultural approach, if categories are to be found through discourse, they should be responded to through education. Education should open linguistic boundaries to give way to the multiplicity, the variety, the dynamics, appropriate in the expression of an individual in constant evolution.

5.2   Modalisation and positioning

In this section, I investigate the linguistic markers when a subject and an object are related. I study the distance which the subject places when writing about culture. This analysis reveals the expression of the subjectivity of the speaker. The linguistic patterns in the corpus are often marked by the use of modals, i.e. auxiliary verbs, as in the following example:

> **I personally** was **very surprised** by the fact that **Americans** would not mind if a bank teller addressed **them** by their first name. (This statement makes reference to the answers in a forum related to the following situation: "*You are cashing a personal check at a bank. The employee reads your name on the check and addresses you with your first name*").

Here the student is expressing his distance from the answers given by his own group (referred to by *Americans/them*) using the modal *would*. Through the use of the adverb *personally*, the student focuses on the difference between himself and others, putting himself in opposition with respect to the generally admitted idea. The assertion of peculiarity is further enforced by the collocation *I personally*. Another modal operator, the superlative adverb *very*, intensifies *surprise* which in this case expresses the unexpectedness of the others' response.

The multiplication of modals in the same sentence acts as a marker of tensions in the representations of culture as a coherent whole. The expression of these tensions varies. The more modal operators are employed within a sentence, the more a "disjunctive" effect is created revealing the distance involved in the subject's positioning. In the following extract, distance is created by the use of reported speech (Charaudeau 1992). The break is achieved in part by the use of graphic markers (here quotation marks):

> The following comment: '[…]', surprised me, because I thought France had a capitalist system.

Having presented an inventory, which is far from exhaustive, of linguistic markers which can be useful for studying the points of view of students in an intercultural approach, I will continue by focusing on the influences of context on the act of enunciation.

6.   The contextual constraints of discourse

Identifying the role of context on discursive production allows for a better understanding of the construction of alterity in Cultura. During individual interviews, the students report their experience both as readers and as writers. To identify the contextual elements which guide the discursive production, I focus on the technical, educational and communicative aspects of the exchange.

6.1   Technology

During the interviews, the students repeatedly specify that they would not have said the same things using other communication tools. In the following excerpts, the students express their awareness of the influence of ITC on discourse production:

> Yeah it's weird like talking to someone over the computer and never being able to see who you're talking to like just talk face to face for once I rely a lot on facial expressions I think they really modify what you are saying.
>
> It would be nice to be able to upload pictures like this is Paris or this is a typical library in Paris or whatever, this is where I live like do you live in dorms or do you live in a house or an apartment? There are some things I wouldn't think to say but like in a picture it would make it clear. And I also think that each post should have threads so like for like in paradox the subject would be like smoking it's so much easier to follow the thread replies 'cause every American student writes something and when they reply to something it's hard to know who they reply to, if someone replies to that.

In the preceding extracts, the limits of using forums are expressed by the students. They regret they cannot access the non-verbal dimension of communication, which deprived them of *facial expressions*. They concede that online writing cannot reveal everything, that communication is more complex than a matter of linguistic markers, and they suggest means to facilitate understanding between students. These examples show that online communication can be useful for linguistics in intercultural education as it can illustrate discourse as a construction depending on an environment.

Many times, the students suggest the use of an instant messaging tool, like MSN or ICQ, instead of the forum. During an interview, to a question related to the use of instant messaging tools, one student answered:

> I guess with an instant messaging type of thing that would be pretty interesting, to find out more about **the people themselves**, because **I feel I don't really know who they are exactly**. Some things about themselves like they are a few people from Spain, some way like to see **who all of them are**, like personal things.

The statement *I feel I don't really know who they exactly are* assumes that speaking about a culture online is not enough to know people. This deficiency, according to the student, is partly due to the communicative tool chosen. This variety in the presentation of the students is also expressed using the lexical field of the self: *the people themselves, who they exactly are, who all of them are*. What is stated here is the expression of multiplicity of the aspects of the self: the one I am, the one I think I am, the one I am told to be, the one I can be, and the one I say I am… For the students, CMC does not facilitate the expression of this multiplicity. In fact, studies have shown that online telecollaboration in multicultural exchanges can lead to tensions and misunderstandings (O'Dowd 2003; Thorne 2006). Therefore the linguistic expressions of the self depend on the tool chosen.

6.2   Educational context

Not surprisingly, the students reveal how the framework of an institutional language course influences their discourse. When they were questioned about whether they participate sincerely in the program, several students explained how the fact the teacher read their written production influenced them. This confession was not, however, easy to obtain at the MIT. Its expression was accompanied by laughter, expressing the embarrassment of the student. For one student, his aim to obtain *credit* influenced what he wrote:

> (…) probably a little because you know that someone else is going to read it someone [laughs] who is going to give you **credit** at some point is reading this.

The frequency of participation by the student was also strongly dependent on the educational context:

> Hummmm probably four times a week because … the **homework** [*laughs*] … so: either four or five times a week 'cause I normally do two days during the week-end and one four days during the week … so probably four or five times a week.

The educational context has an effect on the frequency of participation, influences the content of the discourse produced online as in Cultura, students are expected to be "*cultural specialists*". They must: "Enter into a real dialogue with their cultural partners, exchanging viewpoints, asking questions and answering each other's questions, trying to make sense together of the materials they analyze, thus cooperatively constructing an understanding of each other's culture".[3]

Thus, the students are invited to look for some convergence (*trying to make sense*) in the written words of their partners. This entails a kind of "expected disorder" which the students have to put right. Disorder is normal in a complex world (Morin 1990). Observing disorder should lead the students to question and be cautious of generalizing. In the course of the exchange, as a confrontation with complexity occurs, the participants used an increasing number of question marks, and multi-modal operators. It is in the process of "rationalization", by searching for order, that intercultural tensions occur within a subject who is assigned three roles by the context: (a) the individual – unique; (b) the mediator; (c) the "American"; together with expected "norms" (of online communication, of exchanging) and the "world" (in movement, interconnected…).

---

3.   From Cultura teacher's guide: http://cultura.mit.edu/community/index/cid/81.

These tensions sometimes prove to be difficult to overcome, as for the following student who rarely posted in the forums:

> But you have your fellow students, other people you do know, then you come back to class … so if you do write something outrageous everybody else's going to know about it and also the teacher's going to know about it so sometimes I think that it probably makes me more reserved.

6.3   Linguistic mediation

The language chosen for communication is also an element to be taken into account in Discourse Analysis. When in other contexts, online exchanges often take place in a foreign language, in the forums of Cultura, students use their native language:

> I **really** think it's a good idea because for me to write what I am thinking in French right now would be very tedious and I think my responses would probably be a lot shorter and a lot less informative just because I don't know the vocab so to be able to actually write in English I think is very helpful and then … but you **really** do learn because you have to read the French … when I explained this to my parents they were like 'Wait, you're writing in English?' And like it actually is really helpful because both sides can **really** communicate what they are thinking and then you learn the vocab rather than having to limit what you actually have to say.

With the repetition of the adverb *really,* the student insists on his/her capacity to write the information the way he/she wants to, otherwise impossible for her in a foreign language.

   In addition to the difficulties that most students have, other students have additional difficulties to deal with. This student for instance had been living in the United States for only one year. Since he did not participate in the forums, during the interview I asked him why.

> It's just when it comes to … One day I ask questions and I would have to answer, it's hard. It's just really … **I don't know what to do or what to say or if what I am saying is right**.

Clearly mentioned here is the confrontation between the framing of the program and the reality of an evolving and multiple world where education is a process of internationalisation. The student does not know what *being American means* and his participation is constrained by the framing of the task.

These extracts could show that discourses are influenced not only by the media, but also by linguistic or educational mediations. They also give the researcher a network of links to identify and to follow in order to identify expressions of subjectivity during an online exchange.

7. Discussion and conclusion

The aim of this article was to observe the contributions of linguistics to analyze the "intercultural" in relation to online technologies. The aim was to capture the expressions of subjectivity, which are indicative of how the actors construct interculturality. The analysis gathered, on the one hand, linguistic markers used for building the learners' *points of view* and *positionings* and, on the other hand, it questioned the influence of the context on the development of intercultural awareness. The questions this study sought to address were: What is the relationship to alterity that is constructed during an online exchange with a cultural objective? What are the *discursive positionings* of the students? The study shows that associations by categorization (specific attributes) are constructed in discourse, and that group comparisons were seen to lead to culturalist discourses (i.e. culture only explains what is happening). There is a risk that a comparative methodology affixes a filter (generalizations related to nationality) through which the learner is led to think about others. In an intercultural approach to learning, the learner must be able to escape from this filter in order to distance her/himself and look at things from the outside. This process is quite important, as it contributes to the construction of identification. The study of modality seems to be an effective means of estimating the distance of the enunciator in the expression, construction and enactment of his/her representation of reality. In an online exchange program, the teacher should try to *destabilise* the categorizing process that results from a comparative methodology. For Wieviorka (2001) it is necessary to find the balance between the individual and the collective. The individual needs collective representations to express him/herself, while at the same time he/she can only exist through *distance, disengagement,* and *reflexivity.*

This leads us to a final question: Are there signs of learners' awareness? Our study was able to illustrate the awareness of students of the influences of educational conditions on their discursive production. While the written expression of the discoveries made in intercultural communication can bring the individual to distinguish him/herself from the object under consideration, *mediatisation* is perceived as an influential element in this context. The study of discourse in a digital environment must take into account the influences of the technical environment in the construction of enunciation. Participants appear to think that with instant messaging, the expressions of self and the other would be different. What is important now is to explore what becomes of enunciation with digital tools. What characteristics of the tool can be used for what expression of self and other?

Discourse analysis inevitably evokes the question of changes which occur during the *re*-expression of the studied object. The operation can be infinite. Kerbrat-Orecchioni (2002: 247) suggests that *énoncés*, i.e. the discursive results of enunciation, are like Russian dolls whose exploration never stops. For an intercultural study of online discourse, what is important is to consider interactions and the *intersubjectivity* in relation to contexts (educational, social, technological, etc.). This is what can give the "doll" its uniqueness, its relativity, and its "unpredictable" outline.

References

Abdallah-Pretceille, M. (1986). *Vers une pédagogie interculturelle*. Paris: Anthropos.

Abdallah-Pretceille, M. (2004). *L'éducation interculturelle* (second edn.). Paris: P.U.F, Que sais-je?

Abdallah-Pretceille, M. (2006). *Les métamorphoses de l'identité*. Paris: Anthropos.

Barbot, M.-J. (2005). Les ancrages socio-affectifs: Un défi en formation des enseignants. *Glottopol, 6*, 181–194.

Barbot, M.-J. (2010). Voyages de formation interculturelle et étonnements. *Le Journal des psychologues, 278*, 44–48.

Belz, J. A. (2002). Social dimensions of telecollaborative foreign language study. *Language Learning and Technology, 6*(1), 60–81.

Bakhtin, M. (1970). *La poétique de Dostoïevski*. (Trans. C. Koutcheff). Paris: Éditions de Seuil.

Council of Europe. (2001). *Common European framework of reference for languages: Learning, teaching, assessment*. Strasbourg: Council of Europe.

Charaudeau, P. (1992). *Grammaire du sens et de l'expression*. Paris: Hachette.

Dervin, F. (2009). Approches dialogiques et énonciatives de l'interculturel: Pour une didactique des langues et de l'identité mouvante des sujets. *Synergies Roumanie, 4*, 165–178.

Downes, D. (2005). *Interactive realism: The poetics of cyberspace*. McGill: Queen's University Press.

Furstenberg, G., Levet, S., English, K., & Maillet, K. (2001). Giving a virtual voice to the silent language of culture: The Cultura project. *Language Learning and Technology, 5*(1), 55–102.

Furstenberg, G. (2004). *Using communication tools to foster cross-cultural understanding*. NFLRC Symposium. University of Hawaii National Foreign Language Resource Center. Retrieved from http://nflrc.hawaii.edu/networks/nw44/index.htm.

Goffman, E. (1974). *Frame analysis: An essay on the organization of experience*. London: Harper and Row.

Hall, E. T. (1966). *The hidden dimension*. New York, NY: Doubleday.

Kerbrat-Orecchioni, C. (2002). *L'énonciation*. Paris: Armand Colin.

Maingueneau, D. (2002). Analyse du discours. In P. Charaudeau & D. Maingueneau (Eds.), *Dictionnaire d'analyse du discours* (pp. 41–45). Paris: EDS.

Maingueneau, D. (2002). Positionnement. In P. Charaudeau & D. Maingueneau (Eds.), *Dictionnaire d'analyse du discours* (pp. 453–454). Paris: EDS.

Mangenot, F. (2006). Analyser les interactions pédagogiques en ligne, pourquoi, comment? *Intercompreensão, comunicacão electronica em contextos de educacão linguistica. Teorias e praticas* (Vol. 13, pp. 11–28). Santarém: Editions Cosmos.

Moirand, S. (2004). L'impossible clôture des corpus médiatiques. La mise au jour des observables entre catégorisation et contextualisation. *TRANEL, 40,* 72–92.

Morin, E. (1990). *Introduction à la pensée complexe.* Paris: ESF.

O'Dowd, R. (2003). Understanding the "other side": Intercultural learning in a Spanish-English e-mail exchange. *Language Learning and Technology, 7,* 118–144.

O'Dowd, R. (Ed.). (2007). *Online intercultural exchange: An introduction for foreign language teachers.* Clevedon: Multilingual Matters.

Prensky, M. (2001). Digital natives, digital immigrants. *On the Horizon, 9*(5), 1–6.

Thorne, S. L. (2006). Pedagogical and praxiological lessons from internet mediated intercultural foreign language education research. In J. A. Belz & S. L. Thorne (Eds.), *Internet-mediated intercultural foreign language education* (pp. 2–30). Boston, MA: Heinle & Heinle.

Wieviorka, M. (2001). *La différence.* Paris: Balland.

Web page

Cultura Community site: http://cultura.mit.edu/.

Complex and symbolic discursive encounters for intercultural education in plurilingual times

Julie Byrd Clark and Sofia Stratilaki
Western University / Université Sorbonne Nouvelle – Paris 3

The goal of this chapter is to present some new ways of conceptualizing linguistic competence in relation to intercultural education. With the impact of globalization, immigration, new technologies, and the competitiveness of national and international markets, multilingualism represents the practical norm. It has been deemed a tool for local integration and international mobility. In the school context, the question of a plurilingual and pluricultural identity has also become important and research incorporating language biographies has tended to focus on the subjective view of linguistic and cultural learning and on the significance of the interaction of identities (*Inter*, an indicator of relationship and not of a simple juxtaposition). It is this plurality or notion of *plurilingual* competence that is of issue and holds significance in this chapter, particularly as regards intercultural education. In drawing upon an interdisciplinary approach, which combines sociolinguistic, psycholinguistic, and educational perspectives, we demonstrate how linguistics has much to offer intercultural education today.

1. Introduction

During the past ten years, there has been an increased interest among both researchers and practitioners to look at the relationship between linguistics and interculturality in language education through a postmodernist conceptualization. Much of this interest has been sparked by the emergence of a new knowledge economy, trans-nationalism, mobility, and the impact of globalization in multilingual societies (Byrd Clark 2008a, 2009, 2012; Beacco 2005). As such, language educators worldwide are being called upon to produce effective human capital through intercultural education; that is well-developed people who are critical, independent, life-long learners as well as international or worldly citizens (Byram 2010; Hu & Byram 2009; Hu 2003).

This is particularly evident in Europe where trilingual education and various curricula for third language acquisition have been increasingly implemented around the world, in order to meet the growing demand for multilingualism. With the impact of globalization, immigration, new technologies, and the competitiveness of national and international markets, multilingualism represents the practical norm. It has been deemed a tool for local integration and international mobility. In the school context, and in a similar vein as the chapter by Cuenat & Bleichenbacher (this volume), the question of a plurilingual and pluricultural identity has also become important and research incorporating language biographies has tended to focus on the subjective view of linguistic and cultural learning and on the significance of the interaction of identities (*inter*, an indicator of relationship and not of a simple juxtaposition). However, many of the educational policies, shaping curriculum, continue to reproduce the language-nation-state ideology (e.g. one language, one people), and as such many language education programs struggle with the tensions between finding ways to promote diversity and having to operate under an ideological competence-skills based model of language (Chomsky 1965). This model views language learning as the mastery of "unitary, determinate practices that people can be trained in" (Fairclough 1992:44), rather than viewing linguistic repertoires as plural and multidimensional, shifting in different social contexts. It is this plurality, or *plurilingual* competence, that is of issue in this chapter and that holds significance when we consider how and what linguistics has to contribute to intercultural education today.

The goal of this chapter is to explicitly present some new ways of conceptualizing linguistic competence in relation to intercultural education. In drawing upon an interdisciplinary approach, which combines sociolinguistic, psycholinguistic, and educational perspectives, we demonstrate how linguistics has much to offer intercultural education. In order to do this, we begin by providing a discussion on some of the interrelated concepts that we will be using throughout this paper: symbolic competence, plurilingual competence, and social representations (e.g. Moscovici 1984). Our use of the term *plurilingual* is intricately connected with the term intercultural – meaning "in-between" – in other words between the socially constructed and interconnected "self" and "other". After all, it is through language that we construct notions of self and other. At the same time, we can observe through language uses, the construction of social difference; that is how social processes, such as social categorisation, operate and more specifically, how the "us" and "them" get socially constructed. Plurilingualism and plurilingual practices make these processes more visible. We will connect these concepts to some of the discourses surrounding multilingualism and intercultural education. In order to understand how these concepts and discourses are related to intercultural education, we aim to: (1) provide a historical overview of how language, particularly linguistic competence has been conceptualized (in Europe), and how this conceptualization is continuing to evolve; and (2) contextualize these concepts by presenting a case study on French-German bilinguals (see Stratilaki 2011a). More specifically, based on a qualitative and quantitative analysis of data elicited in the form of questionnaires and semi-structured narrative interviews in French, we explore the conditions and stakes of building intercultural (plurilingual) competence in learners who, because of their language biographies or the educational system, are studying in prestigious institutional school environments in France and Germany.

2. Symbolic competence as a way of understanding intercultural competence

In a world that is both postmodern and hypermobile, languages, identities, and cultures can no longer be seen as static, homogeneous, or nationalized entities. In this chapter, we are concerned with an understanding of intercultural competence, referred to as *symbolic competence* (see Kramsch 2006), which enables social actors to interpret identities, experiences, and practices while navigating through different contexts characterized by cultural complexity (Coste 2004, 2010). This notion of competence likewise permits the social actors to negotiate languages and frames of references in as well as through communication (see Dervin 2012). Having said this, we will analyse this notion of competence from two levels: first, from the macrolinguistic level, we will take into account the perspective of the organisation of curriculum and of individual social trajectories of learning; and second, from the microlinguistic level, in its discursive and interactional reality of the learners' social and linguistic practices. In doing so, we attempt to reveal how the complex plurilingual and pluricultural repertoire(s) of French-German learners takes shape, through typological profiles and by closely examining the constituent components of representations of identity. The results suggest perceiving learners' plurilingual and pluricultural identities as fluid, dynamic, and changing across varied situations, space(s), and time[1] (e.g. Pavlenko & Blackledge 2003).

---

1. In our study, we adopt the definition of Coste of the notion of *plurilingualism*. According to the author: "La notion de plurilinguisme semble désormais bien établie en sociolinguistique et en didactique des langues, avec la distinction elle aussi devenue courante entre plurilinguisme des individus et multilinguisme des territoires, l'un n'impliquant pas l'autre et inversement [...]. Et, surtout, dans le cas de l'anglais, *multilingualism* tend à occuper tout l'espace et à plus ou moins recouvrir les deux dimensions (individuelle et territoriale)" (Coste 2001: 144).

In order to understand the meaning of symbolic competence, and the ways in which we are using this construct, it is important to ascertain how the students in this study see themselves in different contexts, how they talk about their linguistic and cultural practices, how they get positioned in different contexts, and whether the learners' social representations of languages, including their features and status, shape the processes and strategies they develop and implement for language learning and use. We want to understand the significance of multilingualism and multiculturalism for these youth, and one way of doing this is through examining their discursive practices and the different discourses they encounter in their daily lives (e.g. in the classroom, at home, with peers, etc.). We use the term discourse here to represent language practices and social practices that individuals use to make sense of their actions or their social realities by expressing positions and representations (see Fairclough 1995; Labrie 2002). In other words, how individuals use their linguistic resources or different elements of a linguistic repertoire, in relation to societal norms through different interactions and contexts (Byrd Clark 2008b, 2010).

According to Pennycook (2010), multilingualism has become eulogized as one of the cornerstones of modern society. We would argue that although multilingualism has been going on for centuries and does not appear to be a new phenomenon, the ways in which multilingualism has been and is being looked at, and how individuals, including researchers, are positioning themselves around this discourse is significant (Byrd Clark 2008a, 2009; Stratilaki 2009). What is noteworthy and what we hope to exemplify here is that a good deal of the phenomenon, especially with the innovations in communication and information technologies, lies in the ways in which discourses of globalization, particularly the globalized new economy (a distinctive contemporary surge in globalization) and the international linguistic markets are positioning as well as appear to be shifting the value of languages, authenticity, and legitimacy. The value (and valorization) attributed to certain kinds of multilingualism is having a profound impact on people's lives, conditions, and identities, presenting constraints, opportunities and obstacles, while at the same time creating spaces for voices to be heard and listened to, which are observable in everyday social interactions (Byrd Clark 2008b, 2009; Byrd Clark & Labrie 2010; Stratilaki 2010a).

Interestingly, if we look specifically at schools, key questions in immersion programs are concerned with the ways in which multilingual skills and strategies are related to communication and learning of the language registers in L1, L2 and L3, which are required to function successfully in institutional settings, where these languages are being used for the instruction of educational content (e.g. Cenoz, Hufeisen & Jessner 2001). However, as mentioned earlier, language policies continue to reflect the language-nation-state ideology (e.g. Hobsbawm 1990;

Holliday 2010), and as a result, languages are seen as autonomous systems in institutional settings, such as school. What is valued is multilingualism as a set of three distinct parallel monolingualisms, not a hybrid system, in other words, *des monolinguismes dédoublés* (e.g. Heller 1999; Castellotti 2008) or a pluralisation of monolingualism (see Pennycook 2010). This kind of multilingualism demands the management of one's plurilingual competence, of the actual internal heterogeneity (dealing with perceived incursions of one language into another as well as repressing practices like code-switching or language switching).

As a linguistic system is also a part of a symbolic system that draws upon different elements of a linguistic repertoire one can also observe how social practices become meaningful or assigned different value in certain contexts (Byrd Clark & Labrie 2010). Developing symbolic competence has implications for intercultural education as we are looking not only at complex linguistic systems, but how words and social activities have acquired a symbolic value for people. After all, the language(s) and culture(s) of an individual influence and inform the practices on meaning making and interpretation that one brings to each encounter and interaction with different interlocutors. According to Kramsch (2009), multilingual subjects deal with linguistic diversity differently from monolingual subjects, and this is particularly important and sheds new light for intercultural education as symbolic competence highlights the subjective experiences and communicative practices of the participants. One of the dimensions of looking at symbolic discourse competence is through what we refer to as *plurilingualism*. Plurilingualism differs from multilingualism in that plurilingualism is not the mastery of three abstract separate monolingual systems, rather a multiple and fluid transidiomatic practice (Jacquemet 2005). A plurilingual competence then is intricately linked to code-switching as well as to a learner's motivation, engagement, and affect (attitudes) towards languages, cultures, and ways of speaking, as we will see in our upcoming analyses of the data. For example in our study, on the one hand, French-German learners in the Buc school (France), consider bilingualism as the development of a composite inventory, original and complex, in which the different languages in contact interact and combine. Following this perspective, bilingual competence can be perceived as a flexible interaction between languages, associated with linguistic plurality, whereas plurilingual competence is considered as a facilitator for language learning and use. On the other hand, the French-German learners in Saarbrücken (Germany) consider bilingualism as the addition of two separate and equivalent competences.

The conceptual notion of plurilingual competence can be considered as the development of a composite repertoire, original and complex, where the different languages in contact interact and combine. Therefore language alternation could help promote metalinguistic awareness, through the communicative use of more than two languages. According to the *Common European Framework of Reference for Languages*:

> Plurilingual and pluricultural competence refers to the ability to use languages for the purposes of communication and to take part in intercultural interaction, where a person, viewed as a social agent has proficiency, of varying degrees, in several languages and experience of several cultures. This is not seen as the super-position or juxtaposition of distinct competences, but rather as the existence of a complex or even composite competence on which the user may draw.
> (Council of Europe 2001: 260; see also Coste, Moore & Zarate 1997, 2009)

Obviously the scope of language variation is an aspect in which plurilinguals differ greatly from monolingual or bilingual speakers. Thus, plurilinguals exhibit a great linguistic variety measured in terms of plurilingual competence. The present research adopts, therefore, a broader perspective on the conditions for successful language learning and tries to show that in order to understand the dynamics of plurilingual competence it is necessary to examine the social representations of languages and address the question of what discourse functions code-switching serves. This will entail both identifying the social representations of plurilingual competence of French-German learners and attempting to link the linguistic variable of code-switching under consideration to social representations of plurilingual competence, in order to explain the significance of language choice in trilingual education. Therefore, the working hypothesis developed for this research assumes that there is an important place for focusing on the language learning strategies of different learners, namely the role of linguistic distance in L3-acquisition, in code-switching and cross-linguistic influence. It is argued that the interaction(s) between languages can help learners to link the knowledge of the languages they already know or the languages that are being learned and, thus, can foster metalinguistic awareness, which is an important predictor of third language acquisition (e.g. Cummins 2001). As such, the development of plurilingual competence is intertwined with the learners' awareness of the intersections of languages and social representations of plurilingualism. This is particularly important for intercultural education as the learners' do not only have the capacity to gain metalinguistic awareness, but more importantly, they have the potential to develop a reflexive awareness of their own linguistic engagements and ways of being (Foucault 1980) in relation to representations of languages, cultures, and identities. Following these introductory remarks and discussion of key concepts, we will present the initial assumptions and hypotheses of the research. After developing the method and the context of the study, we will then take a closer look at the representations and language uses of plurilingualism by French-German learners. Finally, we will present some future research perspectives for intercultural education.

3. Plurilingual competence, code-switching and trilingual education

Few characteristics of bilingualism have inspired as much academic research as code-switching and its role and function in the interrelation between linguistic forms and sequential organisation of bilingual speech (e.g. Lüdi & Py 2002).

Cook (1992, 1995), Grosjean (1989), Gogolin (1994) and others, have criticised what they call 'monolingual prejudice', 'monolingual habitus' or 'the monolingual view of bilingualism' and proposed the notion of 'multicompetence' to designate a unique form of language competence that is not necessarily comparable to that of monolinguals. In this sense, the language competence of bilinguals should not be regarded as simply the sum of two monolingual competencies, but rather should be judged in conjunction with the user's total linguistic repertoire. Since Grosjean (1985), the alternate use of languages has been attributed to a monolingual-bilingual mode continuum of speaking. A mode is a state of activation of the bilingual's languages and language processing mechanisms. In the bilingual mode, both of the bilingual speaker's two languages are activated, although one to a relatively higher level than the other, whereas in the monolingual mode, only one language is activated and the other is de-activated as far as possible. Evidence for the language mode continuum has been found in adults in experimental settings and in naturalistic settings (Treffers-Daller 1998) as well as in children (e.g. Genesee 1989; Goodz 1989).

In a more recent publication, Grosjean (2001) applies his ideas to trilingual speakers, by pointing out that a trilingual speaker can certainly be imagined in a monolingual, a bilingual or a trilingual mode with various levels of activation. As a result, according to Grosjean, bi/plurilinguals are fully proficient speakers who have specific configurations of linguistic competences that reflect, in part, unique interactions of the languages they know. That is, bilinguals may be shown to exhibit a shared knowledge of what constitutes appropriate code-switching. As argued by Myers Scotton (1990) and Auer (1995) code-switching decisions appear to be governed by pragmatic, rather than syntactic criteria, and therefore it could be hasty to consider switches as no more than merely a discursive proof of lack of competence. As Gumperz (1982) has pointed out, code-switching is one of a number of possible contextualisation cues or communicative resources available for constructing and interpreting meanings in context. Additionally, for Lüdi (2003:175), bilingual speech can be defined as a mode of speaking where rules and norms are activated that overlap single languages and govern the 'grammatical' mixing of elements from different languages. Thus, the study of bilingualism and bilingual competence has grown into a respected research field. At the same time, knowledge of more than one language is now regarded as an imperative accomplishment, both in individuals as well as in institutional settings. The fact that learning strategies as well as communicative strategies are already at the disposal of bilingual speakers might facilitate and accelerate the language learning process. Yet it is only recently that the focus of research studies has shifted onto third language learning in institutional settings, with a specific focus on L3-acquisition and on the plurilingual competence of learners (Cenoz & Jessner 2006; Zarate, Kramsch & Levy 2008; Moore & Gajo 2009).

Given the short history of the field, it is not surprising that trilingualism has frequently been a secondary issue in a range of studies on second language acquisition; it has generally been considered as an extension of bilingualism. Consequently, a focus on the development of instructional settings involving the teaching of more than two languages (L1 + L2 + L3) and the acquisition of plurilingual competence by learners is crucial, especially when we consider the question of the temporary, as opposed to permanent nature of positive effects of plurilingualism on the cognitive development of plurilinguals (e.g. Baker 1996: 142). If we go beyond bilingualism, L3-acquisition and use tends to constitute an independent heuristic direction rather than a borderline case of bilingualism or an analysis of a *dual* L2 competence (e.g. Hufeisen & Lindemann 1998). That this influence between languages might be of a cross-linguistic nature, that any language might exert an influence on another, disregarding the order of acquisition, has often been neglected (e.g. Hufeisen 1991: 16–17). Similarly, Clyne (1997) argues that, whereas in second language learners two systems can influence each other, the contact between three language systems in a plurilingual speaker can develop more forms, that is, apart from the bi-directional relationship between L1 and L2, L3 can influence L1 and vice versa and also L2 and L3 can influence each other. Along the same lines, Moore (2006) and Stratilaki (2010b) stress the importance of representations in the language learning process.

Respecting this pragmatic principle implies that representations of one's mother tongue, the language being learned and the differences between them are associated with particular learning strategies adopted by learners, who construct a representation of the interlinguistic distance between their own language system and those of the languages being learned. Consequently, according to Castellotti & Moore (2002), representation is dual in nature, both static and dynamic. That is, on the one hand, representations are closely related with learning processes, which they either enhance or hinder and, on the other hand, representations are flexible and changing, and can therefore be changed. Moreover, studies on social representations of languages and plurilingualism (Cavalli & Coletta 2002) reveal that learners' representations of interactions between languages are also constructed in relation to linguistic systems, their respective operation, probable similarities and differences and possible relationships between them. From this perspective, it is possible to argue that representations are developed in a complex interaction involving different languages and learners. Within this framework, learners construct their representations of plurilingual competence and their strategies in language uses. It follows that, as already pointed out, plurilingual competence is flexible: that is, it is sometimes difficult for a plurilingual speaker to describe her or his language competences using chronological terminology, since competences usually change over time. In addition, skills within the languages can vary.

4. Social representations of plurilingual competence and language uses by French-German learners

4.1 Hypotheses and research questions

This study focuses on social representations of plurilingual competence and language uses by French-German learners in two instructional settings in Saarbrücken (Germany) and Buc (France). It provides evidence for the positive effects of third language learning on second language proficiency, thus supporting the hypothesis of cross-linguistic influence. The assumption was that the language uses of learners in the Buc school differ from those of learners in Saarbrücken, and, perhaps more importantly, these differences are the result of different representations of learners of plurilingual competence. Indeed, the two situations are intrinsically interesting because they respectively offer a *bilingual* and a *plurilingual view* of the plurilingual competence. On the one hand, French-German learners in the Buc school consider bilingualism as the development of a composite inventory, original and complex, in which the different languages in contact interact and combine. Following this perspective, bilingual competence can be perceived as a flexible interaction between languages, associated with linguistic plurality, whereas plurilingual competence is considered as a facilitator for language learning. On the other hand, the French-German learners in Saarbrücken consider bilingualism as the addition of two separate and homogeneous competences, evaluated according to a model resembling the performance of a native speaker. Whereas bilingual competence is seen as balanced and stable, conceptualised in terms of geographic frontiers between Germany and France and affected by social and historical factors, plurilingual competence is seen as the extent of bilingual competence, which will be referred to here as an unbalanced competence. It must be noted that both institutional settings emphasise positive attitudes towards bilingualism. These hypotheses raise the following basic questions:

1. How do learners define what could be referred to as 'plurilingual competence' in the two schools?
2. Do learners consider themselves as 'bilingual' or 'plurilingual' speakers and why?
3. What is the influence of these representations on the specific strategies that learners use in language learning?
4. What conditions regarding the situation and the type of bi-/plurilingualism noted seem to encourage the use of code-switching?

4.2   Methodological options and data collection

Two main perspectives underlie our research orientations and contribute to providing valuable and complementary insights into representations and language uses of plurilingualism and interculturality (see Dervin 2012). First, we sought to develop experimental research procedures capable of integrating various dimensions in the empirical study of plurilingualism in the two institutional settings, especially through the study of the different *strategies*, which the groups of French-German learners have been developing to deal with three languages in contact. Second, data was collected by informal recorded interviews with bilingual French-German learners. We interviewed female and male students, aged between 16 and 18 years, recruited according to strict selection criteria: namely, according to their answers to a questionnaire which was previously distributed (for more information about the data collection, see Stratilaki 2011b). Interviews were recorded at schools and there was no time restriction. Topics included studies, motivation for language learning and subjects' performance in exams. The recordings were transcribed by the researcher into orthographical French and German. The sample yield data for the years 2001 and 2003 will be used to test our hypotheses.

4.3   The school situation in the French-German Schools in Buc and Saarbrücken

There are three French-German Schools in Europe, known as *Lycées Franco-Allemands* (LFA) or *Deutsch-Französisches Gymnasien* (DFG). The Treaty concerning the foundation of the French-German public high schools was signed in 1963. The establishment of the French-German Baccalaureate (*Baccalauréat franco-allemand* or *Deutsch-Französisches Abitur*) defined the qualification of this diploma and symbolised the reconciliation of the two countries. The first French-German Baccalaureate took place in June 1972 at the French-German high school in

Saarbrücken, Germany, which indicated a successful European integration as far as secondary education was concerned. According to this model of bilingual education, two other partner schools were created, situated at Freiburg-in-Breisgau, Germany (1972) and Buc/Versailles, France (1980). The French-German high school in Saarbrücken was founded in 1961 as an experimental bilingual school. It was the first French-German School in Europe which was organised according to a common bilingual program, in terms of time, curriculum content and teaching, elaborated and accepted by France and Germany. The purpose of the school was to develop bilingualism and biculturalism in French and German.

The two languages of the schools have equal status, that is, both languages are used as a media of instruction. The two languages are also taught as languages (e.g. aspects of grammar and communicative skills). The essential elements of instruction are that different lessons may use different languages with a regular change-over to ensure both languages are used in all curricula areas and that switching languages within a lesson is acceptable. For example, Environmental Studies may be taught in French, or Science and Math in German. In this way, inter-dependence may stimulate cooperation and friendship, as well as learning and achievement. The school ethos is bilingual and bicultural. Such an ethos is created by classroom and corridor displays, notice boards, curriculum resources, cultural events, and extra-curricular activities using both languages in a relatively balanced way. Announcements over the school address system are bilingual French-German. Letters to parents are also in two languages. The staff who work in the dual language classrooms are often bilingual. French-German learners are integrated in some lessons and are expected to respond in the same language. Bilingual teachers ensure that they switch languages to favour language competence in both the target languages as well as the learner's language. A teacher using French will work in close association with a teacher who uses German with the same class. Such teamwork requires teachers to be committed to plurilingualism and pluriculturalism as important educational aims. Additionally, teachers use both languages on different occasions with their students.

French-German Schools contain a balanced mixture of children from more than two different language or dialect backgrounds (e.g. Alsace or Saarland). Therefore, in our analysis, it is important to take into account local realities and exigencies. Bilingual learners are expected to acquire plurilingual competence formally throughout the curriculum, namely through instruction in Spanish (Sciences section) and English (Social and Economic Studies section). That is, all students are expected to learn more than two languages and become plurilingual, though the same level of achievement for the languages taught may not be expected. In both cases, communicative and literacy skills in both languages are likely to receive direct attention in the curriculum. While playground conversations and student-to-student talk in the classroom is difficult to influence or manipulate, the school environment aims to be transparently bilingual. So, the aim of French-German Schools is not just to produce bilingual students. To gain status and to flourish, such schools need to show success throughout the curriculum. The development of plurilingual competence often starts in kindergarten classes. As the kindergarten children move through the grades, metalinguistic awareness is established through the communicative use of more than two languages.

4.4   Analysis and results

To reflect back to our initial stance in this chapter as regards the significance of looking at language and culture as multidimensional and complex social constructs rather than non-static, essentialized entities, (in other words, looking at language as a social practice rather than solely as a system or unidimensional code to be mastered), we focus our analysis on two different yet complex extracts from the French-German bilinguals. We reported earlier that Coste (2001) draws a complex picture of plurilingual and pluricultural competence serving as the goal of future trilingual education at school. He points out that third language acquisition in the school context and trilingual education are complex phenomena, related to a large number of sociolinguistic, psycholinguistic and educational factors. In what follows, the analysis of data will be used to specify the relationship between social representations of plurilingualism and language uses. These samples are significant for intercultural education as we are permitted to see the intricate ways that representations of language and culture are embedded in the ways that the participants talk about their legitimacy and authenticity in claiming their self-identifications. In the following extract, the French-German learners in the Saarbrücken school attempt to define the notion of a bi/plurilingual speaker. In this first extract, we can see how being (and becoming) a "real" bilingual is not only tied to an ideological mastery of two separate linguistic codes but also to essentialized notions of culture. The original version in French and German is integrated in our analysis. The Extracts 1 and 2 have been translated from French and German to English (see Appendix) and are selected on a representative basis of the oral data.

Extract 1

SB-A: For me, being bilingual means knowing and using perfectly two languages knowing all the expressions, all the words signifies also a good knowledge of the two languages, as well as being at the same time capable of **combining the words and switching easily from the one language to the other.** In fact, it's like putting together a French and a German speaker in the same person. Well, feeling at ease in the two languages and in order to feel at ease there are a lot of possibilities which also means having a basic knowledge of the culture…Well being bilingual for me corresponds to an adventure that means to an enrichment. On the contrary, plurilingualism doesn't imply the same knowledge as bilingualism. I think that when we are really bilingual we are more anchored to a language, whereas when we are plurilingual, we **move constantly** between the languages but we stay probably more superficial. Someone who is plurilingual can **speak fluently** a lot of languages but he can make mistakes and can have a foreign accent. Being plurilingual doesn't demand, probably, such a great knowledge of the language but only to be able to **write** and to **speak or to make combinations** in order to learn more Latin or Germanic languages

SB-B: I define 'being bilingual' as someone who knows equally two languages especially as well as **writing** as **speaking**, if it is possible without an accent. He must be able to communicative in the two countries without a problem, he must be able to express himself correctly, he must be able to go to the supermarket without a problem, he must be able to **communicate** with the other people without a problem, he must be able to communicate and partially know the different registers of languages. [He must be able to do] all these in both languages without a problem, concerning **expression**, **vocabulary** and **grammar**, having at least no more problems than a native-like-speaker. Being plurilingual, implies **knowing a lot of languages**, being bilingual is being **plurilingual in two languages**, generally the mother tongue and a second one. It's not exactly the same thing: **when someone is bilingual he is also plurilingual** but when someone is plurilingual he is not necessarily bilingual. I don't know, I think that being bilingual can lead to being plurilingual and personally, yes, I am a real bilingual

Definitions, a speech genre much favoured in schools, constitute an example of decontextualised language use. Learner SB-A considers that language competence is not a stable state and that having to deal with more than one language at a time forms part of the bilingual competence (SB-A: 3). This implies a process whereby SB-A relates the notion of bi-/plurilingual competence and code-switching to his own experiences and knowledge. Thus, for SB-A the development of bilingual competence leads to an enrichment of the individual's language systems and personal life: 'being bilingual for me corresponds to an adventure'. In addition to making his definition of bilingualism more persuasive, activating personal experience affirms the learner's identity as a 'real' bilingual speaker. The final statement in this extract is interesting in that it reveals that SB-A possesses an increased metalinguistic awareness and a considerable knowledge of the proximity and distance between languages. In this sense, the acquisition of languages that are typologically close to French or German can potentially facilitate the process of L3 acquisition. Nevertheless, linguistic distance can also play an important role when focusing on form in order to develop language awareness and learning strategies (SB-A: 14–15). Thus, learners tend to combine languages that are typologically closer to the target language and, in this way, plurilingual competence is seen as a positive linguistic resource for language learning.

Additionally, the double focus on content and form, and the elaborate metalinguistic work of definition provided by learner SB-B may well have a double effect on his communicative means, through which language and content can be integrated successfully (SB-B: 1–12). Therefore, the alternate experience in two languages, demonstrated and magnified through code-switching, could help reinforce complexity and refine the elaboration of the concept of a 'bilingual' or 'plurilingual' speaker. In the example above, switching from one language to the other, goes beyond a mere attempt to translate. That is, it brings attention to semantic differences between the notions of a bilingual and plurilingual speaker and provides us with new information and insights. This cleverly staged code-switching introduces subtle nuances to elicit the meaning of the concept of plurilingualism: with two lexical forms in his bilingual repertoire, SB-B can activate two images, corresponding to two different conceptions of bilingual and plurilingual competence. Bilingual competence is conceived by the learner as stable, and communicative efficiency will therefore be assessed in terms of a monolingual native-speaker discourse. This example illustrates that the representation of bilingual performance is that of full attainment or mastery of two separate languages, which means, for example, that the bilingual speaker SB-B has full command of native-speaker-like language systems L1 and L2 and any systematic deviation can be attributed to a lack of competence (SB-B: 1–6). In this case, errors can be taken as evidence of a deficient language system (SB-A: 12). In this sense, the skills which a plurilingual speaker develops in order to integrate differing language resources into his or her repertoire can be interpreted as transitional (SB-B: 12–13). Another critical factor is the degree of competence/performance in the languages, which will correlate with the image of the speaker as bilingual or plurilingual (SB-A: 11–14). Whilst bilinguals are characterised by a native speaker speaking (SB-A: 1–4), where both systems are considered as developed to ideal speaker competence level, plurilinguals are assumed to have a "foreign" accent (SB-A: 12). As can be seen in Extract 1, both examples illustrate that bilingualism is frequently still assumed to be synonymous with ambilingualism (i.e. native-like competence in both languages), although plurilingualism is seen as a projection of bilingualism, characterised by an unbalanced competence, which can increase difficulties stemming from complexity. The examples also seem to demonstrate the students' motivation for language learning and their desires to develop a plu-rilingual competence.

Previously, we briefly discussed the role of distance and proximity in the de-velopment of plurilingual competence. Such an example (see above) shows the potential for social representations to raise linguistic awareness as well as its pos-sible links with language uses and acquisition (Coste 2002). The next example, in the Buc school, illustrates similar roles for representations of plurilingual compe-tence and adds some new elements for analysis.

Extract 2

B-A: [I speak] with my brother in German, with my sister in French, with my mother in French and with my father in German. It depends on the other: form what language they known better, where I made the experience, in what language it **sounds better** or the **expression is better**, it depends on how I am **feeling**, it always depends on the **people** surrounding me, when we are a mixed group of German and French, we are **switching from one language to the other**, also with those who have grown up as bilinguals, I like French more, because my whole family lives in France. It's easier in German because I was educated my whole life there and most of my friends are German. Bilingual: someone can equally **speak** both languages and he **feels at ease** in both languages

Fragment 2:

I speak only German at home with my parents and my sisters and brothers. It is different when writing. I prefer playing with the words shifting from one language to the other, between French, German and Spanish especially when my interlocutor (friend or classmate) can speak them. Normally, I switch the whole time. In some languages there **are words that express exactly** one thing while in the other language an appropriate word doesn't exist for this or French words with a German end. For instance: his face was afterwards fast 'deformiert' (translation: déformé), afterwards I was really 'boulversiert' (translation: boulversée)

B-B: I prefer communicating in German and in French. I adapt to the **preferred** language of my friends. I **switch** also between German and French. Normal-ly, I speak the language of the person, except if someone asks me to speak the other language in order to learn it or if I don't remember the word. In this case, I explain it in the other language with my friends being perfect bilinguals in my class. I switch the language according to the **subject**, the previous **lesson** or the **persons**

Fragment 2:

Being bilingual demands from the person to **feel at ease** in the two coun-tries, to be able to speak the two languages without hesitation like his mother tongue. The bilingual understands each country, the way of **living** and theoretically he can get used to living in both of them. I believe that **bilingualism goes beyond the knowledge of two languages**

Code-switches are intrinsically bound to draw attention to differences as well as to incorporate aspects that are not included in one language or the other. Therefore, switches can be considered as acting directly on the elaboration of concepts, especially when no semantic congruent equivalents are available (B-A: Fragment 2: 14–15). In other words, there is a positive transfer from second language learning to learning additional languages and the use of these languages in communication needs. The previous example indicates that in situations when the focus is not only on the development of linguistic skills, but also on the transmission of subject contents, there is discursive evidence for cross-linguistic transfer in the development of plurilingual competence when the languages involved are similar in vocabulary, syntax or structure (B-A: Fragment 2: 16–18). That is, learners' representations of the distance or proximity between languages can be far more important than the objective similarities or differences between them.

This approach suggests that plurilingual speakers demonstrate great flexibility in switching strategies, according to the demand characteristics of the situation as well as the fact that plurilingual learners are more effective in using implicit learning strategies than bilingual learners (B-B: Fragment 2: 3–5). In this sense, the two plurilingual learners B-A and B-B are characterised by an enriched experience as language learners which arguably, as illustrated from the Extract 2, helps them choose appropriate strategies and use a variety of discourse strategies for social communication and learning. Moreover, we see that plurilingual learners are more sensitive and responsive to the needs of their interlocutors than bilingual learners (B-A: 5–7; B-B: 1–6). Switches also highlight the idea that plurilingual learners develop hypotheses about linguistic operations and test those hypotheses in a range of settings: plurilingual speakers will thus activate the language network required by the communicative situation. On a more, complex level, this must be taken to mean that the alternate use of languages presupposes a view of plurilingual competence as a complex pattern of proprieties and functions. For instance, in the case of B-B, the notion of bilingualism goes beyond proficiency in two languages. In this perspective, being 'bilingual' implies being also 'bicultural', in terms of being exposed to two cultures, two modes of socialisation, and two national identities (B-B: Fragment 2: 7–10). In other words, the bilingual speaker is defined by B-B as someone who has linguistic competence in two or more languages, and also has a perception of other cultures; in this sense, he is able to develop an understanding of the differences and relationships between his own and an additional culture. That is, bicultural identity is experienced positively as a resource of L3 acquisition, language and cultural learning. Therefore, representations are meaningful and play a crucial role in constructing identity/ies as well as relationships with others and knowledge. We can see in these examples that plurilinguals appear to be individuals who can use two or more languages separately or together for particular purposes with different individuals, in certain contexts (Byrd Clark 2008a; Moore & Gajo 2009).

5. Conclusions and open questions

Social representations of identity and plurilingual competence are essential in third language acquisition, trilingual education and intercultural education. Thus, the development of a symbolic, plurilingual competence on the individual level as a goal of plurilingual education is a complex task. It cannot be provided merely by adding more languages to the curriculum structures and/or incorporated through teaching methods. The interdisciplinary approach advocated here implies that the focus on the similarities and differences between two or more language systems, as known from our observations and analysis of representations of plurilingual competence and language uses in French-German learners in the two institutional settings, seems to be helpful in the overall language learning process. This linguistically oriented approach has strong implications for intercultural education as it can help move us (researchers and practitioners) "away from an overemphasis on national or ethnic identities and cultural differences seen from an objectivist perspective to a more subjective focus on the learners themselves as participants in diversity" as argued by the editors of this book (Dervin & Liddicoat, *Introduction* to this volume). With this perspective, a strong emphasis on metalinguistic knowledge, metacognitive awareness and skills will promote and facilitate further language learning.

To sum up, it is important to acknowledge the unevenness and multidimensionality of plurilingual competence, by pointing out that the plurilingual learner is characterised by a complex competence, which changes according to personal interests, through interactions with diverse interlocutors, geographical mobility and family movements, as well as the educational context. The results also suggest the learner's plurilingual and pluricultural identity/ies are fluid, dynamic, and changing over varied situations, space(s) and time. Therefore, a useful effect of the adoption of a dynamic model of plurilingualism might well be the realization of the need for continuous work towards the development of a plurilingual repertoire by individuals; one that takes into account the impact of social representations, and at the same time, is inclusive and reflects the learners' linguistic practices in everyday life. If we are to acquire a thorough understanding of this complexity of plurilingualism and to develop plurilingual and intercultural education programmes in institutional settings in an era of hypermobility, then we need to expand beyond unidimensional conceptualizations of what constitutes bilingualism, multilingualism, culture and linguistic identity, and support educational policies and practices that take into account the social realities of youth in today's plurilingual and pluricultural world (Byrd Clark 2010). Finally, we need to ask ourselves what it means to be plurilingual and intercultural; merging approaches from language education, applied linguistics and intercultural education has given us the opportunities to do just that.

References

Auer, P. (1995). The pragmatics of code-switching. In L. Milroy & P. Muysken (Eds.), *One speaker, two languages: Cross-disciplinary perspectives on code-switching* (pp. 1–24). Cambridge: Cambridge University Press.

Baker, C. (1996). *Foundations of bilingualism and bilingual education.* Clevedon: Multilingual Matters.

Beacco, J.-C. (2005). *Langues et répertoire de langues: Le plurilinguisme comme 'manière d'être' en Europe. Étude de référence.* Strasbourg: Council of Europe.

Blackledge, A. & Pavlenko, A. (2004). *Negotiation of identities in multilingual contexts.* Clevedon: Multilingual Matters.

Budach, G. & Bardtenschlager, H. (2008). Est-ce que ce n'est pas trop dur? Enjeux et expériences de l'alphabétisation dans un projet de double immersion. *Glottopol: Revue de sociolinguistique en ligne, 11*, 148–170.

Byram, M. (2010). Linguistic and intercultural education for Bildung and citizenship. *The Modern Language Journal, 94*(2), 317–321.

Byrd Clark, J. (2008a). Journeys of integration in Canada's pluralistic society: Italian Canadian youth and the symbolic investments in French as official language. Unpublished doctoral dissertation, The Ontario Institute for Studies in Education of the University of Toronto, Toronto, Ontario, Canada.

Byrd Clark, J. (2008b). So, why do you want to teach French? Representations of multilingualism and language investment through a reflexive critical sociolinguistic ethnography. *Education and Ethnography, 3*(1), 1–16.

Byrd Clark, J. (2009). *Multilingualism, citizenship, and identity: Voices of youth and symbolic investments in a globalized world.* London: Continuum.

Byrd Clark, J. (2010). Making some "wiggle room" in French as a second language/français langue seconde: Reconfiguring identity, language, and policy. *Canadian Journal of Education, 33*(2), 379–406.

Byrd Clark, J. (2012). Heterogeneity and a sociolinguistics of multilingualism: Reconfiguring French language pedagogy. *Language and Linguistics Compass Blackwell Online Journal, 6*(3), 143–161.

Byrd Clark, J. & Labrie, N. (2010). La voix de jeunes canadiens dans leur processus d'identifica-tion: les identités imbriquées dans des espaces multiformes. In S. Osu (Ed.), *Construction d'identité et processus d'identification* (pp. 425–438). Berlin: Peter Lang.

Castellotti, V. & Moore, D. (2002). *Représentations sociales es langues et enseignements*. Stras-bourg: Council of Europe.

Castellotti, V. (2008). Au-delà du bilinguisme: Quelle place en France pour une éducation plu-rilingue? In J. Erfurt, et al. (Eds.). *Ecoles plurilingues – Multilingual schools*. Frankfurt: Peter Lang.

Cavalli, M. & Coletta, D. (2002). *Rapports de diffusion: Langues, bilinguisme et représentations sociales au Val d'Aoste*. Aoste: IRRE-Vda.

Cenoz, J. & Genesee, F. (1998). Psycholinguistic perspectives on multilingualism and multilin-gual education. In J. Cenoz & F. Genesee (Eds.), *Beyond bilingualism: Multilingualism and multilingual education* (pp. 16–32). Clevedon: Multilingual Matters.

Cenoz, J., Hufeisen, B., & Jessner, U. (2001). Towards trilingual education. *International Journal of Bilingual Education and Bilingualism, 4*(1), 1–10.

Cenoz, J. & Jessner, U. (2006). *English in Europe: The acquisition of a third language*. Clevedon: Multilingual Matters.

Chomsky, N. (1965). *Aspects of the theory of syntax*. Cambridge, MA: The MIT Press.

Clyne, M. (1997). Some of the things trilinguals do. *International Journal of Bilingualism, 1*(2), 95–116.

Cook, V. (1992). Evidence for multi-competence. *Language Learning, 42*, 557–591.

Cook, V. (1995). Multi-competence and the learning of many languages. *Language, Culture and Curriculum, 8*, 93–98.

Coste, D. (2001). De plus d'une langue à d'autres encore. Penser les compétences plurilingues. In V. Castellotti (Ed.), *D'une langue à d'autres. Pratiques et représentations* (pp. 191–202). Rouen: Presses universitaires de Rouen.

Coste, D. (2002). Compétence à communiquer et compétence plurilingue. *Notions en Question, 6*, 115–123.

Coste, D. (2004). De quelques déplacements opérés en didactique des langues par la notion de compétence plurilingue. In A. Auchlin (Ed.), *Structures et discours. Mélanges offerts à Eddy Roulet* (pp. 67–85). Quebec: Éditions Nota bene.

Coste, D. (2010). Diversité des plurilinguismes et formes de l'éducation plurilingue et intercul-turelle. *Cahiers de l'Acedle, 7*(1), 141–165.

Coste, D., Moore, D., & Zarate, G. (1997). *Compétence plurilingue et pluriculturelle*. Strasbourg: Council of Europe.

Cummins, J. (2001). Instructional conditions for trilingual development. *International Journal of Bilingual Education and Bilingualism, 4*(1), 61–75.

Dervin, F. (2010). Assessing intercultural competence in language learning and teaching: A critical review of current efforts. In F. Dervin & E. Suomela-Salmi (Eds.), *New approaches to assessment in higher education* (pp. 155–172). Bern: Peter Lang.

Dervin, F. (2011). A plea for change in research on intercultural discourses: A 'liquid' approach to the study of the acculturation of Chinese students. *Journal of Multicultural Discourses, 6*(1), 37–52.

Fairclough, N. (1992). *Critical language awareness*. London: Longman.

Fairclough, N. (1995). *Critical discourse analysis*. London: Longman.

Foucault, M. (1980). *Power/knowledge*. Brighton: Harvester.

Genesee, F. (1989). Early bilingual development: One language or two? *Journal of Child Language, 16,* 161–179.

Gogolin, I. (1994). *Der monolinguale Habitus der multilingualen Schule.* Münster: Waxmann.

Goodz, N. (1989). Parental language mixing in bilingual families. *Journal of Infant Mental Health, 10,* 25–44.

Grosjean, F. (1985). The bilingual as a competent but specific speaker-hearer. *Journal of Multilingual and Multicultural Development, 6,* 467–477.

Grosjean, F. (1989). Neurolinguists, beware! The bilingual is not two monolinguals in one person. *Brain and Language, 36,* 3–15.

Grosjean, F. (2001). The bilingual's language modes. In J. Nicol (Eds.), *One Mind, two languages: Bilingual language processing* (pp. 1–25). Oxford: Blackwell.

Gumperz, J. J. (1982). *Discourse strategies.* Cambridge: Cambridge University Press.

Heller, M. (1999). *Linguistic minorities and modernity: A sociolinguistic ethnography.* London: Longman.

Hobsbawm, E. (1990). *Nations and nationalism since 1780: Programme, myth, reality.* Cambridge: Cambridge University Press.

Holliday, A. (2010). *Intercultural communication and ideology.* New York: Sage.

Hu, A. & Byram, M. (Eds.). (2009). *Interkulturelle Kompetenz und fremdsprachliches Lernen.* Tübingen: Gunter Narr.

Hu, A. (2003). *Schulischer Fremdsprachenunterricht und migrationsbedingte Mehrsprachigkeit.* Tübingen: Gunter Narr.

Hufeisen, B. & Lindemann, B. (Eds.). (1998). *L2-L3 und ihre zwischensprachliche Interaktion: Zu individueller Mehrsprachigkeit und gesteuertem Lernen.* Tübingen: Stauffenburg.

Hufeisen, B. (1991). *English als erste und Deutsch als zweite Fremdsprache: Empirische Untersuchung zur Fremdsprachlichen Interaktion.* Frankfurt: Peter Lang.

Jacquemet, M. (2005). Transidiomatic practices: Language and power in the age of globalization. *Language and Communication, 25,* 257–277.

Kramsch, C. (2006). From communicative competence to symbolic competence. *The Modern Language Journal, 90*(2), 249–252.

Kramsch, C. (2009). *The multilingual subject. What language learners say about their experience and why it matters.* Oxford: Oxford University Press.

Labov, W. (1971). The notion of system in creole languages. In D. Hymes (Ed.), *Pidginization and creolization of languages* (pp. 447–472). Cambridge: Cambridge University Press.

Labrie, N. (2002). Stratégies politiques de reproduction sociale pour les communautés de langues minoritaires. *Sociolinguistica, 16,* 14–22.

Lüdi, G. & Py, B. (2002). *Être bilingue.* Bern: Peter Lang.

Lüdi, G. (2003). Code-switching and unbalanced bilingualism. In J.-M. Dewaele & A. Housen (Eds.), *Bilingualism: Beyond Basic Principles* (pp. 174–188). Clevedon: Multilingual Matters.

Moore, D. (2006). *Plurilinguismes et école.* Paris: Didier.

Moore, D. & Gajo, L. (Eds.). (2009). French voices on plurilingualism and pluriculturalism. *International Journal of Multilingualism, 6*(2).

Moscovici, S. (1984). The phenomenon of social representations. In R. M. Farr & S. Moscovici (Eds.), *Social Representations* (pp. 3–69). Cambridge: Cambridge University Press.

Myers Scotton, C. (1990). Codeswitching and borrowing: Interpersonal and macrolevel meaning. In R. Jacobson (Eds.), *Codeswitching as a worldwide phenomenon* (pp. 85–111). New York, NY: Peter Lang.

Pennycook, A. (2010). *Language as a local practice*. London: Routledge.

Sankoff, D. & Poplack, S. (1979). A formal grammar for code-switching. *Papers in Linguistics, 14*, 3–46.

Stratilaki, S. (2009). Des identités, des langues et des récits de vie. Schèmes constitués ou nouvelles analogies dans la parole des élèves plurilingues? *Glottopol: Revue de sociolinguistique en ligne, 13*, 168–191.

Stratilaki, S. (2010a). Discours sur les langues et catégorisations du plurilinguisme. In G. Veldre-Gerner & S. Thiele (Eds.), *Sprachvergleich und Sprachdidaktik* (pp. 99–114). Stuttgart: Ibidem.

Stratilaki, S. (2010b). Compétences plurilingues et histoires de vie. Nouveaux regards sur les normes à l'école. In D. Abendroth-Timmer, C. Fäcke, L. Küster, & C. Minuth (Eds.), *Normen und Normverletzungen. Aktuelle Diskurse der Fachdidaktik Französisch* (pp. 113–132). Stuttgart: Ibidem.

Stratilaki, S. (2011a). *Discours et représentations du plurilinguisme*. Frankfurt: Peter Lang.

Stratilaki, S. (2011b). Représentations des plurilinguismes et constructions identitaires de la compétence plurilingue, vues du dehors et du dedans. In C. Reissner (Ed.), *Romanische Mehrsprachigkeit und Interkomprehension in Europa* (pp. 31–62). Stuttgart: Ididem.

Treffers-Daller, J. (1998). Variability in code-switching styles: Turkish-German code-switching patterns. In R. Jacobson (Ed.), *Codeswitching worldwide* (pp. 177–198). Berlin: Mouton de Gruyter.

Weinreich, U. (1953). *Languages in contact: Findings and problems*. The Hague: Mouton.

Zarate, G., Kramsch, C., & Lévy, D. (Eds.). (2008). *Précis du plurilinguisme et du pluriculturalisme*. Paris: Edition des Archives Contemporaines.

Appendix

Extract 1

SB-A: Pour moi être bilingue c'est connaître et maîtriser parfaitement deux langues connaître toutes les expressions les jeux de mots signifie aussi: qu'on maîtrise bien deux langues tout en étant capable de les combiner et de passer de l'une à l'autre avec aisance pour en fait, c'est comme si on mettait un allemand et un français dans une même personne... bon qu'on se sent à l'aise dans les deux langues et pour se sentir à l'aise il y a beaucoup de possibilités ce qui implique une petite connaissance de la culture voilà être bilingue représente pour moi une aventure donc un enrichissement. Au contraire, le plurilinguisme n'implique pas la même maîtrise que le bilinguisme quand on est vrai bilingue, à mon avis, on est plus ancré dans la langue tandis que lorsqu'on est plurilingue on jongle avec les langues mais on reste peut-être plus superficiel. Quelqu'un qui est plurilingue sait parler plusieurs langues couramment mais peut faire des fautes et peut avoir un accent plus au moins prononcé. Être plurilingue ne demande peut-être pas une telle maîtrise de la langue mais seulement de savoir se débrouiller avec. À l'écrit et à l'oral, on peut faire des combinaisons pour apprendre plus de langues latines ou germaniques

SB-B: Unter Bilinguismus stelle ich mir vor, dass jemand zwei Sprachen gleich gut beherrscht und zwar sowohl im Schriftlichen als auch im Mündlichen möglichst ohne Akzent. Er muss sich im jeweiligen Land ohne Probleme verständigen können, er muss sich gut und vollständig ausdrücken, er muss ohne Probleme einkaufen gehen, er muss mit den anderen Leuten frei reden können, verschiedene Sprachebenen kennen und zum Teil beherrschen [Erklärung]: familier, courant, soutenu, tout ça in beiden Sprachen, keine nennenswerten Ausdrucks- Vokabular- Grammatikprobleme haben, zumindest nicht mehr Fehler als Muttersprachler machen [Témoignage en français]: être plurilingue signifie maîtriser plusieurs langues, être bilingue c'est être plurilingue avec deux langues, en général sa langue maternelle et une deuxième. Ce n'est pas exactement la même chose : quand on est bilingue on est aussi plurilingue, mais quand on es plurilingue on n'est pas forcement bilingue. Sais pas, je pense qu'être bilingue peut aboutir à devenir plurilingue. Moi, oui, je suis un vrai bilingue

Extract 2

B-A: Oui, avec mon frère en allemand, avec ma sœur en français, avec ma mère en français et avec mon père allemand [Témoignage en allemand], es hängt von den anderen ab: je nachdem welche Sprache sie besser beherrschen. Ich ändere die Sprache, je nach dem in welcher Sprache es sich besser oder schöner ausdrücken lässt, oder nach meiner Laune. Es kommt immer darauf an, welche Leute dabei sind: wenn wir eine gemischte Gruppe von Deutschen und Franzosen sind, dann wechseln wir die Sprache. Auch bei denen, die zweisprachig aufgewachsen sind mag ich lieber Französisch, da meine ganze Familie in Frankreich lebt. Einfacher ist es auf Deutsch, da ich meine ganze Schulzeit dort verbracht habe und die meisten meiner Freunde Deutsche sind [...]. Zweisprachig: man kann beide Sprachen gleich gut sprechen und man fühlt sich in beiden gleich wohl.

Fragment 2
Zu Hause spreche ich nur Deutsch mit meinen Eltern und meinen Geschwistern. Anders ist das im Schriftlichen. Am liebsten spiele ich mit den Sprachen, springe hin und her zwischen Französisch, Deutsch, Spanisch, wenn meine Gesprächspartner sie auch sprechen natürlich. Normalerweise wird dauernd gewechselt. In manchen Sprachen gibt es Wörter, die etwas genau ausdrücken und in anderen Sprachen gibt es kein treffendes Wort. Oder auch französische Wörter mit einer deutschen Endung zum Beispiel: sein Gesicht war danach ganz deformiert [Erklärung: déformé], danach war ich richtig boulversiert [Erklärung: boulversée]

B-B: Je préfère communiquer en allemand et en français. Je m'adapte à la langue préférée de mes amis. J'alterne aussi entre l'allemand et le français. Je parle d'habitude la langue d'origine de la personne, sauf si elle me demande de parler l'autre langue pour l'apprendre ou si j'ai un trou de vocabulaire. Dans ce cas, je l'explique dans l'autre langue. Avec des amis parfaitement bilingues de ma classe, j'alterne la langue selon le thème, le cours précédent, les personnes

Fragment 2
Être bilingue demande à la personne de se sentir à l'aise dans les deux pays, de pouvoir parler les deux langues sans appréhension, comme ses langues maternelles. Le bilingue comprend chaque pays et son mode de vie. Il peut s'adapter aux deux. Je crois que le bilinguisme dépasse la maîtrise des deux langues

Index